Pan's Travail

Ancient Society and History

Pan's Travail

J. DONALD HUGHES

Environmental Problems

of the Ancient Greeks

and Romans

The Johns Hopkins University Press
Baltimore and London

This book has been brought to publication
with the generous assistance of
the David M. Robinson Fund.

Johns Hopkins paperbacks edition, 1996
05 04 03 02 01 00 99 98 97 96   5 4 3 2 1

The Johns Hopkins University Press
2715 North Charles Street
Baltimore, Maryland 21218-4319
The Johns Hopkins Press Ltd., London

Library of Congress Cataloging-in-Publication Data

Hughes, J. Donald (Johnson Donald), 1932–
    Pan's travail : environmental problems of the ancient Greeks and
Romans / J. Donald Hughes.
        p.   cm. — (Ancient society and history)
Includes bibliographical references and index.
ISBN 0-8018-4655-2 — ISBN 0-8018-5363-X (pbk.)
1. Environmental degradation—Greece—History.   2. Environmental
degradation—Rome—History.   3. Civilization, Classical. I. Title.   II.
Series.
GE160.G8H84   1993
363.7´00938—dc20   93-1025

A catalog record for this book is available
from the British Library.

Contents

Contents

Contents

Preface

What is—or was—Pan's travail? Pan is a god of Greek mythology whose origins go back to a time before the alphabet was introduced to his homeland, so it is impossible to say exactly how he was connected to nature at the beginning. But in later Greco-Roman times, perhaps because the Greek word *pan* means "all," he was widely believed to be the god of all nature. "Travail" connotes work as well as suffering, and Pan experienced both at the hands of his supposed worshippers through many centuries. In late antiquity, it was even said that "Great Pan is dead." The Mediterranean environment that Pan symbolized did not die, but it suffered and was diminished. The following pages explore the process and scope of that mistreatment, and also explain how nature exacted revenge: Pan's nemesis.

This book is intended to provide the necessary groundwork for an understanding of the environmental history of classical Greece and Rome. It is written for the general reader, not the specialist, although it is hoped that the specialist will find much of value in it. Many people express surprise that environmental problems existed in the ancient world; they are used to thinking of the environment as an exclusively modern concern. But an examination of the evidence shows that the Greeks and Romans not only faced some of the same predicaments that plague us today but in many cases were aware of them and commented on them. In the chapters that follow, the major environmental problems of ancient times will be discussed in relationship to human culture.

This is a new book, not just a new edition of my earlier book, *Ecology in Ancient Civilizations* (University of New Mexico Press, 1975). Although some of the ground covered is similar, here the focus is more specifically on Greece and Rome, and the areas known to those civilizations and subject to their influence, from approximately 800 B.C. to A.D. 600. Except for a brief discussion of two of the major earlier civilizations in chapter 3, there is no attempt to cover other Mediterranean dimensions, geographically or chronologically. This study gives some attention to the attitudes toward nature expressed in Greek and Latin literature, but the main emphasis is on the treatment of nature by human beings and their technologies. It investigates the latter subjects in greater detail, and takes account of recent work that was not available when the earlier book was written. I believe that most of my conclusions in the earlier work were correct, and that the values of that book are preserved in this one at least in respect to Greece and Rome. But since 1975 I have gathered more information and refined my opinions on many matters treated here.

Parts of the research embodied in this book have appeared as articles in journals or as chapters in edited volumes. Some observations made in those essays are repeated in this book, with credit given in the notes and bibliography, and grateful appreciation is here expressed to the editors and publishers. The individuals who have given me valuable support are too numerous to list here, but special thanks must be expressed to the late Russell Meiggs, to Michael Grant, Niki Goulandris, Eugene Hargrove; to my colleagues in the American Society for Environmental History and the Forest History Society; to my research assistant, Phyllis Corchary, and to my wife, Pamela L. Peters Hughes. The research for this book was supported in part by grants and other aid from the Charles A. Lindbergh Fund, the University of Denver, the Goulandris Natural History Museum, and the Johns Hopkins University Press.

Pan's Travail

One

Introduction: Ecology in the Greek and Roman Worlds

Environment and Classical Civilization

The landscapes of Greece and Italy, and of the other countries once occupied by Greek colonists and the Roman Empire, have suffered greatly from human occupation since ancient times. This has been clear to observers experienced in land use management since the versatile George Perkins Marsh in the mid-nineteenth century, who ascribed the "decay of these flourishing countries" to "man's ignorant disregard of the laws of nature."[1] Similar comments were made by the ecologist Paul B. Sears and the soil conservationist Walter C. Lowdermilk in the early twentieth century.[2] All three of these astute men ascribed the decline of ancient civilizations to environmental problems such as deforestation, erosion, and agricultural exhaustion. Later the geographer Fairfield Osborn also detected in the decline of ancient societies "a contemporaneous deterioration of environment and peoples," of which "the causes were man-made, not natural."[3]

These modern authors wrote, for the most part, before extensive research had been done on environmental changes in the ancient world, but they did not simply ascribe modern environmental degradation to antiquity. They recognized that the Mediterranean

1

basin and neighboring lands have been subject to cycles of devastation and recovery, and that much of the devastation they saw was the result of medieval and modern mistreatment of the natural world. Their intuitive judgments constitute a hypothesis well worth investigating, as this book will show. The Greeks and Romans, like other ancient peoples, did degrade their environments, even though not to the extent of modern times, and it is not unreasonable to connect that process with the decline of classical civilization.

The sight of ruined cities surrounded by ruined land has long been common in the Mediterranean area. When I first visited Greece in the 1950s, the bare, desiccated slopes of Mount Hymettus could be glimpsed between the Doric columns of the Parthenon. That deforestation was first described by Plato in the fourth century B.C.[4] Today the view is becoming less stark as trees planted on the mountain in an immense reforestation project grow larger. But the scene is still common at other archaeological sites, such as ancient Corinth where there has been little change since antiquity. And it is worth noting that on Hymettus so little soil remained after centuries of erosion that in many places holes had to be dynamited in the limestone to allow pine seedlings to be planted.

All around the Mediterranean, ancient ports have been landlocked by erosional sediments, a fact mentioned by ancient writers. In the former Roman provinces of North Africa, the wide avenues and impressive buildings of cities such as Lepcis Magna, Sabratha, and Thamugadi, which once exported wheat and olive oil, stand empty within a Saharan landscape that could not support such populations today without the importation of large amounts of water. The irrigation systems of the Carthaginians and Romans, which once made this arid region blossom, depended for their effectiveness on watersheds whose forests have disappeared. The Libyan government is bringing sections of the desert under cultivation by mining the water that has been underground since the last Ice Age, but this fossil water will be exhausted in the foreseeable future, and another cycle of civilization may end because its environment will have been depleted. While it would be incorrect to blame the ancient Greeks and Romans for all the defects of the present-day Mediterranean lands, since they have been subjected to successive pressures in medieval and modern times, it seems clear that the ancient peoples in many instances initiated a process of wearing away the environment that had supported them. This environmental degradation was set in motion by economic, military, and religious factors. It is useful to inquire into the relationship among these causal factors to understand how they brought about environmental changes that impinged in turn upon human societies.

The Role of Ecology in History

When Amphipolis, a northern colony of Athens, fell to Sparta during the great war between the Greek city-states, "the Athenians were greatly alarmed. . . . The main reason was that the city was useful to them for procurement of timber for ship-building."[5] This comment by Thucydides is only one of countless references in ancient texts to the importance of nature in the course of human history. No ancient general could fight a war, no leader could conduct diplomacy, no reformer could advance a political program, without consideration of the land and its resources. A modern student of the ancient world who wishes to understand the motivations and the actions of people such as these must consider the environment within which they occurred. Robert Sallares said it well: "Any ancient historian who has not immersed himself or herself fully in the problems of ecology can have, at best, only an extremely limited comprehension of the course of history in Classical antiquity."[6] Humans are a species within an ecosystem, so that the condition of the ecosystem as it changes through time influences the direction and development of human affairs. Ecological analysis is, therefore, a crucial means of gaining understanding of human history.

Environmental history, as a subject, is the study of how humans have related to the natural world through time. As a method, it is the application of ecological principles to history. By definition, therefore, it requires familiarity with more than one of the artificial fields into which learning has been divided ever since Aristotle. Ecology is a natural science; history straddles the boundary between the social sciences and the humanities. In addition, to do

3

environmental history properly requires the knowledge of much that is usually considered to lie in such provinces as agriculture, archaeology, botany, climatology, economics, geography, geology, philosophy, technology, zoology, and so on, and the search for useful synthesis.

It has often been remarked that the word *ecology* derives from Greek roots, *oikos* meaning *home* or *house*, and by extension the whole inhabited Earth, and *logos* meaning *reason* or *study*, a common suffix used to indicate a particular science. A survey of all surviving Greek literature shows that a word for ecology (which would have been *oikologia* or something like it) was not coined in ancient times, although significant ecological ideas occur in the writings of philosophers such as Aristotle and Theophrastus, especially in Theophrastus's use of the word *oikeios* to indicate the relationship between a plant species and the environment where it characteristically flourishes.[7] Credit is given to Ernst Haeckel for first using the word *oecologie* in 1866.[8] Haeckel was familiar with the classics and may have had in mind Theophrastus's use of *oikeios*.

Ecology is the study of the interrelationships of organisms with their living and nonliving environments. This study can emphasize either a single species, or the systems within which species live. Species ecology concentrates on the environmental relationships of one species. When *Homo sapiens* is the chosen species the study can be called human ecology; environmental history is an application of human ecology in this sense, and that is what this book attempts to do for the ancient Greeks and Romans. Systems ecology is the study of the relationships of all organisms within a defined area. Such an interacting group of organisms, with its environment, is called an *ecosystem*. An ecosystem can be as small as a pond or as large as the biosphere, the entire complex of the living Earth. In this book, the ecosystem studied is the Mediterranean area, defined broadly both as a basin and a climatic zone, since it was the setting of most of the history of the Greeks and Romans. Historians, interested as they are in human culture, must never forget that on other levels processes are going on that affect humankind profoundly.

Environmental history is significant because it gives perspective to the more traditional concerns of historians: war, diplomacy, politics, law, economics, technology, science, philosophy, art, and literature. Every one of these subjects is connected in essential ways with nature, with the use and meaning of the natural environment. In this book, environment will be understood to include the Earth, with its soil and mineral resources; with its water, both fresh and salt; with its atmosphere, climates, and weather; with its living things, animals and plants from the simplest to the most complex; and with the energy received ultimately from the Sun.

Ancient Environmental Problems

The fact that many of the problems of human ecology as they are now understood also existed in classical times should not come as a surprise. In the chapters that follow, the most vital environmental problems that affected the Greeks and Romans will be discussed: deforestation and overgrazing, which removed vegetative cover; erosion of the land; destruction of wildlife; pollution of air, land, and water; depletion of resources; agricultural decline; and manifold urban difficulties such as food and water supply and sewage disposal. All these problems will be considered in the context of the natural environment of the Mediterranean basin. The city, for example, cannot be discussed in isolation from the countryside upon which it impacts and upon which it depends, for both are part of the same ecosystem. Because of this, it is necessary to analyze the components and dynamics of the Mediterranean ecosystem (chapter 2).

The relationship of the Greeks and Romans to the natural environment was determined in part by their characteristic mental constructions of nature, the topic of chapter 4. The actions of people, after all, did reflect their perceptions and values, even if many of these were confused or contradictory. Ancient attitudes varied from worship of nature to curiosity, desire for prudent use, and greed leading to wasteful exploitation. The Greeks and Romans were seldom deliberately destructive, and they often ameliorated the condition of the world in which they lived by planting parks and gardens and by protecting certain areas. At the same time, natural and economic forces could distort and overwhelm reason, custom, and religion. People were not, and are not, always aware of the long-term results of their actions in the natural world. Intending to sustain balance, they nevertheless upset it. If ancient people adversely affected the natural environment within which they lived, and they certainly did, it is reasonable to suspect that they may have helped to bring about the "decline and fall" of their own civilizations. The end of the Roman Empire, and of the ancient world in general, therefore had an ecological dimension. This is the subject of the final chapter, but it is foreshadowed in much of the discussion throughout the book.

The Sources of Evidence
for Ancient Environmental History

The evidence on which this ancient environmental history depends comes from a wide variety of sources. Much information can be derived from ancient literature of many different types, including both poetry and prose, and from papyri and inscriptions. Ancient Greek and Latin history, philosophy, drama, epic and lyric poetry, scientific and technical treatises, correspondence, and legal documents contain numerous references to environmental problems, although only a few include extensive discussions. The richness of this line of evidence is not as well known as it should be, since only a few modern historians of the ancient world have concerned themselves with it until recently.

Archaeology is another key source of information about the ancient environment, particularly more recent classical archaeology. Earlier work in this field concentrated on the recovery of works of art and monumental architecture, but now, emulating work in other areas of the world, archaeologists in the Mediterranean have turned to ecological data. There is much more to be done. Studies of whole countrysides, including agricultural settlement, industrial sites, commercial ports, urban patterns outside the monumental centers of cities, and the systematic collection of animal and plant materials, have broadened the base for interpretation of the problems discussed in this book, and will undoubtedly continue to do so. Among the best of these surveys are those of Messenia by William A. MacDonald and associates, and of the southern Argolid by Tjeerd H. Van Andel and associates.[9]

A further significant category of evidence comes from scientific studies that provide information on environmental changes during the historical period. Paleobotany, paleoecology, paleoclimatology, and similar specialties have gained new tools in recent years and are making immense strides in understanding. Palynology, the study of pollen deposits, combined with radiocarbon and other methods of dating, has enabled the reconstruction of the succession of vegetation during ancient times at many points within the Mediterranean region. In the not-too-distant future, a much closer correlation of this information with historical events, and with the mass of data being gathered on past climatic changes, will be possible. It is to be hoped that conferences at which historians, archaeologists, and scientists in these last-named fields can talk to each other and share their results across disciplinary lines will become more usual in the future. At the moment, it must be said that for some areas and in some spans of time sufficient evidence allows us to form a convincing picture of what was occurring, but for most times and places too little is known. Additional study of this whole question will prove rewarding, adding critical pieces to the puzzle of world environmental history, an understanding of which is crucial in providing perspective to today's ecological crisis. The purpose of this book is not to prove that environment determined the events of history, but to examine the ways in which human activities and the environment interacted in positive and negative ways.

Two

The Environment: Life, Land, and Sea in the Mediterranean Region

To understand Greek and Roman environmental problems, it is necessary to place them in the context of the special environment in which they occurred and with which they interacted. Fernand Braudel, in his magisterial study of early modern Mediterranean history, pointed out that the environment was not just a background for the human drama, but an actor—or, it may be said, a considerable number of the cast—in the play.[1] It is important to examine the constituent elements and dynamics of the environment at the outset, since they will be present and active throughout this study. As Braudel remarked, "Woe betide the historian who thinks that this preliminary interrogation is unnecessary, that the Mediterranean as an entity needs no definition because it has long been clearly defined [and] is instantly recognizable."[2] This comment is as applicable to the ecosystem as it is to geography. It is essential to understand ecological processes in order to know how human beings affect them and produce environmental problems.

The predominant setting of the Greek and Roman civilizations was the Mediterranean basin, an area dominated by the sea that gives it its name. It includes adjacent parts of Europe, Asia, and

Africa. This zone can be defined in several ways: culturally, histori-
cally, physiographically, climatically, and so on, but for our purposes it is best to regard it as a biogeographical region. Greek
civilization was almost entirely a Mediterranean phenomenon, although Alexander the Great and his successors temporarily extended it east as far as India and Central Asia. The Romans, also
a Mediterranean people, dominated a significant area north of the
Alps for a longer period of time. But the centers of both societies,
and the bulk of their territories and populations, were always in
the Mediterranean basin.

The Mediterranean area can also be described as an ecosystem,
a changing community of animals and plants together with the
physical surroundings on which they depend: the earth, water,
atmosphere, and the fluctuating flow of energy. Human beings
interact with, affect, and are affected by all the components of this
ecosystem. The Mediterranean ecosystem contains many smaller
communities of living organisms that could be considered, with
their physical settings, to be separate ecosystems, but the entire
region possesses enough common characteristics to make it a useful
unit of study. It differs significantly from the rest of the three
continents on which it impinges: Europe north of the Alps, the
Africa of the Sahara and further south, and the vast land mass of
Asia to the east. It is a region that has felt the results of human
actions as long and as extensively as almost any place on Earth.

Climate

When historical environmental changes are noted, the question
often arises as to whether they are the results of climatic alterations
(discussed further in chapter 11). Climate gives the Mediterranean
area its most recognizable character. Although the zone extends
from the rainy Adriatic to the margins of the African desert, the
general impression of the climate is agreeable: sunny and dry, but
moderated by sea breezes. Visitors from less fortunate lands have
often found it attractive, even seductive. The "land of the lotus
eaters" was, after all, a Mediterranean place that travelers found
too bountiful and seductive to leave. Nonetheless, at certain times

9

and in certain places the region can be dangerously hot, cold, or stormy, affecting human activities such as sea transport and agriculture.

The Mediterranean climate is unique among the Earth's climates. It is relatively dependable, with two distinguishable seasons: a long, hot, dry summer extending from April to October, and a mild but sometimes rainy, windy winter the rest of the year. The summer is longer in the southern and eastern parts of the basin. People have deferred to the two faces of the year by making summer the time for travel, especially by sea—and the time for war—and winter the season for peace, cultivation, and staying home.

Average rainfall is typically between 15 and 35 inches per year, almost all of it in winter. Still, the wet season is not constantly rainy, because most of the precipitation comes in a few heavy downpours. The total amount varies greatly from year to year; one year may bring twice the normal amount, another only half. It also differs from place to place. Port Said, Egypt, in the dry southeast annually averages 2 inches of precipitation, while Crikvenica, Croatia, on the northern Adriatic coast, measures 181 inches, some of which falls as snow. Mountain ranges catch the moisture-laden winds that tend to blow from the west, producing orographic precipitation, leaving the eastern slopes in a dry "rain shadow." For example, Corcyra on the western edge of Greece has an average of 52 inches per year, while Larissa, east of the Pindus massif, receives only 20. Mountains often breed thunderstorms in the summer, and flash floods can roll down otherwise dry riverbeds.

The nearness of the sea moderates the temperature in many places around the Mediterranean. Using Fahrenheit, the difference between the average temperature of the hottest and coolest months is often only 25 degrees, and between day and night about 14 degrees. In Palermo, Sicily, there is no month with an average temperature below 50 degrees, and near sea level anywhere in the Mediterranean, temperatures below freezing are quite rare. Summer temperatures of 80 degrees or 90 degrees in a maritime climate are fairly oppressive, so that the afternoon nap is a common custom in Mediterranean lands. Winter snow is a brief novelty, except in the mountains. The higher one climbs, the colder it is likely to get, so that shepherds wear heavy cloaks with good reason. The tallest peaks are snowcapped all winter, although usually not in summer; glaciers occur only in the Alps and Pyrenees.

Winds The Greeks personified the winds and often portrayed them as winged figures: Boreas, the North Wind; Notus, the South; Zephyrus, the West, and so on.[3] They did not agree on the names or number of them; Athens' Tower of the Winds has reliefs with the names of eight, but Aristotle distinguished twelve.[4] The character and prevalence of the winds varied from place to place.

In the summer, a cool air mass with high pressure prevails over western and central Europe, pushing winds of dry continental air across the Mediterranean Sea toward the Sahara and the deserts of Asia, where heated air is rising. These winds are generally northwesterly, but northeasterly on the North African coast and in the Aegean. In ancient Greece, they were called *etesian*, or annual winds. When not too strong, etesian winds assist sailing unless one happens to want to go northeast, and they make it important to choose harbors that are sheltered from that direction. Around large land masses such as Spain and Asia Minor, sea winds tend to blow inland, especially during the day, to replace heated air that is rising.

In winter, low-pressure cells form over the Mediterranean and move eastward with the global circulation of air at latitudes between 30 and 45 degrees north, and the jet stream shifts into the region, bringing westerly or southwesterly rain-bearing winds. Aristotle called Lips, the Southwest Wind, a "wet wind."[5] But the warmer air over the sea rises and colder continental air rushes in from Europe in the form of dry northerlies that are often violent. Among local names for these are *mistral* in the Rhone valley and *bora* along the Dalmatian coast. Air attracted by the same lows from Africa in the form of the *sirocco* is much hotter, and bears a heavy load of sand and dust from the Sahara. It picks up moisture as it crosses the sea, and can produce rain that is red from the dust. Where the continental air roars down the mountainside as a *föhn* (a dry wind that heats as it descends), as it does on the north side of the Atlas Mountains of North Africa, it is reminiscent of a blast furnace.

11

Outdoor Life   The Mediterranean climate is conducive to open-air activities for much of the year. The Athenian Ecclesia, or Assembly, conducted its business outdoors, as did several other political bodies. Theaters had no roofs, and athletes competed nude in gymnasiums and stadiums. Temples had their altars outside, and marketplaces were surrounded by airy colonnades. When the owners could afford it, houses were built around open courtyards that were arranged to be shaded in the summer and to take advantage of solar heat in the winter. The Greeks and Romans were fond of an active life lived out-of-doors.

Mediterranean light, given the lower levels of pollution in ancient times, was noted for its clarity and brilliance. This makes understandable the attention given to lines and shadows in architecture, such as the use of fluted columns and sculptured reliefs.

The Mediterranean Sea

Since the sea is the dominant geographical fact that ties the Mediterranean lands together and gives them a shared character, it is appropriate to discuss it before the land. The Mediterranean is the world's largest inland sea, with an area of almost a million square miles (1,143,000 if the Black Sea is included). It penetrates far into the land mass of Europe, Asia, and Africa, forming islands, peninsulas, bays, inlets, straits, and isthmuses. There is an intimate interplay between sea and land; the Mediterranean area has a strongly littoral aspect. The sea extends 2,300 miles from Gibraltar to the Levantine coast, with an average width of 500 miles from north to south. Its presence at 30 to 45 degrees latitude, where similar climatic zones occur elsewhere in the world, is responsible for the great extent of the Mediterranean climatic zone proper. Mediterranean-type climates in California, Chile, South Africa, and Australia are limited by mountain and desert barriers.

Compared with the larger oceans, the Mediterranean is not extremely deep. Its average depth is about 5,000 feet, as against 12,500 feet for the world's oceans. But it cannot be called a shallow sea; except in the Adriatic, its continental shelves are narrow, and the sea bottom has many ridges and chasms. The greatest depth, 16,706 feet, is in the Matapan Trench of the Ionian basin.

The Mediterranean is almost landlocked; its single natural connection with the rest of the world's oceans is through the Strait of Gibraltar, or Pillars of Heracles (Hercules), where the water is only 9 miles wide and 1,200 feet deep. A result of this almost complete separation is the relative absence of tides within the Mediterranean Sea, since the gravitational pull of the Moon and Sun can act only on the comparatively small volume of water in the basin itself. The tidal range exceeds 3 feet only at Gibraltar itself and on the east coast of Tunisia, and the average throughout the basin is 4 to 6 inches.[6] The connection to the outer sea is extremely important, however, because the rate of evaporation of water at the surface of the Mediterranean is exceptionally high, amounting to 57 inches per year, which is the same as 150,000 cubic yards per second. Rainfall replaces only 27 percent of this loss, and an additional 6 percent is replaced by rivers such as the Nile, Ebro, Rhone, Tiber, and Po. Another 6 percent comes from the Black Sea through the Bosporus and Dardanelles, leaving the vast majority, 61 percent of the Mediterranean's water budget, to be made up by the Atlantic. A surface current flows inward through the strait along the North African coast. Underneath, a smaller and slower current of heavier, saltier Mediterranean water flows into the Atlantic at a depth of about 1,000 feet.

The high evaporation rate of the Mediterranean makes it much more saline than the oceans. It is not getting more salty, however, because the outgoing current carries an amount of salts equal to that being concentrated by evaporation. The water that enters the Mediterranean comes only from near the surface of the Atlantic, which is warmer than the depths, and it is further heated by the sun in the Mediterranean itself. The sea is therefore the warmest large body of water at its latitude, reaching as high as 88 degrees in August off the coast of Libya. There is no major temperature gradient between water near the surface and in the depths; the temperature of the deep Mediterranean is 55 degrees. At times in geological history, the straits have been closed and the sea dried up almost completely. Salt deposits on the sea bottom indicate that this last happened about 6 million years ago, when there were no human beings to witness it.

The floor of the Mediterranean is covered by a layer of yellow-brown sediments about 9,000 feet deep. These are predominantly lime, with some clay and sand, intruded upon by extensive salt beds. Underlying these strata is another of blue mud. Fine riverine muds overlie the strata near river mouths, and their deposition is strongly affected by erosion caused by human activities.

The Mediterranean Lands

The Mediterranean basin has varied patterns of land, but in most places it is mountainous, with rugged and complex ranges. Between them are sheltered valleys and occasional alluvial plains. The typical aspect of the landscape in this region is that of a sea backed by mountains. In many places, such as Mount Athos or the base of the Maritime Alps, the mountains fall directly into the sea. The only extensive flat regions are found north of the Black Sea and along the dry eastern section of the coast of North Africa.

Mountains and Vulcanism   The peaks themselves are not unusually high, but they appear bold and beautiful because their entire rise from sea level is so visible. The highest mountain in Greece is Olympus, at 9,568 feet. In Italy, Monte Corno in the Apennines is almost exactly as high, but Etna on Sicily rises to 10,902 feet, and Monte Viso, a high point of the Alps near the Mediterranean, reaches 12,602 feet. Spain has the Pyrenees in the north and the Sierra Nevada in the south, both of which exceed 11,000 feet in elevation. The Atlas Mountains of North Africa reach 13,671 feet inland at Mount Toubkal, Morocco. Eastward are found Mount Sinai (8,649 feet) in Egypt, Mount Lebanon (10,129 feet), and the Taurus Range of southern Asia Minor (12,251 feet). East of the Black Sea in Georgia (ancient Colchis) rises the highest peak of all in the region, Mount Elbrus in the Caucasus, 18,481 feet high. But it is the number and extent of the mountains of the Mediterranean, rather than their elevation, that is most impressive.

The high relief of this zone is due to the interaction between two huge continental masses, the northward-moving African Plate and the Eurasian Plate. In their collision over a period of millions of years, smaller plates split off and squeezed between them, and mountains were thrust up as strata were folded and deformed. Most of the present mountains of the Mediterranean region were raised in this process during the Tertiary Age of the Cenozoic Era. Earthquakes, often of disastrous intensity, can be expected from year to year. In this tectonically active region, the heated magma of the Earth's mantle sporadically finds its way to the surface and creates volcanoes. Etna, the highest Mediterranean volcano, has erupted frequently, "shooting hot, unapproachable floods of flame."[7] Others of note are Vulcano itself and the almost constantly active Stromboli, two islands in the Lipari group north of Sicily.[8] Vesuvius is famous for its burial of Pompeii and other neighboring towns. Several of the Aegean islands are volcanic, including Melos, Lemnos, and Thera (Santorini). The latter had a catastrophic eruption that destroyed most of the island and which can now be dated to the 1620s B.C. Through deformation and vulcanism, many deposits of useful and valuable metals and minerals were formed.

Rocks and Soil Due to the forces just described, the Mediterranean lands present a complicated geological aspect; in some places, series of strata have actually been turned upside down. The oldest exposed rocks are parts of the underlying continental plates, which are composed of crystalline rocks such as granite, sometimes metamorphosed by pressure and heat into gneisses. Other much deformed rocks called ophiolites are the remnants of former undersea ridges. Sedimentary rocks are widespread. The most characteristic rock of the Mediterranean basin is limestone, calcium carbonate precipitated from seawater in the form of the shells of sea creatures.

Soils are largely formed from the parent material, that is, the underlying rock. Since limestone predominates in the Mediterranean basin, calcareous soils are common. Because the climate is relatively dry, xeromorphic soils are prevalent. Two typical soils of this type are *terra fusca* and *terra rossa* (black earth and red earth); the former develops under forest cover and the latter under deforested conditions. Both are rich in clay and rock debris. Places with volcanic soils were noted for their richness; Theophrastus said that the soil of the volcanic island of Melos was "wonderfully productive, for it is good both for grain and olives, and fairly good for vines."[9] Except where erosion has occurred, and as long as water is available, Mediterranean soils tend to be well suited to agriculture.

Living Communities: Plants and Animals

An amazing variety of living things flourishes in the Mediterranean ecosystem. Various parts of the basin support different communities of plants and animals, interacting with one another.[10] Each community is adapted to its particular location and climate; as Strabo noted, humans and animals are shaped by the same climatic factors.[11] The number of Mediterranean plant species greatly exceeds that of the areas immediately to the north and south. Greece alone, for example, has 6,000 flowering plants, compared with 2,113 in Britain, which has twice Greece's land area. One reason for the diversity in the Mediterranean zone is that it escaped the glacial sheets of the Ice Age, which scoured northern Europe as recently as 11,000 years ago.

Plants   Mediterranean vegetation occurs in life zones whose limits correspond roughly to a combination of elevation and latitude. Each is affected differently by the activities of human beings. The lowest of the zones, from sea level to about 3,000 feet in elevation, contains the typical vegetation of the Mediterranean climatic zone proper. Before human interference, this was for the most part a belt of forests dominated by pines and evergreen oaks, with dense stands of broad-leaved trees near watercourses.

Also at this elevation occurs the most distinctive plant association of the present-day Mediterranean basin, the *maquis*, a brushy cover of hardy shrubs that varies from sparse to impenetrable.[12] The bushes or small trees of which it is composed rarely exceed 25 feet in height. Maquis often establishes itself after forest removal and can be a sign of disturbed habitat, but in many districts it is the climax, that is, the biotic community that perpetuates itself

16

under the prevailing conditions of soil and climate. The most prominent species are broad sclerophylls, which are evergreen trees with leaves adapted to drought by thick hairy, leathery, oily, or waxy coverings. Maquis plants also survive in dry conditions by having long root systems, high osmotic pressure, and the evergreen ability to utilize winter moisture. All the species possess adaptations that enable them to reestablish themselves after fire, by recuperating rapidly, sprouting from buried root crowns, germinating from seeds that respond to heat or spread into a burned area on the winds or by other means and find bare or scorched soil a congenial place to germinate.[13] Typical maquis plants are holm and kermes oaks, junipers, arbutus, laurel, myrtle, tree heather, rockrose, broom, mastic tree, and rosemary.

In harsh locations, or after repeated destruction by clearing, browsing, or fire, maquis is replaced by *garigue* or "rock heath," a tough, low community of shrubs that are often spiny.[14] These are rarely more than 20 inches high, and therefore often lower than the rocks among which they grow. Among the more than 200 common garigue plants are many spice-bearing herbs such as basil, garlic, hyssop, lavender, oregano, rosemary, rue, sage, savory, and thyme. Their pleasant odors waft far out to sea, especially during the spring flowering season.

Where the conditions are even more extreme or overexploited, not even garigue survives, and a winter grassland or "steppe" occurs.[15] It has many annual species that grow in the cooler, moister half of the year, and perennials that grow from rootstocks, tubers, or bulbs. Like the garigue, the grassland blooms in spring before the desiccating winds of summer. Species that survive grazing do best here; most prevalent are asphodel, mullein, sea squill, thistle, and members of the buttercup, composite, grass, legume, lily, mint, mustard, parsley, pink, and rose families.

The deciduous forest zone occurs, where rainfall permits, above the true Mediterranean zone just described, and extending upward to around 4,500 feet, and is sometimes called the upper Mediterranean zone. The dominant trees are deciduous oaks, elm, beech, chestnut, ash, and hornbeam. These forests are seen most often in the mountains of the northern and western parts of the basin;

17

elsewhere they have been eliminated by human use over the centuries, or in some districts this life zone may never have been present.

At even greater altitudes the Mediterranean mountain zone, or coniferous forest zone, extends upward to treeline, which is found at about 7,100 feet in the Maritime Alps, 7,500 feet on Mount Olympus, and 9,350 feet in the Atlas Mountains. In undisturbed conditions, a high forest of pine, silver fir, cedar, and juniper flourishes here, interspersed with open meadows. This is the zone of the famous cedar forests of the eastern and southern Mediterranean.[16] Precipitation is higher in this subalpine zone, taking the form of snow in the winter and thunderstorms in the summer. The growing season, limited by winter cold rather than dryness, takes place in the summer.

Above treeline is an alpine tundra of dwarfed plants and lichens. Tiny flowering plants are adapted to a short summer growing season, during which they must bloom and set seed quickly before frosts return. On the bare rocks of the summits, snow may persist until the hottest part of the summer. Glaciers are virtually nonexistent on the Mediterranean mountains proper, although present on more northerly ones, such as the Alps, that border the basin.

To the south and east, the limits of the Mediterranean zone are set by deserts. Largest is the Sahara, which reaches the shore of the sea in parts of Egypt and Libya. Elsewhere, there are the large Syrian and Arabian deserts, and a smaller one in central Turkey. Rainfall varies from zero to 1 inch, and as a result there are vast stretches where no plants are visible. But plants have evolved stratagems to survive in more marginal situations. Long root systems, reduced transpiration, extremely short life cycles that are triggered by water, and devices to reduce palatability can be observed in various desert plants. The common genera of plants in the desert life zone are anabasis, artemisia (sagebrush), astragalus, atriplex, centaurea (thistle), convolvulus, ephedra, halogeton, haloxylon, origanum, retama, stachys, tamarisk, varthemia, and zygophyllum (caltrop). In oases and along better-watered wadis, including places where there is water not far below the surface, more hydrophytic plants can grow.

Animals The dominant vegetation, or flora, in each of the zones just described supports an assemblage of animal life, or fauna, that is characteristic of that particular zone. Plants are the food producers of every ecosystem, and all animal life, including the human species, depends on them. Some animals, the herbivores, consume plants directly, while others, the carnivores, prey on other animals. All animals and plants, before and after they die, may provide nutriment for decomposers such as bacteria, molds, and microscopic animals. Species do not destroy one another when they eat each other; they maintain a fluctuating balance of numbers. Among the ancients, Plotinus recognized that predators and prey are equally necessary to biodiversity, the abundance of different kinds of life essential to the world.[17] The variety of animals found in the aboriginal Mediterranean basin was even greater than that of plants, so that it is impossible to list them all. Just as people have changed plant communities in the basin, most notably by removing the forests, so have they also changed the distribution of animals by altering their habitat, reducing their numbers, causing extinction, and by deliberately or inadvertently introducing domestic or other exotic species. This process will be discussed more fully in chapter 6. The primeval fauna of the Mediterranean was of the Palearctic type characteristic of Europe, with the addition of some species more representative of Asia and Africa. There were a number that occurred only in the local area, although a lower proportion than among plants.

Some of the wild mammals that were present in the Mediterranean region when humans arrived were herbivores that are relatives of domestic animals such as goats, sheep, cattle, swine, donkeys, and horses, although their domestication probably took place in areas outside the basin. Large herbivores such as bison and deer ranged the forest. The hippopotamus was common in the Nile and other African and Asiatic rivers, and the desert margins had a fauna with similarities to that of Kenya and Tanzania in modern times. Smaller plant eaters are ubiquitous, including rabbits, hares, mice, voles, porcupines, and squirrels.

What ecologists call the next trophic level consists of animals that eat other animals: the carnivores and insectivores. The larger

19

predators include lions, leopards, lynxes, hyenas, jackals, foxes, and wolves, then present on the European side of the sea as well as the Afro-Asiatic. Omnivores such as the bear and Barbary ape eat both animal and vegetable foods. There are smaller carnivores such as wildcats and weasels, and insectivores like the hedgehogs, shrews, and bats.

The Mediterranean ecosystem includes a variety of reptiles and amphibians. There are several kinds of tortoise, both herbivorous and insectivorous. Snakes of many species, both poisonous and nonpoisonous, prey mostly on small animals, helping to keep their numbers under control. Small lizards such as the insectivorous gecko and chameleon, including one poisonous species, can be found. The huge carnivorous crocodile sprawled on the banks of rivers in Africa and Palestine. Amphibians, including the frogs of Aristophanic fame, toads, newts, fire salamanders, and others, as a rule insectivores, are found near water.

The ancients were familiar with many species of birds, and used them for divination, which indicates that they observed them carefully. Like other animals, birds can be herbivorous; some, such as finches, pigeons, and sparrows, are seed eaters. Others are carnivorous: eagles, owls, hawks, and other raptors. Some specialize in carrion: vultures, ravens, and magpies, for example. Great numbers are insectivores, and this makes them important to the ecological balance; to list only a few, there are swallows, thrushes, warblers, nightingales, starlings, and the crested hoopoe. The migratory habits of birds provide transfers of matter and energy into and out of the ecosystem at various times of the year. There are summer visitors (oriole, warblers), winter visitors (short-eared owl, gulls), commuters between the northern and southern Mediterranean (avocet, wryneck), and year-round residents (buntings, wall creeper). One Mediterranean bird, the rock dove, adapted to human buildings and has spread around the world as the common pigeon.

A notably large fraction of the animals in the ecosystem is made up of insects, whether one thinks of number of species, number of individuals, or total biomass. They perform many functions in ecological processes. Many of them, from bees, beetles, butterflies, and moths to the musical cicada, cricket, and locusts, eat plants.

Insects that consume animal material include praying mantises, wasps, hornets, and some beetles. Literature pays attention with good reason to lice, fleas, flies, and mosquitoes, which include human blood in their diets. Various species of ants are herbivorous, some carnivorous, and some practice mold agriculture or aphid pastoralism. Numerous insects, such as the dung beetle, assist in process of decomposition.

Among other herbivorous arthropods are the wood louse and millipede. Centipedes, spiders, and scorpions are predominantly insectivorous. Snails and slugs, which are land molluscs, are destructive to plants but serve as food for predators, even humans at times. Annelids such as earthworms also perform the helpful function of soil aeration and fertilization, although the ancients did not discover this.

Aquatic Life The various climates, water depths, degrees of salinity, and benthic forms of the Mediterranean Sea provide a variety of habitats for aquatic life. Here life depends on food producers such as algae and phytoplanktons, and also on nutrients washed down from the land. More than 500 species of fish are found in the sea, along with algae, corals, shellfish, and sponges. Most sea life is found in the upper layers where light penetrates. The western basin has a greater variety of species than the saltier eastern one. The total quantity of marine organisms, however, is not particularly large compared to the oceans, either in number of species or in the total weight of living organisms per unit of volume of seawater. This is the result of several factors: high salinity, the barriers to entry from other seas, the relative lack of volume in river flow, the narrowness of the continental shelves that are nurseries of fish populations, and the fact that the lack of a temperature gradient in this relatively warm sea is not conducive to the cold vertical currents that favor the production of phytoplankton.

It should not be supposed that Mediterranean fisherfolk found their work unprofitable. In ancient times fishing was a significant economic activity, although catches were mostly destined for local markets. There were 120 species of economic importance, from sharks and rays to eels, sardines, and anchovies. Flounder and sole

21

lurk on the sea bottom. Tyrian purple dye, made from the murex or rock whelk, was once a principal product shipped from the Phoenician coast.[18] Large quantities of sponges, brought up by divers, were exported from Greece.

Mammals of the Mediterranean waters include whales, seals, and dolphins, all of which count as predators of other animal life of various sizes. Birds are well adapted to depend on the sea, whether frequenting the shore (snipe, sandpiper), the surface (gulls, terns), or diving under the surface (cormorants). There are numerous other seabirds including grebes, pelicans, and puffins. Several species of sea turtles, which are marine reptiles, were found.

Lower animals of the salt water are numerous, interesting, and some of them are considered delicacies and sought after by fisherfolk. There are crustaceans (barnacles, shrimp, prawns, lobsters, crabs); molluscs, including monovalves (limpets, tritons), bivalves (oysters, mussels, clams), and cephalopods (squid, octopus, nautilus); echinoderms (starfish, urchins, sea-cucumbers); and coelenterates (jellyfish, sea anemones, sponges, coral). Some of the latter were confused with plants by the ancient Greeks and Romans.

Rivers and lakes provided freshwater habitats for ecosystems composed of many species. The eels of Lake Copais in Boeotia were famous in the time before that large body of water was drained. Other fish in the lakes and streams include carp, perch, and catfish. Anadromous fish such as the salmon-trout and sturgeon were known to spend most of their lives in the salt water, but ascended rivers to spawn. The hippopotamus and crocodile have already been mentioned; the Nile was a major ecosystem with many fish, and like other fresh waters, supported a huge population of aquatic birds, including ducks, geese, ibises, herons, and egrets.

Conclusion

The Mediterranean ecosystem is large, productive, and complex. Powered by the energy of a sun that is relatively seldom obscured, the yearly cycle of weather allows plants to grow, and they, depending on the sun's energy for photosynthesis, produce food for the whole interacting structure of the community of life. Its setting is a unique mixture of mountainous, unstable land, and a tideless, omnipresent inland sea.

One can hardly imagine this cradle of civilizations without human inhabitants, but for most of its geological history, that was its condition. Then, for a long and formative time, the human species was simply one of the strands in the web of the ecosystem, held in delicate relationship to all the other strands, physical and biological. But humankind changed that relationship. The various activities adopted by the growing numbers of human beings: hunting, fishing, gathering, forestry, agriculture, pastoralism, mining, industry, and urbanism, began and accelerated the process of unbalancing the ecosystem. This process will be investigated in the following chapters. Balance is, in the long run, essential to human survival. Balance need not mean the absence of change, however. The ecosystem is resilient and can absorb and adapt to change of certain kinds, and to a certain degree. To search for an analogy, one can say that its balance is not like that of a pyramid, solid and immovable without destruction. It is not the unstable balance of scales, where a weight added on one side must be compensated for by an exactly equal weight on the other in order to keep the arm from swinging out of true. It is the living balance of an eagle in flight, which can compensate for changes in the currents of air by altering the position of its wings and tail. But even an eagle cannot survive a tornado. Beyond limits that exist in the arrangement of nature, the ecosystem cannot maintain or recover its productivity and its ability to support human activities. The ancient Greeks and Romans reflected at times on those limits, but never established exactly what they were. Neither has modern science, although it has come much closer. Sometimes the Greeks and Romans inadvertently exceeded the limits of the natural system that supported them, and they suffered as a result. It is in the interest of modern society to treat the experience of the ancients as a kind of experiment, to attempt to see what mistakes were made and what the results of those mistakes were, not only to understand the distant past, but also to comprehend the far more rapid, extensive, and dangerous experiment in imbalance upon which contemporary humankind has embarked.

Three

Ecological Crises
in Earlier Societies

I n light of the present state of knowledge of fossil and genetic evidence, it seems that the human species evolved outside the Mediterranean basin, most likely in East Africa.[1] There, in an abundant ecosystem, early humans subsisted as omnivores, gathering useful plants, catching fish and crustaceans, and hunting mammals. Sometimes they were prey, too, but their ability to invent hunting tools eventually made it possible for them to kill the largest and most dangerous animals. They made hand axes from stones and discovered the uses of fire for cooking, keeping warm, and driving wild animals. They devised the spear and the spear-casting lever (atlatl), the fishhook, and later the bow and arrow, using materials such as wood, antler, bone, and stone. This level of material culture is called Paleolithic (Old Stone) Age. It was the culture humans brought with them when they arrived on the margins of the Mediterranean Sea hundreds of thousands of years ago, and further developed as they lived there through the long millennia of the Ice Age. The earliest way of life of the human race was this culture of hunting, fishing, and gathering. It endured for most of prehistory, indeed for more than nine-tenths of the time that humans have existed, and lay importantly as tradition, ritual, and custom below the civilized veneer of the classical societies.

Culture and technology, which represent adaptations to the natural environment, undoubtedly became more complex and potent as time passed. They enabled humans to make ever more sweeping changes in the ecosystem, although not to live outside it. Early humans were dependent in a very direct way on the natural environment for their daily food, drink, clothing, and shelter. Their total numbers and the size of their groups were therefore limited. Too many people could not crowd into a small territory without depleting the food supply and consequently either starving or being forced to leave. A natural balance was thus maintained between human numbers and the carrying capacity of the local environment.

The Role of Tradition   This balance was also supported and maintained by an oral tradition, complete with stories embodying customary views of the world, creation, the gods, animals, methods of hunting and gathering, and principles of family relationships, initiations, birth, and death. The broad characteristic outline of this tradition, even though these people had not as yet developed systems of writing, can be surmised through archaeology, the surviving evidence of their art, and comparative ethnography. Those who shared this tradition tended to look at the world as a place animated with spirits and spiritual power. This was true of animals and plants, but also of rocks, springs, rivers, and mountains. Therefore, these people regarded the universe as a sacred realm where everything was alive and conscious, including the Earth and the sky. They approached animals and plants respectfully, killing them only when necessary, and honoring them with ceremonies even after they killed them. They treated themselves not as separate individuals, but as integral members of a tribal community, with the duty to provide the group with food, protect it against enemies, and seek power for it from the spiritual side of nature through visions, disciplines, and the repetition of rituals. Certain tribal members favored by experiences of closeness to other

living creatures became shamans, identifying with animals, wearing
their skins, horns, and skulls, and dancing with the movements of
the animals they impersonated. All members of the tribe venerated
the tribal elders because they contained the memory, accumulated
knowledge, and wise judgment of the community.

When each of these traditional convictions is examined, its
ecological function can be seen, in that it helps the tribe to adapt
to the local environment and use it without destroying it. For
example, the hunter had an incredible respect for the prey, and a
great degree of knowledge of the animal. Surviving Paleolithic
carvings and paintings reflect this. The hunter got ready for a hunt
by chanting, washing, and abstaining from food, sex, and the use
of certain words, such as the true name of the animal that was the
object of the hunt. Then the hunter prayed to assure the animal
that the tribe had great need for its flesh and would treat it with
homage and gratitude, and to urge it to give itself willingly. The
animal was stalked, slain with as little suffering as possible, and
the dead body treated with ceremonies to honor it. So treated, it
was believed that the animal's spirit would consent to being reborn
and killed again for the benefit of the tribe. We can find ancient
literary evidence for certain common rules that would have encouraged conservation, such as one that forbids taking a mother bird
together with its eggs or young.[2] Others cautioned the hunter not
to kill more animals than were needed, not to waste meat, to leave
at least a male and female so that an entire herd would not be
destroyed, and not to kill the first one seen of the species that the
hunter was seeking. There was also a widespread belief that animals
were protected by a watchful god, a Lord or Lady of Wild Animals,
who would reward good hunters and punish reckless ones.[3] Compa-
rable beliefs and methods were characteristic of gatherers in their
treatment of plants. Many tribes maintained annual patterns of use
that left parts of their hunting and gathering territories undisturbed
for long periods, allowing the species there to recover.

Ecological Crises of the Paleolithic Age   Early hunters and gatherers
were not wandering nomads in the usual understanding of the
term; most often they inhabited home territories whose topogra-

phy, vegetation, and wildlife they knew very well. Their subsistence, population, and health depended directly upon the condition of the local ecosystem. The hunting-gathering economy provided feedback in both short and long terms. Taking too many animals or plants of a critical species resulted in reduction of numbers or even extinction in the tribal hunting range, a memorable disaster for the tribe. Such events had occurred in the past history of every group, and they became part of traditions that were preserved. Prohibitions against indiscriminate slaughter appeared and were strengthened as the eventual result of repeated experiences of this kind.

The Paleolithic period had its ecological crises, however. In spite of traditions that taught rudimentary conservation, the hunters and gatherers could not leave nature untouched. Their traditional taboos would never have developed if mistakes had not been made, and in any case traditional teachings are notably resistant to change even when alteration in social, economic, and ecological conditions demands it. They persist even after they have become destructive.

Hunting and domestication altered the zoological picture. It has often been maintained that the pressure of Stone Age hunting drove many of the larger animals of the Pleistocene period to extinction, or at least acted together with the climatic change at the end of the Ice Age to hasten their disappearance. Some of the animals that vanished from the Mediterranean ecosystem at that time were rivals of humans as predators, or predators upon humans, such as the cave bear and cave hyena. Others were huge herbivores, such as the mammoth and rhinoceros, good sources of food, but not amenable to preservation through semidomestication, as the reindeer was. The present range of the domestic reindeer has climate and vegetation quite similar to the environment of more southerly Europe during the glaciation, and the way of life of their herders could easily have evolved from that of the Paleolithic hunters by a long process of association in which people came to control the movements of the herds and to protect them. The dog became the first true domesticate of these early times. Its wolflike ancestor was an animal that lived in packs, whose attachments shifted to human groups that adopted puppies.

Fire was certainly "the first great force employed by man."[4]
Hunters periodically set fire to forests, brushlands, and grasslands
in order to drive animals and to encourage the growth of grass as
a source of food for the grazing animals that were often their
quarry. This often resulted in the destruction of woodland and its
replacement by grassland over large areas. But early hunters were
aware of times and places to set fires so that they would be most
suited to their purposes. They wanted to avoid anything that would
harm their hunting territories. Fire is a natural phenomenon, and
in areas that are not burned periodically, lightning can start fire-
storms, so judicious burning may have served as a preventive
measure. Although hunters and gatherers made important impacts
on ecosystems, they intended to maintain and often succeeded in
maintaining balance with them. Indeed, they had little choice in
the matter, since if they damaged the local ecosystem, they would
suffer.

The Invention of Agriculture:
The Neolithic Age

The domestication of animals and plants caused such a radical
change in humankind's relationship to the natural environment
that it is justifiably called the "Agricultural Revolution," even
though the process took thousands of years during the Neolithic
period (New Stone Age). As a result, two new life styles appeared:
the settled agricultural life of farmers and the pastoral way of
herders.

Farming   Farming began independently at least twice in different
parts of the lands neighboring the Mediterranean Sea. There is
evidence of experimentation with planting and harvesting near
pools of water left after the annual flood of the Nile in Egypt after
12,500 B.C., but this effort appears to have been abandoned by
9500 B.C.[5] Numerous farming villages appeared in the Levant and
the northern margins of Mesopotamia between 7000 and 5000 B.C.
There the major crops were barley, wheat, and legumes. Even
before plant domestication, people in Palestine and elsewhere had

used stone-edged sickles to reap wild grain. The early planters also used simple hoes and digging sticks, disturbing the soil to a certain extent.

In many ways, the heritage of hunter-gatherers persisted in the new age. Hunting continued as a means of supplementing the food supply. The reverence formerly felt for wild species was maintained and extended to the domestic ones that had become the sustenance of life. In the large agricultural village of Çatal Hüyük in Anatolia, for example, murals of bulls in black and red decorated the walls and the skulls and horns of bulls, covered by clay and painted with geometric designs, projected from the walls and floors.[6] Domestic sheep and goats were honored in art along with wild leopards and vultures. The Mother Goddess, enthroned between animals or shown in the posture of giving birth with her arms raised in benediction, may well have personified the fertile, life-giving grain. In agricultural societies studied ethnographically, grain was given the title of "Mother." Hunting rituals gave way in the calendar to festivals of planting and harvest. Farm animals were honored as prey species had been, particularly mighty ones like the bull, with its evident strength and fecundating potency. The act of slaughter for food became the supreme form of sacrifice.

The domestication of plants improved the dependability of the food supply and made a more concentrated population possible, but it also required a settled community to care for the growing crops. Much later, the Greek philosopher Theophrastus reflected on this development: "It is mankind, alone among all living things, to which the term 'domesticated' is perhaps strictly appropriate."[7] Humans began to build houses in villages, becoming more sedentary. Farmers selected seed after the harvest for planting in the following year, and in this way new varieties of food crops evolved. Material technology changed irrevocably; stone was worked into smaller and more finely shaped forms. Village dwellers invented pottery, useful for storage and cooking as long as it did not need to be carried very far; hunters would have rejected it because it was heavy and breakable.

With agriculture, human populations became larger and more concentrated, but they did not become healthier. Physical anthropologists have discovered that the farmers of the New Stone Age were shorter than the hunters of the Old Stone Age, suffered more from bad teeth and bones, caught more communicable diseases, and died at an earlier age on the average. This was true both of males and females.[8] A choice had been made, no doubt unconsciously, in favor of quantity of human numbers over quality of human life, at least as far as health and longevity are concerned. It has therefore been suggested that "the agricultural revolution may prove to be the greatest mistake that ever occurred in the biosphere—a mistake not just for *Homo sapiens*, but for the integrity of all ecosystems."[9]

Pastoralism   Another way of life originated when some people, rather than following herds of grazing and browsing mammals just to hunt them, began with help from the already domesticated dog to protect them from predators and control their annual movements. Most herders were not nomadic wanderers, but practiced transhumance, that is, the alternate movement of herds to higher summer and lower winter ranges. Pastoralism developed first in the Near East with goats and sheep, and later with cattle, pigs, and donkeys.[10] These animals are all at home in ecotonal country where grassland, brushland, and forest interpenetrate. Weaving was a useful invention for clothes and also for material to make tents for portable shelter, replacing the animal skins used by hunters.

Ecological Crises of the Neolithic Age   Human ability to change and control the natural environment greatly increased with the agricultural revolution. One of the first problems of agriculturalists was to find suitable soil for cultivation. In limited areas, they could plant seed where flooding and deposition of mud had left clear ground. But in most places, land that would support crops could also support wild vegetation, and did so until it was cleared. More and more land was opened for agriculture, which meant the breaking of grassland sod or the felling and burning of forests. When farmers burned to clear land, they observed that the ashes temporarily enriched the ground. Sometimes, as the soil lost its fertility, they shifted from one place to another. Forests also provided firewood and building materials, and those closest to Neo lithic villages were used up for these purposes. With the removal of plant cover came erosion, so that the hilly districts where farmers have practiced subsistence agriculture for 10,000 years or so are now desiccated, rocky, and almost denuded of useful herbage. These effects were slow and cumulative, and farmers who stayed permanently in the same area tried to find ways of countering them by caring for and restoring the earth. On hillsides, they built terraces to reduce erosion. They learned to let the land lie fallow for one or more years between crops. They discovered the use of manure and other fertilizers, and found that planting legumes enriches the soil for other crops. Neolithic farmers learned by trial and error, and managed to remain in balance with the changing environment for long periods of time.

The herders became a force that could destroy vegetation. They often started fires to open forests for their animals and to encourage the growth of grass. As soon as sheep were domesticated, the danger of overgrazing appeared, since they eat grasses and herbs, roots and all, and their sharp hooves tear up the sod. Goats not only browse most kinds of shrubs, but climb right up into trees to eat the foliage, and they eagerly consume seedlings, thus preventing forest regeneration. Cattle munch all the palatable green things they can reach, including leaves on the lower branches of trees, and herders would lop off higher branches for them to eat. Baring the soil by overgrazing accelerated erosion. The movement to different pastures spread the damage, but made it less intensive. Balancing the destructive effects to a certain extent was the return of nutrients to the soil in the form of manure.

The people of the agricultural villages and pastoral herds were conscious of the passing of the seasons, and carefully watched the rising and setting of the Sun, Moon, and stars. They realized that human beings have a place in the unity of nature, and that they needed to cooperate with natural cycles if they wished to survive and prosper. Human numbers in the Neolithic period were relatively small, even if they were greater than they had been in the Paleolithic. It was still possible for people living close to natural cycles, dependent upon the annual crops and the increase of the herds, to maintain a balance with the ecosystems of which they were a part.

The Rise of Cities: The Bronze Age

Mesopotamia and the Levant   The first cities appeared in a large swath of the Near East that stretches from the Levantine shore of the Mediterranean Sea to the head of the Persian Gulf, including the valleys of the Jordan, Orontes, Euphrates, and Tigris rivers. Except for some montane margins and the Mediterranean coastal sections, this area would be desert were it not for the rivers and the irrigation they make possible. The so-called Urban Revolution that brought cities into existence was made possible by a changed relationship between human beings and the environment, based on a more intensive agriculture using two new inventions: the plow and systematic large-scale irrigation. The fertile, sandy soil of Mesopotamia was easily turned by the ox-drawn plow. The rivers provided the needed water, but their flow was so undependable that their control demanded major irrigation works. This new agriculture enabled a much larger human population to live in expanded settlements, and many people no longer had to work on the land, so that specialized occupations flourished in the cities.

Building materials for urban centers were determined by their availability in the natural environment. In the Levant, mountains had abundant supplies of stone and timber. But many of the earliest cities arose in the flat, alluvial land of Mesopotamia, where there was no stone or metallic ore, and almost no trees large enough to be useful for construction. Metal, stone, and wood were brought in by trade, but were expensive, so the native materials—reeds and, most abundant, clay—were used in ordinary construction. The urban dwellers raised mighty works of baked and unbaked clay bricks: temples, shrines raised on lofty ziggurats, palaces, and thick city walls. But the systems of canals that brought water to the fields constituted their most extensive and labor-consuming achievement. These works of irrigation conquered sections of the land and won rich sustenance from its basic fertility. Thus a Mesopotamian king felt justified in listing the construction of a new canal, along with the defeat of his enemies in battle, as the major events of his reign.

Copper and bronze metallurgy appeared as the early cities developed, and the period (approximately 3000–1000 B.C.) has been called the Bronze Age for that reason. Some of the earliest metal objects were formed from copper and copper alloys that occur naturally in metallic form around the Near East. In the search for additional supplies, metalworkers turned to smelting copper oxide ores, adapting techniques from pottery firing to obtain the high heat that was necessary. In the process, they discovered alloys of copper (called bronze of various kinds) that were superior in hardness and the ability to keep an edge. The preferred bronze, eventually, was an alloy of copper and tin. Since tin was the rarer of the two metals, it was often imported over long distances. Household utensils, decorative and ceremonial objects, and armor and weapons came to be made of bronze.

The attitude of city-dwelling people toward the natural environment shows a striking change from that of the hunter-gatherers, early farmers, and herders. It is as if the barrier of city walls and the rectilinear pattern of canals had divided urban human beings from wild nature and substituted an attitude of confrontation for the earlier feeling of cooperation. This attitude can be traced in Near Eastern literature from early Sumerian times down through Akkadian and Assyrian writings, which often use the image of battle to describe the new relationship with nature. In creation myths, Nature was represented as a female monster of chaos who was confronted and overcome by a hero-god. It was only through the conquests made by the gods, and the constant labor of their human followers, that the natural chaotic state of the universe could be overcome and order established. The order of the city, with its straight streets and strong walls, and the regular pattern of canals in the countryside, were believed to be an earthly imitation of the heavenly order that the gods had established. The orderliness of the stars and planets was admired by the Mesopotamians, who identified them with their gods and developed astronomy and mathematics to a sophisticated level.

The *Epic of Gilgamesh*, perhaps the oldest extant long poem, reveals the urban Mesopotamian sense of the distinction between the tame and the wild, between civilization and wilderness, and shows an attitude of hostility toward untamed nature. Enkidu, the hairy man of the wild, first appears in the poem as a friend and protector of beasts, but he is a nuisance and even a menace because he releases animals from hunters' traps and warns them away from hunters' ambushes. When Enkidu had been tamed, his former animal friends feared him and fled. Entering the city of Uruk, he met and struggled with King Gilgamesh, who became his close friend. Together they went on a quest for cedar wood in the far mountains. The forest was a sacred grove protected by the wild giant Humbaba, and his defeat and death at the hands of the two heroes was a symbol for the subjugation of the wilderness by the city. Gilgamesh promptly cut down the cedar trees and carried them off to Uruk to use in building a palace for himself. The proper effort of mankind toward wild things, in the view of the Mesopotamians, was to domesticate them. They added native animals such as the onager and the water buffalo to the cows, pigs, sheep, and goats already tamed by their ancestors. Animals that could not be domesticated were hunted mercilessly; Gilgamesh is said to have killed lions simply because he saw them "glorying in life."[11]

Environmental Problems of Mesopotamia and the Levant   Flooding was a continual danger for the Mesopotamian cities. The Tigris and Euphrates rivers rose over their banks unpredictably, destroying settlements and fields, perhaps one reason why these people regarded nature as chaotic. Cities accumulated mounds and rose above the plain and, if they were lucky, above the floods. The temple dwellings of the gods were raised high on platforms, and then even higher on the step-pyramids called ziggurats. The system of canals and dikes served both for irrigation and flood control.

But the silt and mud carried by rivers and canals settled out rapidly. Constant dredging was needed to keep the canals flowing, and the excess material piled up along their banks until the canals were 30 feet or more above the surrounding fields, so that the ditches could no longer serve to drain the land and were a danger in time of flood. Salinization, the accumulation of salts in the soil as a result of water evaporation, is a danger wherever irrigation is practiced in dry climates, and it was unfortunately prevalent in Mesopotamia. Irrigation water, carried into low-lying areas, was allowed to evaporate, and over the years in this land of low humidity and scanty rain, the salts accumulated. The conditions of poor drainage also made it difficult to correct the situation by leaching salt from the fields. Ground water became increasingly saline. Farmers tried to adapt to the changing conditions by planting the more salt-tolerant barley instead of the vulnerable wheat. But in extreme cases, cultivated plants were unable to grow in salinized soil. Such areas had to be abandoned, while new sections were brought under irrigation and cultivation until they in turn suffered the same effects. A survey by Thorkild Jacobsen and Robert Adams found evidence of increased salinity and declining yields in southern Mesopotamia between 2400 and 1700 B.C., and they identified these as contributing to the breakup of Sumerian civilization.[12] The famous cities of ancient Mesopotamia are now desolate mounds in a desert environment, and photographs taken from space show that the fertile land occupies a remnant of its former extent. These effects are not the result of climatic change or of warfare, although both have occurred through the centuries. They represent a true ecological disaster caused by human actions. In Mesopotamia, above all other regions, there is the clearest relationship between environmental degradation caused by humans and cultural decline.

Egypt

Egypt existed as an autonomous civilization from before 3000 B.C. to after 1000 B.C., and during that period maintained a relatively consistent pattern in economy, government, religion, and ecological viewpoints and techniques. It is likely that the stability of Egyptian civilization was the result of the sustainability of Egypt's ecological relationships. Karl Butzer remarked, "It has become difficult to ignore the possibility that major segments of ancient Egyptian history may be unintelligible without recourse to an ecological perspective." He added that the history of flood-plain civilization in the Nile valley offers a test case of human-land relationships.[13] But a further observation must be made: the ecological attitudes and practices of the Egyptians were rooted in a world view that affirmed the sacred values of all nature, and of land in particular.

Egypt, although one of the first societies to develop cities, was predominantly agrarian rather than urban.[14] Agriculture remained the foundation of Egyptian civilization, and urban centers were not sharply separated from the rural landscape. This can be seen in the absence of fortified walls. Representation of walled cities in early art indicates that they existed in predynastic times, but with the unification of the so-called Two Lands under the god-king (pharaoh), need for them disappeared except in frontier areas, and at times when central authority broke down. Thus it is agriculture that manifests the characteristic ecological relationships of Egyptian civilization.

Dependability of the Egyptian Environment   The sustainability of Egyptian agriculture was made possible by the annual flood of the Nile and the deposition of fertile alluvial soil containing phosphorus and other minerals and traces of organic debris brought down from the mountains and swamps of lands further south. Herodotus, observing that the soil of Egypt had been formed by river sediment, pronounced Egypt the "gift of the Nile."[15] An early inscription said that the Nile "supplies all the people with nourishment and food."[16] The climate was dependable, and although there was little rain, the river supplied the water needed. Their environment encouraged the Egyptians to think of processes of nature as operating in predictable cycles. The Nile flooded its banks at the same time every year, bringing moisture and new soil to the fields. As Pliny the Elder remarked, "In that country the Nile plays the part of farmer."[17] The only fertile land was what the river watered in the long, narrow valley floor of Upper Egypt and in the broad, flat Delta of Lower Egypt.

Of the world's great rivers used in early times for flood agriculture, the Nile was most regular, but not completely predictable.[18] Disasters occurred when a high flood washed away irrigation works, storage facilities, and villages, or when a low river failed to water or fertilize the "black land" adequately.[19] Lapses in sustainability occurred when the Nile failed, and invaders took advantage of weakness produced by flood or famine. Egyptian history is punctuated by difficult times when pharaonic government collapsed, and these "intermediate periods" have been correlated with anomalies in the average level of Nile floods.[20] But traditional patterns of culture, including environmental relationships, reasserted themselves after these intervals with tenacity: "The Nile never refused its great task of revivification. In its periodicity it promoted the [Egyptians'] sense of confidence. . . . True, the Nile might fall short of its full bounty for years of famine, but it never ceased altogether, and ultimately it always came back with full prodigality."[21] The natural regime provided the environmental insulation necessary for a sustainable society, but the positive efforts of the Egyptians were also necessary.

The Sacred View of Nature Egyptian religion held as sacred the forces of nature that assured sustainability, and urged the people to cooperate with rather than to interfere with them. The world to them was a place of system and regularity, qualities attributed to Ma'at, goddess of balance. More than just a goddess, she embodied the order that harmonized apparent antitheses in nature. Gods and pharaohs alike were expected to act in accord with her principles. Egyptian creation myths display the idea that the world, with everything in it, is the expression of a creator, or creators, that acted in congruence with the harmony that Ma'at represents. The yearly Nile inundation reenacted creation, with the "primeval hillock" appearing to view above the sinking primordial waters. The first land emerging from the flood promised renewed life in the coming agricultural season.[22]

The orderly movements of the heavens were evident to the Egyptians, whose sky was so seldom clouded. Re-Harakhte, the sun-god, appeared every morning and crossed the sky to his western harbor, and the movement of his path to north and south showed the passage of the year. The stars marked hours and seasons; when Sothis, star of the goddess Isis, rose just before the sun, it was a sign that flood time was at hand. As above, so below: the sky-goddess Nut arched her body above her fertile consort, the male earth-god Geb, in perfect balance. When the stars, the children of Nut, showed the proper season, then Geb's children, the plants, bore fruit. It is interesting to note the reversal of identifications common in other societies, where Earth is usually feminine and Sky masculine. The principle in Egyptian myth was a balance of sexual roles, not the dominance of either. Deities often occurred as balanced pairs of male and female, like Geb and Nut. Sometimes the pairs balanced two sides of the feminine, such as kind Hathor and angry Sekhmet, who could be transformed into each other; or two aspects of the masculine, for example, Horus, hero-god of fertile land, and his counterpart, the desert-god Set, enemies whose battles ended in reconciliation and peaceful co-rule.

The land was a god, and therefore sacred, and all its aspects were gods. Osiris, widely worshipped, embodied vegetation. The annual cycle of flood, planting, harvest, and fallow was mythologically portrayed as his birth, growth, death, dismemberment, burial, and resurrection, so that every stage of the agricultural year repeated an event in the life of Osiris. Hapi was god of the Nile. Bringer of fertility, though male, he was portrayed with breasts to show his power to nurture. He was called "Father of the gods" because they depended on the Nile for offerings or existence. For example, he suckled Osiris, helping to resurrect him in a myth standing for the reliance of vegetation on the Nile flood. So when the river rose to its appropriate level, people rejoiced at the advent of the god. In the words of a pyramid text, "They tremble, that behold the Nile in full flood. The fields laugh and the riverbanks are overflowed. The gods' offerings descend, the visage of the people is bright, and the heart of the gods rejoices."[23]

Farmers who cared for the earth carried on long-established traditions. It was believed that hoeing, properly done, was an act of veneration of the earth-god. The round of the agricultural year had a numerous series of festivals honoring the recurrence of natural events. Originated by villagers in Neolithic times, these celebrations were later institutionalized. At the harvest festival of Min-Amun in Thebes, for instance, Pharaoh cut the first sheaf of wheat and a bull was led in procession. "For the Egyptians the ideal society on Earth . . . was a fundamental reflection of a divine order," observed Barry Kemp.[24]

Sacred Science, Sacred Technology The sciences of geometry and astronomy, and sacred records (hieroglyphics) were marshaled to ensure the dependability of relationship to the environment. Geometry, necessary to reestablish field boundaries when markers had been swept away in the flood, was not a mundane skill, but a hallowed occupation believed originated by the god Thoth and entrusted to trained scribes. Temples were located according to geomancy and oriented to important points in the revolutions of the Sun and stars. Papyri containing these arcane branches of knowledge were kept by scribes in the House of Life, the temple library.

Irrigation was a form of sacred technology shown in art as an activity of the pharaoh and the gods themselves. Indeed, canal building was believed to be a major occupation of those in the blessed world beyond death. Some scholars maintain that the absolute monarchy of the pharaoh grew out of the need to marshal labor and direct hydroengineering on a national scale.[25] This seems supported by the first-dynasty Scorpion-King Mace Head, which shows the king digging a canal, and the fact that "Canal-digger" was an important title. It is true that all Egyptian males except the nobility and priesthood were obliged to perform corvee or compulsory labor, ostensibly for the pharaoh, during the agricultural fallow season, from two to four months a year. This was expended on great public works, both monuments and structures for water control and distribution. But recent research has discovered that most irrigation work was supervised by local officials, and Butzer states that the small provinces called nomes developed as local irrigation units.[26] Irrigation increased the cropland area beyond that originally flooded by the Nile. The two types of land were kept distinct. Local laborers dredged channels, dug ditches, built earthen dams, constructed dikes and basins, and raised water with buckets, activities that were considered parts of a holy occupation. Major projects sponsored by Pharaoh were commemorated

as good works; inscriptions boast, "I brought the Nile to the upland
in your fields so that plots were watered that had never known
water before,"[27] and "I caused the water of the Nile to flood over
the ancient landmarks."[28]

Environmental Problems in Egypt   In spite of Egypt's sustainable
agriculture, environmental problems appeared. One, ironically,
was a result of the success of the Egyptians in producing the ancient
world's most reliable food supply. Even the most dependable
system will fail with overpopulation. When population increased
to a level that required every year to show a good harvest, an
abnormally low harvest would bring famine. Works of art such as
the causeway of Unas at Sakkara show people starving, their ribs
prominently visible. Egypt suffered because fat years were interspersed with lean ones, and population had peaks and valleys as
a result. Governmental officials tried to even out fluctuations of
supply and demand by storing surplus in good years and distribut-
ing it when harvests failed. The story of Joseph's interpretation of
Pharaoh's dream, and his advice to build granaries to prepare
for hard times, reflects the actual situation in Egypt.[29] The store
chambers of the Ramesseum, built at the order of Ramses II, could
have held 590,000 cubic feet of grain, enough to support 3,400
families for a year.[30] In difficult periods, prices fluctuated. In the
fifty-five years between the reigns of Ramses III and Ramses VII,
for example, emmer wheat rose from eight to twenty-four times
base price.[31] At times, famine relief had to be distributed over large
districts.[32] Even so, Egypt remained a breadbasket of the ancient
world, exporting wheat and barley with few interruptions.

The Egyptians' joy in their environment can be sensed in their
representations of activities such as plowing and hunting. Apparently, there was little realization that nature was being damaged in
the process. For them, Earth was unchanging: time ran in cycles,
not along an inexorable line. Changes, some harmful, nonetheless
happened, including salinization, deforestation, overdevelopment,
and habitat destruction.

Egypt suffered less than Mesopotamia from salinization because
the Nile flood leached salt from the soil. But salt deposits occurred

in irrigated areas above the flood line and were serious in the Fayum, an oasis below sea level.

Deforestation was a major problem, which may seem surprising because most of Egypt was not forested land. But although more than 90 percent of the country is desert, the watered land had sections full of trees. Before clearing, the Nile valley supported an evergreen forest of fig, jujube, acacia, and other species. Pollen analyses in the Delta show that there were many wetland plants including trees.[33] This changed as cultivation extended. Tomb paintings show trees being cut to clear land. Egypt had supplies of firewood and fine woods for carving and cabinet making, but few tall, straight trees, and had to import timber from Phoenicia and other lands to the north. Egyptian ships reached Byblos as early as 2650 B.C. to obtain cedar, juniper, fir, pine, and other timber for construction. Cedar wood from Mount Lebanon was called "a wood which [the God] (Amun-Re) loves," so that journeys undertaken to secure it were believed to be commanded by the god.[34] In the Middle Kingdom, as excavated tombs in Lebanon show, Egyptian influence dominated the Phoenician coast through political and cultural forces that followed the timber trade. In the New Kingdom, the same area was conquered outright. In Egypt itself, in addition to cutting for fuel and other purposes, pasturing of domestic animals depleted the vegetation.

The reverence of Egyptians for sacred trees acted against total deforestation. Trees were worshipped, and deities were shown in tree form. Isis, for example, was symbolized by a tree with breasts from which Pharaoh received milk. The tree of life portrayed in mortuary paintings with the deceased bowing low before it or drinking from a spring of water at its base was not just imaginary. Trees such as *ished* and palm were planted in temple gardens beside sacred lakes and tended by priests and their servants. The planting of a tree was considered to be a good work that aided the soul. Great trouble was taken to plant and water trees near tombs and mortuary temples such as the terraced monument of Hatshepsut.[35] Officials and affluent citizens planted gardens and groves, and Pharaoh had plantations of valuable species for royal use. Sycamore trees were exempted from taxation. The king rewarded his subjects

41

for planting trees along roads, canals, field boundaries, and other places, and tree farming became an art and science.

The need for wetlands, plants, and wildlife in sustaining the ecology of this land threatened by desert is evident. But the habitats of wild animals, birds, and aquatic creatures shrank, perhaps so slowly that few people noticed what was happening. Eventually "the almost total disappearance of large game" from the Nile valley, "with increasing importation of captured animals for symbolic hunts by the nobility, argues for eradication of the natural vegetation."[36] Even such a ubiquitous plant as papyrus became less prevalent, though it did not totally disappear from Egypt before the end of antiquity.

Animals were sacred to the Egyptians. They were regarded as visible manifestations of deities: the jackal of Anubis, the lioness of Sekhmet, and many others. Groups of animals were kept in temple precincts, and when they died were mummified and accorded honorable burial. Tens of thousands of mummies have been found in special vaults: Horus hawks, Thoth ibises, Bastet cats, and so on. Worship did not, however, prevent wild animals from being hunted; still less did it save them from the effects of habitat destruction. In predynastic times, as petroglyphs attest, Egypt possessed a variety of species as rich as that now found in East Africa. But by the end of the Old Kingdom, elephant, rhinoceros, wild camel, and giraffe were missing or rare. Barbary sheep, lion, and leopard were still present, but in reduced numbers. Some of this depletion was due to climatic change, since the Sahara did not dry to its present aridity until well into the Old Kingdom. But some was also due to deliberate destruction; Amenhotep III boasted of killing 102 lions by his own hand; lions were the prey of kings.[37] By the Middle Kingdom, the ranges of antelope species had been limited and their numbers decimated.[38]

The abundance of birds, particularly waterfowl, once astonishing in Egypt, a "land of whirring wings," was gradually reduced.[39] Nobles enjoyed bird hunting in marshes, but there were fewer marshes as drainage proceeded. Inscriptions say that Ramses III gave over 426,000 waterfowl to temples, including 9,350 per year to the Temple of Amun at Thebes alone. Some of these became part of temple flocks, while others were offerings; sacrifice in Egypt consisted of the presentation to the gods of prepared food dishes that were consumed by priests after the ceremony. Egyptian bird life, diminished but not destroyed by the ancients, is today at a low ebb. The ibis is scarcely seen, and of fourteen species of duck in ancient Egyptian art, only one now breeds there.[40] A similar fate awaited the fish. Some were protected; it was forbidden even for Pharaoh to fish in sacred temple lakes. A stele from Abydos reports the words of Ramses IV: "I ate nothing I should not eat, I did not fish in the sacred lake, I did not hunt with the bird-net, I did not shoot a lion at the festival of Bastet."[41]

Environmentally, Egypt at the end of the ancient period was much changed, but still productive and full of life. The Nile continued to bring annual floods, with sufficient water and sediment in most years to guarantee good crops. Grain, other foodstuffs, and crops such as flax for linen and papyrus for paper, were usually abundant enough to meet Egypt's needs and to be exported as well. Egypt was not lacking in environmental problems such as gradual loss of natural vegetation and wildlife, but in every case where the influence of the realization of the sacredness of the Earth and living creatures was felt, it helped to mitigate damage and to preserve life and the environment.

Egypt was in most respects self-sufficient, so that the Egyptians were content with their land. Some modern writers interpret this contentment as an attitude that was "insular and self-satisfied."[42] That this was not the case is clear from the vigor with which they pursued the timber trade abroad to obtain a necessary resource in which they were not well supplied. At home as well, they understood their relationship to the land to be governed by the gods and by sacred principles derived from Ma'at, the universal order that controlled the pharaoh and even the gods themselves, and harmonized the people with their natural environment.

Conclusion

The environmental history of earlier human societies in the Mediterranean basin or peripheral to it is presented here as background to Greece and Rome, which followed and were in many important ways influenced by them. Paleolithic and Neolithic lore and life-ways formed traditional patterns that persisted at least in part into the classical period and helped to determine Greek and Roman treatment of the natural environment. The civilizations of Egypt and Mesopotamia were in contact with the Greeks and Romans throughout their formative period, and the latter tended to regard the former as alien, but wise and learned civilizations. Therefore it is to be expected that they would reflect their influence in terms of environmental attitudes and practices, as in other aspects of their culture. There were differences too compelling to ignore, however. Egypt and Mesopotamia were river-valley civilizations that grew up in regions of large deserts; the Greek and Roman homelands lacked very large rivers and were located in the Mediterranean climatic zone. Their environmental setting, and their responses to it, were therefore distinct.

Four

Concepts of the Natural World

The period of the classical Greek and Roman civilizations was a long and creative time during which an immensely varied number of ideas developed and flourished. Some of these concepts were supportive of a balanced human relationship to nature, and others were not. To understand how environmental problems developed in antiquity, we need to look at the ancient cultures' attitudes toward the natural world.

Traditionally, the Greeks and Romans regarded the world as a sacred place where the gods of nature, who shared some human qualities, were present. Thus it would be expected that they would treat the environment with awe and care, and this was true to a considerable extent. With the appearance of philosophers who questioned or denied the activity of the gods in the world, the older attitudes weakened. The new thinkers rejected traditional mythological explanations of the world and insisted that the human mind could discover the truth about nature through reason. The varying pictures of the world offered by reason included some beautiful images of the Earth as a living organism, and other views in which chance and materialism produced what is seen. Various ethical systems either provided strong motives for conservation, or left humans free to exploit the environment.

A few of the best minds were keen observers of nature who insisted on making their explanations consistent with what is actually seen. This enabled them to begin the process of scientific inquiry. Virtually all of these writers assumed too easily that the inner workings of the human mind are congruent with the outer workings of the universe, and many of them shared an antipathy to experiment, which limited their discoveries and sometimes led them into fallacious speculation. In spite of that, the discoveries of ancient philosophers and scientists were many and impressive, and they made a tentative start in the ecological field of inquiry.

To what extent do the attitudes of people toward their environment, and their knowledge of it, determine the kinds of environmental problems they will have, or the ways in which they will approach them? Ideas, however unrelated to reality they may sometimes be, are not entirely irrelevant to the way in which people act in the world and toward natural objects.

Nature as the Sphere of the Gods

The people of the ancient Mediterranean felt that nature manifested the activities of the gods, whether they perceived the gods as personifications of natural forces, as the Greeks characteristically did, or as *numina*, mysterious presences in the natural world, as the Romans tended to do before they adopted Greek ideas on these matters. Any natural phenomenon could be seen as the result of a god's operation. Therefore any human activity that affected the environment could be seen as attracting the interest of or provoking the reaction of some god or goddess, and ought to be undertaken with caution.

Gods of Nature   All the major gods had associations with nature, and many of the minor ones were divinized natural features such as winds and rivers. The Greek god of the sky was Zeus (a cognate of the Roman Jupiter), who "sometimes shines brightly, sometimes rains."[1] When a mighty thunderhead advanced across the Mediterranean landscape, it was perceived as the presence of the father of the gods, who made the wind blow, hurled the lightning, and spoke in the thunder. Of a particularly foul spell, Homer said, "Zeus rained the whole night through."[2] Myth said that Zeus had divided the natural world between himself and his two brothers, Poseidon, who took the waters as his portion, and Pluto, who reigned in the regions underground. Demeter was the personification of growing grain; the Delphic oracle spoke in literal fashion of "scattering Demeter forth, or gathering her in."[3] Even the gods associated most closely with aspects of human life had deep connections with nature; the religious tradition did not distinguish sharply between human beings and the rest of nature. Athena's oldest concerns were the olive tree, owl, and serpent. Aphrodite stirred passions not only in human beings, but also in "birds that fly in air and all the many creatures" of land and sea.[4] The music of Apollo (called the "mouse-god" by Homer) charmed a "tawny troop of lions" along with "dappled lynxes" and fawns in the mountain forest, causing them all to dance with delight.[5] Asclepius healed through the intermediaries of snakes and dogs.

Certain gods had preeminent roles in nature. First was Earth herself, Gê or Gaia, *Mêtêr Pantôn, Terra Mater*, "oldest of gods," mother of gods, humans, and every living thing.[6] Her worship was immensely ancient, and can be traced far back into the Stone Age. Her creative womb bore all that is, including first of all the sky, according to Hesiod, and all it contains. Many of her offspring were monsters; her fecundity had a dark side. The ancients believed they were born from her, nourished by her, and returned to her at death: "Mistress, from you come our fine children and bountiful harvests; yours is the power to give mortals life and to take it away."[7] She was honored as having her own law, a natural law deeper than human enactments and beyond repeal. Her law is not the justice of human morality; it is simply the way things are. "Earth is a goddess and teaches justice to those who can learn, for the better she is served, the more good things she gives in return."[8] Who treat her well receive blessings; who treat her ill suffer privation, for she gives with even-handed measure. Earth forgives, but only to a certain point; when the balance tips and it is too late, famine, disease, disaster, and death ensue. For example, a fragment preserved in a late source surmises that Themis, goddess of law,

47

Gaia's daughter and alter ego, planned the Trojan War with Zeus in order to thin out the overpopulated tribes that were oppressing the surface of Mother Earth.[9]

Another important Greek nature deity was Artemis, *potnia therôn* ("lady of wild things"), adopted into the Roman pantheon by assimilating Diana to her. She was paradoxically both huntress and protectress of wild animals, and her character and roles will be discussed in chapter 6. Her worship involved practices of conservation by hunters and others, and initiation rituals that introduced children to such practices, giving them the sense of close identification with animals and their tutelary goddess. Though myth called her a virgin, in Ephesus she was shown as a fertile, multiple-breasted mother of animals, her body covered with images of such creatures as lions, deer, cattle, and bees.[10]

As Greco-Roman religion developed, Pan was recognized as universal god of nature. This results partly from etymology, since *pan* means "all" in Greek, so that a primal god of herd animals, "soft streams," "close thickets," "snowy mountains and rocky peaks,"[11] became Great Pan, the "all-god," nature personified, who ruled "all things" (*ta panta*, the closest word in ancient Greek to what is today termed the "natural environment"). An Orphic Hymn calls Pan "Green power in all that grows, procreator of all."[12] Thus the "travail" of Pan in the title of this book represents the depletion of the natural environment through everything it suffered at the hands of the Greeks and Romans.[13]

Divination   Since nature was full of gods, natural events could serve as the medium for discerning their intents. To a skilled augur, birds of many kinds, singly or in groups, bearing prey or flying free, on the left or on the right, were ways that the world of nature displayed the plans of the gods. In the sound of thunder or the rustling of leaves the gods' words could be heard by those who knew how to listen. There were skeptics even in Homer's time, but they were regarded as improvident fools. Eurymachus, in the *Odyssey*, remarked, "Many birds there are that fare to and fro under the rays of the sun, and not all are fateful," when a seer had predicted from the encounter of two eagles that Odysseus would soon return.[14] The result of this untimely rationalism was that the doubter failed to take warning and was killed by the angry husband when he returned. Not only did the gods send birds, but could also take their forms: "Athena and Apollo of the silver bow in the likeness of vultures sat upon the lofty oak of father Zeus."[15]

Sacred Places   Both Greek and Roman religions had a strong sense of locality. The presence of gods was felt in places of natural attractiveness and traditional associations. For example, Socrates knew a spot on the banks of the Ilissus stream where the North Wind had carried off Orithyia, princess of Athens; there was an altar to Boreas there.[16] Both great gods and lesser spirits haunted wild, beautiful locations such as springs, caves, groves, and places with panoramic, inspiring views. Specific features of the landscape had their particular deities; rivers had gods, springs had nymphs called *naiads*, and lakes had *limniads*. There were *oreads* for mountains, *napaeae* for valleys, and *leimoniads* for meadows. Groves of trees and their associated deities will be discussed in chapter 10.

The love of the ancients for their native lands is well known; they thought of their own territories as central and particularly blessed by the gods.[17] Virgil addressed his country, Italy, with the images of the old agricultural religion: "Hail, great mother of harvests! O land / Of Saturn, hail! Mother of men!"[18] The sacred places where gods were manifest turned the map of a local territory into a holy text that could be read by those who knew the alphabet of landforms and watercourses.

Each sanctuary had a location and orientation that was dictated by the natural setting, especially features that could be perceived as bodily forms including feminine breasts and hollows and masculine promontories. The oracular temple of Delphi was located in a spot commanding one of the most spectacular scenes on Earth, looking up at the "shining cliffs" of Mount Parnassus and down a deep gorge to a distant blue gulf. The healing shrine of Asclepius and its great theater are set within a comforting natural amphitheater at Epidaurus. The mountain view from Zeus's oracle at Dodona is majestic. Vincent Scully showed that ancient sacred architecture was always erected with full awareness of, and adaptation to, its

49

natural context.[19] The sacredness of the place, it was felt, existed before it was dedicated or a temple constructed there, and anything built or done there had to take cognizance of the powers present in Earth and sky.

Wilderness was known to the ancients as a place with few human inhabitants or none at all, *eremos* in Greek or *solitudo* in Latin. But the gods were present there, and when they invaded the human world, it was often out of wilderness that they seemed to come. High mountains were revered as sacred spots; sometimes a throne, and often an altar, was erected on a summit for Zeus or another deity. Olympus, highest mountain in Greece, was home to the gods of the upper world, but many other mountains had their own patrons. Apollo haunted Parnassus, and "mountain-born" Dionysus roamed the forest on its flanks. Poseidon held forth with Athena on the high cape of Sunium. There is a Hill of Ares (Areopagus) in Athens, though it was no longer a wild place in classical times. Mount Helicon sheltered the Muses, goddesses of the creative arts. One of Pan's sanctuaries was on Mount Parthenium. But Artemis outdid all the others; when her father Zeus allowed her as a girl to choose her own presents, among the requests he granted were all the mountains in the world.[20]

Roman Religion   Roman religion followed its own course even though it shared some sources with Greek religion, and in later times exhibited great openness to Greek myths and religious practices. Romans were not without reverence for wild places, and went so far as to personify mountains like "Father Apennine" as gods in their own right. But Roman religion had a strongly agricultural flavor, reflecting the early observances of farm families close to the land who depended on the orderly cycles of nature for subsistence. The numerous Roman religious festivals followed a calendar based on the round of activities of the ancestral farm, from the hanging of the plow on the boundary marker in the Compitalia in January to the festivals of Saturn and Bona Dea, deities of the soil, in December. This agricultural element was not foreign to the Greeks, but was prominent among the Romans. Roman gods were associated with the natural environment, and they were myriad. Their hierarchy ran from great deities such as Mercury, god of flocks, to local spirits of springs, such as Juturna. The Romans possessed gods of the farmhouse and storehouse (the *penates*) and of the fields (the *lares*). A god or goddess was the growing spirit of every major crop: Ceres of grain, Liber of wine, and so on. Beyond that, every major and minor activity of the farm had a deity that could be invoked for its success, such as Vervactor for the first plowing, Repacator for the second, Imporcitor for harrowing, Insitor for sowing, and even Sterquilinius for manuring. On the margins of cultivated lands lurked Silvanus and other wild gods of the forests.

Nature, Justice, and Pollution   Both Greeks and Romans perceived order and balance in nature. They felt that the gods, or a principle of justice that even the gods had to obey, operated to keep everything in its correct place, spatially and temporally. "The immortals have appointed a proper time for each thing upon Earth, the giver of grain."[21] When everything holds its proper time and place, then all is right on Earth and in heaven, and justice reigns. To overstep the bounds and to attempt to change the natural arrangement of things is to do injustice and to upset the gods. The Greeks in particular thought that rearranging land and sea was a prideful challenge to Zeus, who had ratified their limits when he divided the world with his brothers. For example, when the people of Cnidus tried to dig a canal through the neck of land that connected them to Asia Minor, the workmen suffered many injuries from flying rock splinters. Seeking the reason, they sent an inquiry to the oracle of Delphi and received an uncharacteristically clear reply: "Do not fence off the isthmus; do not dig. / Zeus would have made an island, had he willed it."[22] They stopped work immediately. When the Persian king Xerxes invaded Greece, it was regarded as evidence of the pride that goes before a fall that he had a bridge of boats built across the Hellespont, turning sea into land; that he caused a canal to be cut through the Athos peninsula; and that his huge army "drank rivers dry" and set forests on fire. When the Colossus of Rhodes fell in an earthquake, it was believed the gods were angry at human presumption, and an oracle forbade its reerection.[23]

Pollution was a most egregious violation that was believed to bring divine punishment on the polluter. An impressive list of taboos against pollution of various kinds can be culled from traditional texts.[24] Pollution was for the Greeks and Romans a qualitative concept, not a measurable phenomenon. The Greek verb *miaino*, the noun *miasma*, and the adjective *miaros* all have the connotation of "bloodstain," and they imply ritual impurity. Similarly, the Latin *polluere* and *pollutus* carry a moral and ceremonial sense along with the meaning of sullying with filth. The early Greek poet Hesiod cautioned his hearers against urinating or defecating in springs or rivers, a prohibition that occurs as part of a long list of magical injunctions. Rules like this embody the astute response of the ancestral Greeks to experiences with disease and poisoning. Such taboos contain fossilized wisdom, the result of sound precautions in the past which were given the authority of religious sanctions such as avoiding affronts to river-gods. Deliberate pollution aroused public wrath, as when the emperor Nero bathed ostentatiously at the intake of the Aqua Marcia, one of Rome's aqueducts.[25]

For the ancients, the natural environment was endowed with living divine presences who maintained its order and resisted the ill-considered actions of human beings. Because of this, many felt that acts of social injustice could bring environmental punishments, and that the gods could manifest their wrath in natural disasters: "And even as beneath a tempest the whole black earth is oppressed, on a day in harvest-time, when Zeus pours forth rain most violently, when in anger he grows wrathful against men that by violence give crooked judgments in the place of gathering, and drive justice out, reckoning not on the vengeance of the gods; and all their rivers flow in flood, and many a hillside do the torrents furrow deeply, and down to the dark sea they rush headlong from the mountains with a mighty roar, and the tilled fields of men are wasted."[26] Justice was seen not only as fairness among people, but also as keeping proper relationships among people, the natural environment, and the gods, so that the whole universe might stay in balance. The balance was maintained not only by punishments but also by rewards. Though sometimes capricious, the gods responded with good gifts when people acted in ways pleasing to them and cared for the environment wisely. The way in which nature, under the aegis of the gods, responds to care, good leadership, and justice is told beautifully in a simile from the *Odyssey* that is a companion piece to the one from the *Iliad* just quoted: "Lady, no one of mortals upon the boundless Earth could find fault with you, for your fame goes up to the broad heaven, as does the fame of some blameless king, who with the fear of the gods in his heart is lord over many mighty men, upholding justice; and the black Earth bears wheat and barley, and the trees are laden with fruit, the flocks bring forth young unceasingly, and the sea yields fish, all from his good leading; and the people prosper under him."[27]

Sacrifice was made to the gods, usually in the form of the slaughter, cooking, and eating of domestic animals, although wild animals were sometimes offered. Bloodless sacrifices, such as the pouring of wine, oil, milk, or grain, or the presentation of fruit, cakes or cheese, were also made. Many of the ancients believed that sacrifice was a gift to the gods in expectation of benefits, or in thanksgiving for them. The Latin phrase was *do ut des*, "I give (to you) so that you will give (to me)." Comparative ethnography also suggests that sacrifice was a form of common meal shared with the god, since most of what was offered was consumed by the worshippers. The substance sacrificed often represented the god. Since the number of victims in a Greek or Roman sacrifice was sometimes in the hundreds, the effect on the environment through killing animals, consuming fuel, and releasing smoke into the atmosphere must have been considerable. Sometimes sacrifice or prayer was used as a way to avoid the environmental protections that religion otherwise afforded to sacred places and their inhabitants, as for example in the all-purpose prayer that Cato advised landowners to make "to the god whom it may concern" in order to gain permission to cut down trees in a temple grove.[28]

Oneness with Nature Ancient religion recognized the essential oneness of humankind with nature. This idea is most notable in mystery cults such as the initiation ceremony at Eleusis, in which thousands saw and heard the enactment of the myth of the goddess

Demeter and her daughter Persephone, who had been seized by Pluto and carried off to his underworld kingdom. In agonized search for her beloved child, Demeter caused all crops to stop growing, threatening the destruction of human life and the end of sacrifices to the gods. Zeus finally decreed that the daughter should be restored to her mother if she had not eaten anything in the Underworld. Since she had tasted only four tiny pomegranate seeds, a compromise was reached: Persephone would spend four months each year underground, during which the crops would not grow, but for the other eight months she would live with her mother, who would then cause seeds to sprout and Earth to be clothed in living green.[29] The myth signified the origin of the seasons, the four months underground being the dry season between the grain harvest and planting when little grows in Mediterranean lands. But the mysteries of Eleusis also identified the life and death of men and women with the dying and rising of vegetation and its goddesses in the never-ending cycle of being: people die and, like seeds, are buried in the earth. But as seeds send forth shoots in response to healing moisture, the initiates of the mysteries would flourish again and live a happy life in the other world.

Orphism and Pythagoreanism: The Living Earth   A more intellectually developed recognition of oneness with nature was found in the Orphic mysteries and their refinement by philosophers and religious teachers such as Pherecydes, Pythagoras, Philolaus, and Empedocles. Orphic cosmology envisioned the organic unity of the world and the cyclical interplay and balance of the elements and creatures within it: a strikingly ecological conception. Orpheus is shown in art and literature as expressing the harmony of nature; when he played the lyre and sang, he was quickly surrounded by animals and his song awakened sympathetic attraction even in trees. Pherecydes, reputedly the teacher of Pythagoras and the first to write about nature and the gods, says that the three first principles were Time (Chronos), Life (Zas), and Earth (Chthoniê).[30] The latter two through their union created the world as a great winged Tree of Life of which all creatures were parts.[31] Like some modern

environmental philosophers, he considered the whole Earth to be
a single living organism.

The Pythagoreans, who adopted the Orphic world view, were
pantheists who held that the universe is spherical, animate, en-
souled, and intelligent.[32] All things share the same elements, so
that no creature comes out of nothing nor is it finally destroyed,
but there is a constant process of recycling. But this natural cycle
was balanced and harmonious, not chaotic. Philolaus defined harmony as "a unity of mixed elements that are various, and an
agreement of elements that disagree."[33] The Pythagoreans believed
that harmonies could be expressed as mathematical proportions.
Since all living things, including humans, have a common origin
and natural ties, and are formed of the same components, including
the soul, they taught, all are related and should be treated with
respect. They forbade killing animals or plants, as well as eating
food "that has had life," that is, that required killing an organism.[34]
Thus they were more than simply vegetarians, since they banned
eating beans and many other plant foods along with meat. Many
foods could be consumed without killing, so far as the ancients
knew, such as milk, cheese, honey, wine, oil, fruits (as long as one
did not eat the seeds), and leafy vegetables. The strongest reason
they adduced for not killing was that all living things have the
same kind of souls, and that after death these souls pass into other
bodies. Some "become lions, such as make their lairs on the hills,
. . . or they become laurel trees with goodly foliage," said Empedocles, and he added, "In the past I have been a boy and a girl, a
bush, a bird, and a silent water-dwelling fish."[35]

Plato, who followed the Pythagoreans in many respects, used
this doctrine of metempsychosis as the basis of his famous Myth
of Er.[36] Elsewhere he gave a systematic account of the theory that
the cosmos is "a living creature, one and visible, containing within
itself all living creatures which are by nature akin to itself." This
great living creature is "endowed with soul and reason."[37] The
Stoics also held that the cosmos is sentient, rational, and pervaded
by harmony in which all living things partake. The cosmos was
deemed self-sufficient because it nourishes and is nourished from
itself.

It is worth noting that the idea of Earth as a living organism has been revived in modern times as the result of rational scientific inquiry into atmospheric chemistry and other phenomena by James Lovelock, who chose the name of the ancient Greek earth-goddess Gaia for his hypothesis. "Any living organism a quarter as old as the Universe itself and still full of vigor is as near immortal as we ever need to know. She is of this Universe and, conceivably, a part of God. On Earth she is the source of life everlasting and is alive now; she gave birth to humankind and we are a part of her."[38]

Esthetics and the Enjoyment of Natural Beauty

There can be no doubt that the Greeks and Romans delighted in the wild and cultivated beauty of Mediterranean landscapes. Flashing sea, rocky islands, and waving forests, all seen in the clear Mediterranean light, made patterns that were reflected in art and celebrated in literature.

The subjects of painting included landscapes, and animals in motion. Though the nonceramic painting of the Greeks is almost completely lost, it can be deduced from literature and Etruscan and Roman adaptations that it included portrayals of nature. The walls and floors of Pompeii and other Roman cities were covered with renditions of trees, mountains, seascapes, lifelike birds, mammals, and creatures of the sea. Architecture and sculpture also adapted motifs from nature. Leaves, flowers, and heads of animals were repeated in roof ornaments and column capitals. Sculptors have been justly praised for their portrayals of the human body, but they also exercised their skill on other aspects of the natural world. The bulls, wild boars, lions, the elegant horses of the Parthenon, the vaulting deer of Artemis, olive trees, and fountains carved in stone all seem endowed with life.

Poetry and prose also voiced a love of nature. Homer constantly used such epithets as "Chalcis with its beautiful streams," "Pelion of the waving leaves," "Antheia with deep meadows," and countless others that are possible only for a writer who admires natural beauty and knows his reader does the same.[39] Many Homeric similes depend on nature's power to move the human mind: "Even as in heaven about the gleaming moon the stars shine clear, when the air is windless, and mountain peaks and high headlands and glades appear in view, and from heaven breaks open the infinite air, and the shepherd rejoices in his heart."[40]

Lyric and dramatic poets sang praises of the beauty of land and sea. Sappho depicted a meadow pasture with spring flowers and breezes.[41] Euripides is credited with this fragment: "Dear is this light of the sun, and lovely to the eye is the placid ocean-flood, and the Earth in the bloom of spring, and wide-spreading waters, and of many lovely sights might I sing the praises."[42] A school of pastoral writers in Hellenistic Alexandria, of whom Theocritus is best known, adopted a romantic style of nature description emphasizing the bucolic delights of the countryside. As for the philosophers, Plato often voiced his admiration of nature, notably near the beginning of the *Phaedrus*, where Socrates remarks, "Upon my word, a delightful resting place, with this tall spreading plane-tree, and a lovely shade from the high branches of the willow. Now that it's in full flower, it makes the place ever so fragrant. And what a lovely stream under the plane tree, and how cool to the feet!"[43] In the section of the *Critias* concerning Atlantis, Plato described mountains as both beautiful and useful.[44]

Roman writers often followed this Greek tradition, but the Romans had their own more pragmatic tradition of agricultural writing in Cato the Elder, Varro, and Columella. Direct statements of enjoyment of the environment with which they were familiar were common among the Romans; for example, Cicero observed, "If we have dwelt some time amid mountains and forests we take delight in them."[45] Pliny the Younger added, "There is nothing that gives either you or me as much pleasure as the works of nature."[46] Many Latin authors had moved to Rome from country towns, which helps explain the depth of their feeling for rural settings. Two lines from Virgil typify his landscape description: "For now the farmhouse gables are smoking in the distance, / And larger shadows fall on the lofty mountains."[47]

The glories of a nature wilder than farmland also were sung by Roman writers. "How fair the sight of . . . fir-trees, mountain-born, / And beauteous lands that owe no debt or wage / To implement of man!"[48] Virgil exclaimed. He added, "May I love the streams and the forests!"[49] Elsewhere he described streams tumbling down rocky canyons, and loved to name mountain peaks.

Appreciation of natural beauty is one reason given for the many ascents of high mountains that are recorded in Greek and Roman times. Rome's most famous mountaineer was the emperor Hadrian, who "climbed Mount Etna to see the sunrise, which is many-colored, it is said, like a rainbow."[50] Hadrian also ascended Mount Casius in Syria by night, in order to be there to see the sunrise, and narrowly escaped being struck by lightning.[51] A mountain in Pontus was the scene of his third known climb. Hadrian was far from alone in climbing Etna; he had been preceded by the philosopher Empedocles, Seneca's friend Lucilius the Younger, and an unknown number of less famous tourists.[52] Etna was a usual goal of the able-bodied visitor to Sicily. As Strabo remarked, "Near Centoripa is the town of Aetna, . . . whose people entertain and conduct those who ascend the mountain; for the mountain-summit begins here."[53] Pausanias's guidebook to Greece gave advice to travelers on various routes to the summit of Mount Parnassus.[54] Besides the esthetic motive, there were two other reasons given for climbing mountains: they were high places where the gods could be worshipped, and they were observatories of interesting phenomena—places where knowledge could be gained.

Nature as the Theater of Reason

Greek philosophers invented the idea of nature (*physis*) as everything that exists in the world outside human culture (*nomos*), and regarded it as a proper object of rational investigation. Beyond simply admiring nature, they tried to understand it. This task was first undertaken by the natural philosophers, who wondered what the basic building blocks of the universe were, and how they were put together. We have two cryptic statements from the philosopher Thales: "All things are water," and "All things are full of gods."[55] As an illustration of the latter assertion, he pointed to the lodestone and its mysterious attraction for iron. Thus he may have attempted to distinguish matter and energy as the primal entities.

Others advanced air, fire, and earth as basic elements, alone or in combination. Various kinds of motion were postulated as producing the changes seen in nature, or the reality of motion and change was denied. These philosophers shared a common assumption about the natural world, that is, that it can be understood by the human mind because it possesses a rational order of its own. As Aristotle was to put it, "Nature does nothing in vain."[56] Some early thinkers made rationality a creative force in their views of the universe; Heraclitus called it *logos* (reason) and Anaxagoras called it *nous* (mind). But the result of the excursion of the Greeks into natural philosophy was to develop a series of mutually exclusive systems of explanation, all of which seemed rational, but none of which could defeat the others. It is impossible to speak of a consensus among the Greeks on the natural environment.

Plato developed an eloquent view of cosmological unity, but for the most part he made human society rather than the natural environment the object of inquiry. A few lines after the lyrical description of nature quoted earlier, Plato made Socrates add that trees and open country would not teach him anything, since he was interested only in what he could learn from men in the city.[57] Socrates' ethical search was concerned with establishing an absolute standard of justice between human beings. Even so, Plato's writings are full of insights about the relationship between human beings and nature, the environmental problems that arise in that relationship, and possible solutions.

Aristotle returned to the investigation of questions about the natural world, using a more systematic and inductive method than the natural philosophers had discovered. He gathered from his research that the living and the nonliving merged with one another in gradual stages, thus preserving the dominant Greek view of the universe as a living, harmonious system. But Aristotle's scheme was hierarchical. He thought that making sharp distinctions between classes of beings was difficult; for example, he wrote, "In most of the other animals can be discerned traces of the psychical modes which attain their clearest differentiation in man."[58] And yet, as Anthony Preus explained, in Aristotle's view "there is one ultimate ruler, and each level is subordinate to the next higher level, as in an army."[59] Aristotle asserted that plants exist for the sake of animals, animals for the sake of man, and that inferior men are natural slaves of the superior.[60] This doctrine supports human use of nature in any way that is conducive to human good, and it has been extremely influential in the history of Western environmental philosophy. Aristotle himself would not have justified the misuse of animals or their senseless slaughter, but others later derived from his teaching that animals and plants are of lower orders subservient to human needs the corollary that animals and plants have no purpose of their own and no inherent right to existence.

Aristotle's student Theophrastus did not accept the idea that other creatures exist to serve humankind. He did not deny that there is purpose in nature; he found the purpose of an annual plant, for example, to be the production of seed to provide for a new generation. But the purpose of things in nature, he maintained, is not always evident. Theophrastus undertook "to determine the conditions on which real things depend and the relations in which they stand to one another" through careful observation rather than the facile assigning of final causes.[61] His philosophy might have given birth to an ethics of consideration for other forms of life, had it been more influential, but he had few followers.

Quite a different concept came from Leucippus and Democritus, who maintained that the world is purely physical, composed of indivisible particles (atoms) whose movements are purely mechanical and governed by accident. This view denied the idea of design in the universe, but in itself had the rational consistency so characteristic of Greek thought. According to Epicurus, whose cosmology followed Democritus, there is no creator and nature works through blind physical cause. His ethics, based on anthropocentric hedonism, held little promise as a caution against environmental damage. Still, some Epicureans supposed that animals and plants could not have been created for human use, because so many people are fools, and there is not enough human intelligence in the world to make creation worthwhile, anyway. Through the poet Lucretius and others, Epicureanism became influential among the Romans.

But the Romans were more profoundly influenced by the Stoic school, founded by a Cypriot named Zeno and taught in Roman times by the slave Epictetus, his student Arrian, and the philosopher-emperor Marcus Aurelius. Like the Epicureans, the Stoics were materialists. But they held that the cosmos has unity, order, and cyclical development, and is animated by a fiery soul of which all individual souls are fragments. Nature is designed by divine reason, as Cicero explained: "Unless obstructed by some force, nature progresses on a certain path of her own to her goal of full development. . . . In the world of nature as a whole there must be a process towards completeness and perfection. . . . There can be nothing that can frustrate nature as a whole, since she embraces and contains within herself all modes of being. . . . Since she is of such a character as to be superior to all things and incapable of frustration by any, it follows of necessity that the world is an intelligent being, and indeed also a wise being."[62] Within this world, humans are bound to act with justice, which is a compact between humans. The Stoics accepted Hesiod's dictum that "human beings have no compact of justice with irrational animals," and Aristotle's hierarchy of plants, animals, and man.[63] All decisions regarding the environment, therefore, should be made with respect to the possible effect on other humans. The argument of the Stoics on this point with the Neoplatonists, who were even more Pythagorean than Plato had been, was over the question as to whether beasts are rational or not; the Neoplatonists claimed that they were.

Neoplatonism's exponents were Philostratus, the eclectic Plutarch, and especially Plotinus. In some respects they followed Pythagoras more closely than Plato. Plotinus held that the universe is the expression of the One, the ground of being. The cosmos is informed by a World-Mind and animated by a World-Soul. As nature unfolds from the One, there is less unity and more individuation, but every being still contains every other being. So far, so good. But bare matter, the Neoplatonists taught, is the source of evil. Since the body is matter, the body is evil (*sôma sêma*, "the body is a tomb," was a common saying of theirs). The proper course for a human soul was to purify itself of matter and rise toward spiritual union with the One. The natural environment, as material, tied the soul to the lower world and the body and should

61

be rejected as a delusion. Injunctions of these Neoplatonists may sound "environmentalist" but they are really intended to help the soul escape from attachment to the physical world. Early Pythagorean rules about diet and against sacrifice were relaxed among the Neoplatonists as concern for pure spirit and the next world replaced reverence for life.

The Roots of Ecological Science

Although ancient thinkers never used the word "ecology," they originated inquiries that would today be called ecological. Thus they were forerunners of the science of ecology, even if their ideas reached fruition only in modern times.

The Presocratics   The philosophical grounding for ecology is the notion of the world as a biological system within which cycles of interaction and change occur. This idea can be found in the surviving fragments of Empedocles, who held that all things share the same elements, so that there is a constant process of interchange in which no creature comes out of nothing nor is it ever finally destroyed.[64] This might today be compared to the flow of energy and matter in an ecosystem. Empedocles conceived of the universe as an endless recycling. "There is no birth in mortal things, and no end in ruinous death. There is only mingling and interchange of parts, and it is this we call 'nature,'" he wrote. "When these elements are mingled into the shape of a man living under the bright sky, or into the shape of wild beasts or plants or birds, men call it birth; and when these things are separated into their parts men speak of hapless death."[65] Anaxagoras enunciated a similar idea: "Nothing exists apart; everything has a share of everything else."[66]

Anaximander seems to have intuited a relationship between evolution and predation. He wondered how human beings, who are weaker than many other animals, and who spend a long childhood in a defenseless state, could have survived in earliest times. He decided they had originally grown as embryos in a fishlike state that protected them from predators.[67] Empedocles added the idea of natural selection. Believing that all creatures arose from a mixture of the elements, he stated that only those whose structure fitted their purpose had survived, while those with an odd assortment of parts had perished.[68] He speculated as to why various animals and plants prefer different environments, though his answer is unclear: one source says he thought that animals whose nature was fiery "flew up into the air," another that they became aquatic to cool off their inner flames.[69] Empedocles puzzled over the roles of climate, moisture, and soil in plant growth, attempting to work out a concept of harmony between organisms and environment.

Herodotus, who had a wide-ranging interest in natural history and often repeated fantastic stories about animals and plants without necessarily believing them, pondered the relationship between predators and prey. He noted that timid animals that are eaten by others produce young in abundance, while predators bring forth only a few offspring, thus achieving a balance of numbers.[70] This idea was repeated by Plato, who credited it to Protagoras.[71]

The Peripatetics Aristotle, whose "philosophical emphasis is clearly the natural world" and whose "starting point . . . was biology and the notion of organismic development and function," was interested in the relationships among living things and between them and the physical environment.[72] He observed, "All things are ordered together somehow, but not all alike—both fishes and fowls and plants; and the world is not such that one thing has nothing to do with another, but they are connected."[73] It is this principle that makes the study of ecology possible, and Aristotle's own observations on ecological relationships, contained in his biological writings, were so intelligent that he has been given credit for introducing "ecologic considerations into scientific literature."[74]

Aristotle noted the food preferences of various species, and the competition "between such animals as dwell in the same localities and subsist on the same food," particularly when supplies run short.[75] The lion and civet will compete for meat, and the kite will steal food from the raven. "Thus we see . . . their mutual friendship or enmity is due to the food they feed on and the life they lead."[76]

Modern ecologists explain fluctuations of animal populations as resulting from reproduction, predation, availability of food, and climate. Aristotle gave a description of a spectacular population increase among mice and subsequent population crash in which he noted all the important factors. To help explain this, he reported what might be called an experiment in population ecology. A female mouse "in a state of pregnancy was shut up by accident in a vessel containing millet seed, and after a little while the lid of the vessel was removed and upwards of 120 mice were found inside it." He went on to recount a plague of mice that appeared suddenly, devouring all the crops. The predators, including foxes, ferrets, and pigs, were active but ineffective in thinning the numbers, until heavy rains fell and the mice disappeared at once.[77] Theophrastus made similar observations, but attributed the population drop to disease.[78] Other ecological relationships described by Aristotle include territoriality among mammals and birds and animal behavior such as competition and dominance within species, migration, and hibernation. He discussed symbiosis, including parasitism and commensalism, through examples including the pinna (a mussel) and a small crab, the "pinna-guard." "If the pinna be deprived of this pinna-guard," he said, "it soon dies."[79]

Theophrastus, whose most important surviving scientific treatises deal with plants, was the most consistently ecological ancient writer.[80] He observed that a plant flourishes best in an "appropriate place" (*oikeios topos*), which now might be termed its "habitat" or "site."[81] He distinguished plants adapted to environments that were arid (xerophytes), moist (hydrophytes), and saline (halophytes), and to various soil types. He discussed the effects of slope, exposure to wind and sun, and elevation on conditions in small areas (microclimates) and the plants that grow in them, and noted that mountains provide an unusual variety of environmental conditions.[82] He saw that plants of limited distribution (narrow endemics) can be associated with particular mountains or isolated marshes. He did not consider plants only as individuals, but investigated the effects that they exercise on one another when growing in groups, thus taking a step toward the concept of the ecosystem. Theophrastus classified plants into four groups by habits of growth: trees (*dendra*), shrubs (*thamnoi*), subshrubs (*phrygana*), and herbs (*poai*). It is possible to see in these categories a workable classification for Mediterranean plant associations: forest, maquis, garigue, and steppe (grassland). He also described how plants compete or cooperate with, and parasitize, one another, and their interactions with animals. He was particularly interested in the process of cultivation and human effects on plants in general, including extinctions, and effects of removal of vegetation on climate. More than half of Theophrastus's botanical writings deal with ecological observations. In many cases he anticipated terms that would become part of the lexicon of scientific ecology. In other cases, his ideas have to be corrected in the light of more recent work, but it is hard to fault a writer of such rationality and good sense.

Strato of Lampsacus and Demetrius of Phalerum, students of Aristotle and Theophrastus, were instrumental in founding the Museum of Alexandria, a research institution under the sponsorship of the Ptolemies. Not only was it connected with the greatest library in the ancient world, but it possessed a botanical garden with plants from many parts of the world, including India. There was also a zoo with a diverse study collection of animals and birds (see chapter 6).[83] There is, unfortunately, no surviving evidence of ecological research at the museum or similar institutions of the Hellenistic Age.

The Romans   The Romans were fascinated by Greek science, although they added little to it. Pliny the Elder's *Natural History* is an amazing collection of unusual facts and fictions, some from his own observations but most from earlier writers such as Theophrastus. Roman agricultural writers made a number of useful comments that bear on ecological subjects, but they cannot really be called *students* of ecology.

Theories of Environmental Influence

The idea that the natural environment has a formative influence on peoples and civilizations is an important theme in intellectual history. The earliest extensive consideration of it came from the school of Hippocrates. The work entitled *Airs, Waters, Places* investigated the effects of different environments on human health, both physical and mental. The writer believed that one must understand nature as a whole to understand the human body and soul. The climate, seasons, and prevailing winds of a place, the drinking water, and the topography and exposure, the writer maintained, determine to a great extent the physique, temperament, intelligence, and therefore the culture of the people who live there, along with the characteristic diseases to be expected among them. The same environmental factors affected the growth of domestic and wild animals and plants in each region. The Hippocratic author's pioneering environmental studies were based on careful observation of the regions discussed.

Thucydides saw that environment had notable effects on history, including warfare. The thin, dry, unrewarding soil of Attica, he thought, had made that land unattractive to potential invaders and thus saved it from conquest and depopulation. Its relative safety made it a refuge for victims of war from elsewhere, the numbers of people exceeded the capacity of the land to feed them, and Athens was forced to send out colonies to relieve population pressure.[84] Democritus saw the environment as a teacher, believing that many advances in human civilization resulted from observing habits of other animals. People learned weaving from spiders and singing from birds, and built houses of clay because they had watched swallows at work on their nests.[85]

Environmental Determinism   An extreme form of the idea of influence is environmental determinism—that human life and culture are completely shaped by environmental forces. In ancient times, the most popular variety of this doctrine was astrology, which taught that human life was controlled by the changing positions of stars and planets. The climatic zones of the Earth were considered to be under the influence of diverse zodiacal constellations and planets, accounting for the differences in peoples and animals found there.

Another type of environmental determinism held that the Earth is growing old and decaying, with dire results for humankind. Hesiod presented this idea in his myth of the Five Ages, in which

Earth became less fertile and human life shorter as the Golden Age gave way to Silver, Bronze, and Iron ages.[86] Lucretius also gave currency to the doctrine of nature's senescence. Earth is eroding, and if she is a mother, then like human mothers she will become barren, while mankind's monuments will fall into ruin; no permanent improvement can be expected, since history is a process of decline.[87]

But environmental determinism had an optimistic side, too. Some Romans, for example, explained their rule over other peoples by appealing to Rome's superior environmental situation. If nations are formed by their environments, then the nation with the best environment must inevitably be foremost and possess a natural right to rule. People have a tendency to see their own lands as central and pleasant, so it is not surprising that Aristotle had made a similar claim in behalf of the Greeks.

Nature as Ennobling Influence   A further positive application of the idea of environmental influence was the notion that people who live closer to nature are morally superior to those in urban centers. This is the theme of the *Euboean Discourse* of Dio Chrysostom, who described the visit of a shipwrecked traveler to a hunter's family in the wilds of a large island. The hunters were self-sufficient, living on what they obtained directly from nature. After describing their idyllic home, where they lived in natural honesty, hospitality, and unspoiled nobility, the author brought them to a city and into contrast with the corruption of "civilized" society.[88] Similar sentiments are found in Roman poets who liked to escape to the countryside. Horace, Martial, Juvenal, and others did so in the firm conviction that they were not simply shunning human society but were exposing themselves to the good influences of nature, choosing their company more wisely, and finding living space enough to recover their essential humanity. "There's no place in the city for a poor man to get a little peace and a chance to talk."[89]

Human Effects on Nature

Counterposed to the idea that the natural environment determines the expression of human nature is the idea that humans can change the environment. The second idea is as old as the first in classical authors; Homer's poems resound with the sound of axes and falling trees. It was the opinion of Anaxagoras that human beings were cleverer than beasts in manipulating the world because they had hands rather than hoofs or paws.[90]

The Positive View Most often the impacts on the natural world are shown in a positive light; Sophocles gave the chorus in *Antigone* a hymn to sing in praise of humankind's ability to control other creatures and change the Earth, although it ends with an ironic twist: humans can cross the sea and plow the soil, snare birds and beasts, and tame the horse and mountain bull. They know speech and thought, and how to avoid frost and rain, but not how to escape death, or to prefer justice to evil.[91]

From Hesiod on, writers lauded agriculture, believing that through it human beings were improving Earth by creating ordered patterns of beauty as well as producing food. Like Anaxagoras, Cicero praised the cleverness of human hands and the many things they could do, including agriculture, domestication of animals, building, mining, forestry, navigation, and hydrology, and concluded with this insight: "Finally, by means of our hands we endeavor to create as it were a second world within the world of nature."[92] Strabo believed that people worked in partnership with nature to rectify the deficiencies of the environment, as in Egypt, where the hydraulic technology of the Egyptians assured that the land could be irrigated even when the Nile flood failed to reach its usual height.[93]

Stoic philosophy saw our ability to change the environment as resulting from humankind's participation in the rational, creative life of the natural world itself. The design of the world, Seneca noted, included provision for human activities: metals, for example, are hidden in the earth, but we possess the ability to discover them.[94] Human beings were the natural caretakers of Earth, and its creatures were placed in their custody. Well-planned efforts make the Earth more beautiful and serviceable for human purposes; in this view, beauty and utility are synonymous. Humans improve plants and animals through domestication. In the same way, the extension of civilization was seen as making up a defect of the wilderness, which was a "haunt of beasts" or "barren waste."

The Negative View   On the other hand, human impacts could be seen as environmental damage. Herodotus felt that mighty works like bridges and canals demonstrated *hubris* and infringed on the natural order. In one of the most perceptive analyses in ancient times of human impact on the earth, Plato described the deforestation of Attica and the resultant soil erosion and drying of springs, so that "what now remains compared with what then existed is like the skeleton of a sick man, all the fat and soft soil having wasted away, and only the bare framework of the land being left."[95] Change was not regarded as an automatic good by the Greeks; many of them reached the conclusion that Earth under humankind's hand was undergoing degeneracy, not progress.

Some Romans made similar observations. Cicero maintained that "the products of nature are better than those of art."[96] Others were aware that human activities often produced results neither beautiful nor useful. Pliny the Elder complained that people abuse their mother, the Earth.[97] The idea that meager crops could be blamed on an aging Earth was attacked by the wise agriculturist Columella, who placed the blame for nature's infertility not on some supposed senescence or changing climate, but on poor husbandry.[98] A good farmer knows how to restore soil to fertility, but those who misuse the land should not be surprised when the result is diminishing crops and sterility. Horace scorned "the owner contemptuous of the land."[99] Pragmatic Roman attitudes could encourage wise use of resources, with an eye to sustained returns in the future.

Conclusion

To return to the question that was raised at the beginning of this chapter, to what degree did the ideas held by the Greeks and Romans about nature affect their practical treatment of Earth and its living inhabitants? There is no simple answer. Some protection was undoubtedly afforded to the environment by religious beliefs and rituals. Hunters spared some animals, particularly the young of wild creatures, because gods and goddesses like Artemis and Pan were thought to punish their killers. Sacred groves of trees were saved by prohibitions against cutting them. Major changes of the landscape were avoided because they were believed to challenge the gods and bring on their vengeance. Animism in general entailed an "enchantment" of nature that made people think twice before harming it. Philosophy encouraged the rational use of the mineral, vegetable, and animal realms. Scientific thinkers not only pointed out problems, but sometimes suggested solutions.

There remains the undeniable fact that the natural environment incurred considerable damage at the hands of the Greeks and Romans. This damage was not as serious or widespread as that which has occurred in modern times, and some areas of the Mediterranean survived with relatively little impairment. But the harm was more than one might expect from people who held the views that were discussed in this chapter, views that were for the most part positive. Why was this so?

The pattern of Greek and Roman attitudes toward, and ideas about, the natural environment is extremely complex. In this chapter it has been possible only to touch on a few major themes in religion, philosophy, science, and literature. The information that survives from the ancient world inevitably has a social bias. The people who left evidence of thought on these subjects were the upper classes of their respective societies, the intellectuals. In spite of the fact that these writers were also often landowners and farmers with intimate knowledge of the Mediterranean land, they do not necessarily reflect the characteristic set of mind of ordinary people, peasants, woodcutters, herders, hunters, fisherfolk, miners, and laborers. Obviously the latter group outnumbered the former, and their actions had an immeasurable impact on the environment.

Religion permeated all levels of society, and it can be assumed that the common folk were more traditionalistic and therefore more likely to preserve the practices of the deep past than questioning philosophers were. The overwhelming environmental orientation of ancient religion was toward preservation of the natural order. Still, it is characteristic of human beings to evade religious prescriptions when it is in their self-interest to do so. It is possible that tree worshippers might have preserved a few sacred trees while they were cutting down whole forests for fuel. Custom provided sacrifices and prayers that could be used to atone for invasion even of a sacred grove. Some of the mystery religions taught the oneness of human beings with the universe and nonviolence toward other forms of life, but they also stressed purity of soul and escape from the physical world. Religious agnosticism and doubt trickled downward in later classical times, and the spread of Christianity weakened the older nature religion.

The philosophers were a tiny minority in any century, and they disagreed with one another intensely. Facing a period of time that spans 1,200 years, it is hard to make meaningful generalizations about them. Of course they had influence far beyond their numbers, and doctrinal schools of philosophy such as the Pythagoreans, Stoics, Epicureans, and Neoplatonists had multitudes among their followers. Many Roman emperors were Stoics and they were in a position to apply their philosophy in a way that would affect widespread areas of the Mediterranean basin and beyond. Stoic ethics taught that human beings should remain in the jobs they had been assigned by fate, performing them well with responsibility to all. Occasionally there were attempts to carry philosophical systems into practice in a few short-lived utopian communities. But it is almost impossible to identify a general pattern of environmental effects deriving from the competitive philosophies of the ancient world.

Ancient religion, or some forms of philosophy, could well have provided constructive environmental attitudes. But these would not have been effective in environmental conservation without knowledge of the workings of nature and the effects of human actions. There were places where a body of traditional knowledge, the result of centuries of trial and error, survived. One of these was among subsistence farmers, whose practices often reflected successful adaptations to the ecosystems they had to live within or perish. They took fairly good care of the land as long as their own lives were not disrupted by war, which was unfortunately often. Science in general, and ecology in particular, had only a small beginning among the Greeks and barely survived among the Romans. It would have been difficult, then, to decide which practices were likely to bring the best results when an environmental problem appeared for the first time, or was exacerbated in the course of time from a tolerable level to an intolerable one.

It must be assumed, therefore, that the course environmental problems took in the ancient world was not chiefly the result of the concepts of the natural world held by the Greeks and Romans. It was also, and probably more prominently, the result of the technology they inherited and developed; the population levels they reached at various times; the agricultural and other economic measures they took to feed, clothe, and shelter themselves; and the common patterns of their rural and urban lives. Only through studying the interaction of all these factors will it be possible to move toward an understanding of the ecological failure that underlies the decline of ancient Mediterranean civilization.

Five

Deforestation, Overgrazing, and Erosion

No environmental problem of the Greeks and Romans was as widespread and prominent as the removal of forests and the ensuing erosion. In a passage of the *Critias* that has been quoted often, and deservedly so, Plato observed that the mountains of his homeland, Attica, were heavily forested not long before his own time, but had been laid bare by the cutting of timber and by grazing. The result was serious erosion that had washed away the rich, deep soil and consequently dried up the springs and streams that formerly existed there.[1] Strabo complained that the forests near Pisa, once fine, had been exhausted for shipbuilding and, at the time he was writing, for the construction of buildings in Rome and villas of "Persian magnificence" in the surrounding country.[2] Other authors record that wood of good quality, especially large trees useful for ships' masts and temple roof beams, had disappeared from many areas and had to be sought in less accessible mountains.[3]

The reason for concern at the disappearance of trees was the predominance of wood as the basic material for buildings, tools, machines, means of transportation, and fuel. For many of these purposes, substances obtained from mining such as metals, coal, and oil, are used in modern times. In ancient times, bronze and iron were less utilized, and the fossil fuels were rare enough to be curiosities. So important was wood that its name (*hyle* in Greek, *materia* in Latin) was a synonym for "substance" or "material."

Consumption of Wood

Wood and its carbonized product charcoal were the primary ancient fuels in households, public facilities such as baths, and industries, producing both heat and light. (This subject will be discussed more fully in chapters 7 and 9.) Consumption as fuel constituted the most extensive use of wood by far, accounting for perhaps 90 percent. Metal refineries and pottery kilns used prodigious amounts, placing great pressures on the forests. While some forestland was doubtless managed as coppice, where stems and branches are taken out selectively and the forest allowed to regenerate and provide a sustained yield, it is hardly a coincidence that the areas around ancient mining centers became among the most deforested. Towns and cities also demanded the constant services of woodcutters, charcoal burners, and haulers who brought fuels to marketplaces on the backs of mules or donkeys. For example, Phaenippus made twelve drachmas a day, quite a large sum, by keeping six donkeys busy carrying firewood into Athens.[4]

Lumber for use as building material was a fundamental article of trade in the ancient Mediterranean. Much of this commerce was carried on by water, and allowed the users of timber to tap supplies along coastlands and rivers. Logs were floated down natural watercourses or canals to ports, and there loaded on merchant ships. A typical lumber port would be located near the mouth of a river with a mountainous, forested watershed, like Thessalonica in Greece, Luna or Ravenna in Italy, or Colchis at the eastern end of the Black Sea. Those without major rivers had the mountains right at their backs, like Antandros in Asia Minor and Genoa in Italy. Rome imported much timber from outside Italy, but a large proportion of the city's supply came down the Tiber River from the highlands. The entry point was located at the Porta Trigemina.[5] The wood market was in the Porticus inter Lignarios, near the docks.[6] From this place, lines of carts carrying long logs of pine or hr made the streets shake, according to Seneca, and Juvenal added that the innocent stroller in the streets at night ran the risk of being maimed by a wide-swinging tree trunk.[7] Governments encouraged the timber trade through privileges, tax incentives, and advantageous leases and conditions of sale.[8]

The use of wood most often mentioned in ancient literature is shipbuilding. From keel to mast, almost everything in a ship came from trees, including pitch to caulk the vessel. This applies to merchant vessels and warships alike, although authors give more attention to warships. Attempts to secure supplies of timber for the latter play a major role in ancient diplomacy and warfare. When Histiaeus of Miletus founded a colony in Thrace, the Persian Megabazus warned King Darius that the area was valuable because it had "abundance of timber for building ships and making oars" and therefore made Histiaeus too powerful. In the Peloponnesian War, to give a second example, one of Athens' main purposes in launching the Sicilian Campaign was to conquer a source of shipbuilding timber.[9] Later in the same war, the Persian governor of Asia Minor helped the Spartans win by giving them access to the forests of Phrygian Mount Ida and advising them "not to be discouraged over a lack of ship's timber, for there is plenty of that in the King's land."[10] Timber was also used for war machinery such as siege engines, and for other military purposes. Detachments of soldiers were sent to cut wood for fortifications and fuel.[11] Deliberate destruction of forests, usually by fire, was a common tactic in warfare; to give one instance, the Persians under Xerxes burned the woods during their invasion of Greece. It is quite clear that warfare was continually affected by timber supply, and in turn war was a major force in the process of deforestation.

Methods and Technology of the Timber Industry

Literature and inscriptions give considerable information, if limited in quantitative data, on the process of forest exploitation among the Greeks and Romans. Loggers took great pride in their work; a grave inscription on Mount Parnes announces, "I never saw a better woodcutter (*hylotomon*) than myself."[12] Such men knew the forests

75

well; in his works on plants Theophrastus often took advantage of the expertise of lumbermen from areas that supplied the Greek timber trade, including Macedonia, Mount Ida, and Arcadia. Columella advised a landowner who wanted beneficial use from his forests to have his overseer instructed by "a good forester" who would not "refuse to impart to one desirous of learning them the principles of his art."[13]

Trees were cut with double- or single-bitted axes, long metal saws with set teeth, and wedges, tools similar to those used as late as the mid-twentieth century. Smaller trees could be uprooted by digging with shovels. The branches were then lopped off, and the logs pulled out by oxen or other draft animals. Large logs might have pairs of wheels attached to them to make hauling easier. After they arrived at a place where they could be at least partly prepared, logs were cut into sections of transportable length and perhaps split into thick beams and planks. Theophrastus, guided by the experience of woodcutters he knew, gave directions for splitting pine and fir logs in the best way so as to take advantage of the grain.[14] Those to be used as masts were kept whole. The emperor Tiberius ordered larches brought from the Alps, one of which measured 120 feet long.[15] Finally, boards of the desired length and thickness could be sawn, with one man standing below, either in a pit or under a supported log. In the later Roman Empire, sawmills powered by water might have been used; there is no direct evidence of this, but a poet describes a water-mill driving a saw to cut marble in fourth-century Gaul, and such a machine could easily have been adapted to timber.[16]

Other Causes of Forest Removal

Clearing for Agriculture   The removal of forests to make room for farming was a prominent feature of ancient history, and will receive further consideration in chapter 8. New farms were established in forested regions without necessarily cutting all of the trees, at least not at once. Older farms often reserved sections as woodlots. Agricultural writers commend several ways of "reducing a wooded area to an arable state."[17] The axe and saw were part of regular farm equipment. Trees were uprooted or cut down, the useful parts removed and the rest burned and the ashes plowed under as fertilizer. Trees that grew naturally on a plot were used as indicators of crops that would do well if planted there, although wise farmers knew that good forest sites were not always suited for other crops. Pliny remarked, "A soil in which lofty trees do brilliantly is not invariably favorable except for those trees: for what grows taller than a silver fir? Yet what other trees could have lived in the same place?"[18]

Overgrazing One of the most consistent and widespread forces of environmental degradation in the ancient Mediterranean basin was the grazing of domestic animals. The largest portion of the land area, unsuited to cultivation, was used as pasture. Even some areas that would have been arable were devoted to grazing by owners of large tracts, especially in Italy. But perhaps the worst effects of grazing were in making deforestation permanent and exacerbating erosion. As Varro complained, "Grazing cattle do not produce what grows on the land, but tear it off with their teeth."[19] Such a statement ignores the positive function of animals in manuring the land, and it is true that grazing animals, by themselves, will not destroy a mature high forest, although goats do climb into trees to eat foliage. But grazing can make a disturbed situation worse, and shepherds often deliberately disturbed the forests.

The four major species in Greco-Roman grazing were cattle, sheep, goats, and swine. Each has its own dietary preferences, and together they form a synergistic partnership that is destructive to virtually all vegetation within reach. Cattle prefer grass and leaves, leading herders to cut tree branches or whole trees to let them graze. Swine especially like acorns, chestnuts, and beechnuts, so swineherds drive them into the forest where they destroy the means of reproduction of the trees. Sheep eat grass right down to the soil and also pull up the roots of all but the hardiest plants. Shepherds set fires to burn other vegetation and encourage the growth of grass. Goats are most destructive of all, and their ability to eat almost anything is proverbial, but given the choice they prefer woody plants such as bushes and young trees. Thus, in areas where the forest has been cut down, the grazing of animals, goats in particular, prevents forest regeneration. Herds of goats browsed almost everywhere in the Mediterranean, and they were adaptable, prolific, and easy to care for, the "poor man's cow." Goats and sheep together can strip a hillside bare, opening it to erosion, driving away competing wildlife, and forcing the whole ecosystem to regress down the scale of succession and energy. Wise limitation of numbers could have prevented this, but such limitation was almost never practiced. If one herder left any vegetation untouched by his flocks, it would no doubt have been used the same season by others.

The ancients observed that goats could damage plant cover. Plato knew how controversial the goat was, proposing an argument between a man who thought it a valuable animal and another who regarded it as a destructive nuisance.[20] The comic poet Eupolis wrote a play with a chorus of goats, and had them bleat a list of their favorite foods:

> We feed on all manner of shrubs, browsing on the tender shoots
> Of pine, ilex, and arbutus, and on spurge, clover, and fragrant
> Sage, and many-leaved bindweed as well, wild olive, and lentisk,
> And ash, fir, sea oak, ivy, and heather, willow, thorn, mullein,
> And asphodel, cistus, oak, thyme, and savory.[21]

This could well serve as a botanical list of the most typical plants of the maquis, the Mediterranean scrub-forest ecosystem, and it should be noted that a number of timber trees are included on the goats' bill of fare. They were usually consumed while young and small. The significance of pastoralism is not that it destroys high forests but that it makes permanent what destruction went before. The effect of goats may be judged from the following statement of J. R. A. Greig and J. Turner in the early 1970s: "In a place not far from Kopais we saw woody plants regenerating vigorously in a goat-proof enclosure, effectively demonstrating that the present sparse vegetation is due to grazing."[22]

The grazing of sheep, goats, and, to an extent, cattle, involved transhumance, the annual shift to moister pastures with a later growing season in the mountains during the dry summer. As a result, mountain vegetation was consumed at the time it was growing, and with the prevalent overgrazing, erosion was always a danger. In addition, manure was lost to the farms during the summer months. Animals could still be grazed at lower elevations in the summer, but only if pastures were irrigated, and the scarce water was often needed for other purposes.

Fire Ancient writers knew that the destruction attendant upon pastoralism included fire to clear brush and forests. Virgil said as much in a simile of the *Aeneid*:

Just as, in summer, when the winds he wished for
Awake at last, a shepherd scatters fires
Across the forests; suddenly the space
Between the kindled woods takes fire, too.[23]

These fires, as well as wildfires started by lightning or volcanic eruptions, usually burned until they reached a barrier or were put out by rains; they would not be fought unless they threatened a settlement. Fires during the long, dry Mediterranean summer are often catastrophic and bare the slopes to erosion, though the plants are adapted to fire and show remarkable powers of recovery if not prevented by grazing.

Urbanization Ancient writers were aware that cities stood where forests had once flourished. Speaking of the disappearance of *thyon* trees from Cyrene, Theophrastus remarked, "There was an abundance of those trees where now the city stands, and people can still recall that some of the roofs in ancient times were made of it."[24] Ovid said, "Here where now is Rome, the world's capital, were once trees . . . men lived in huts of which there were few to be seen."[25] Place names often preserved the memory of forests that had been encompassed by the growth of cities and towns. An Athenian fortress was designated Peuke ("Pine"). The Caelian Hill, one of the seven on which Rome was built, was originally called Querquetulanus ("Oak Hill"), and the Viminal was named for osier-willows (*vimina*, or "Willow Hill"). A place on the Campus Martius was called Aesculetum, "Oak Grove," after *aesculus*, the

79

Italian or winter oak. The Aventine Hill was once "covered with trees of every kind . . . but the whole place is now covered with buildings including, among others, the Temple of Diana."[26] Of course the effects of urbanization were more far-reaching than the simple clearing of sites for cities; through the ever-extending tentacles of the timber trade, the needs of the city for wood grasped and denuded forests many miles away.

The Process of Deforestation

It would be interesting to know exactly which areas of the Mediterranean basin were deforested and at what times. Classical writers give the impression that the devastation was extensive, since they describe places as wooded which were not so in later times, or mention forests that had disappeared in their own day. Most of the land surface was covered at one time, however far in the past, by forests of various types. Pliny said there once was a forest of giant trees in Egypt, and Diodorus chronicled the passing of the rich forests of Spain and his homeland, Sicily.[27] "In those days," asserted Livy of fourth-century B.C. Italy, "the Ciminian Forest was more impassable and appalling than were lately the wooded defiles of Germany."[28] Livy himself would have found precious little forest where Fabius's army had marched with such difficulty against Hannibal two centuries earlier. Traces of vanished forests persist in names of places that once played a part in the lumber trade, such as Elatea ("Firtown"), Pityoussa ("Pineville"), Castanea ("Chestnutburg"), and Xylopolis ("Timber City").[29]

Exploitation of forests began near centers of demand, such as cities and mining districts, and proceeded into more isolated places as time went on. The environs of Athens were mostly bare by the fifth century B.C., and the nearby island of Euboea, where the relict forests suggest abundant original growth, produced only inferior timber once the requirements of the silver mines at Laurium had stripped it of accessible wood. Forestlands that were more easily reached were cleared first. Lowlands lost their trees before the mountains, and forests near rivers were exploited before those farther away. The areas most praised as sources of good timber in classical times tend to be mountainous regions with heavier than average rainfall: Macedonia, the Alps, Illyria, the Atlas Range, the southern coast of the Black Sea, and Corsica may serve as examples. But it would be misleading to suggest that the progress of forest removal was steady and cumulative. Some forests were leveled, grew again, and were reharvested more than once. Although forests were seriously depleted in ancient times, not all of them were destroyed, and the area remaining in forest was undoubtedly larger than that existing in the late twentieth century.

Literary sources are not the only evidence for forest history. In recent years, much interesting information has come from palynology, the study of pollen grains contained in deposits of dust, soil, and mud. Pollen is well preserved under certain conditions, and the grains from various plant species are markedly different in shape, so that scientists can recover from a column of accumulated material such as lake sediments or cave-floor deposits a record of the relative abundance of pine trees, say, or grain, over a long period of time. The deposits can be dated by the radiocarbon method, although there is a margin of error sufficient to make it often difficult to relate changes in vegetation to specific historical events. Even so, general observations can be made, and in the future more exact knowledge can be expected. Pollen diagrams make it clear that forest history is far from simple. In a single region, forests may have become established and then been removed many times. In northern Greece, for example, paleobotanists have discovered a pattern indicating that forests survived best in settled times, but when invasions occurred, peasants moved into refuge areas in the mountains, cleared the forests and planted fields of wheat and barley. When conditions became more stable, they abandoned these retreats and moved down to the richer plains, allowing forests at higher elevations to recover.[30] Because movements of peoples occurred often over the centuries in Macedonia, this cycle was repeated several times there. On the other hand, palynology also shows that forests persisted in parts of the north down to medieval times, whereas they were gone in some populated areas of southern Greece as early as the Middle Bronze Age. For example, pollen cores from Messenia in the Peloponnesus show that pine woods had disappeared from coastal areas near Pylos by the Middle Bronze Age or early in the Late Bronze Age.[31] Textual evidence such as treaties between Athens and the Macedonian kings shows that in classical and Hellenistic times the city had to depend on the forested north for timber.[32]

Not all Mediterranean forests were exploited in ancient times; the most remote mountains, particularly those located on strategic borderlands, escaped. One such forest in Greece, which has apparently remained untouched since time immemorial, has been discovered in the Rhodope Mountains north of Drama near the Bulgarian frontier. A national park of 585 hectares (1,450 acres, or 2.26 square miles) was set aside by the Greek Republic in 1975 to protect a portion of this unique forest of beech, fir, Norway spruce, and other trees, with its rich population of birds and mammals.[33] Among the birds found there are the capercaillie, golden eagle, and black and griffon vultures; mammals include bear, wolf, lynx, red and roe deer, and chamois. The scenery is exquisite, with mountains, gorges, streams, and waterfalls.

Effects of Deforestation

The most common results of deforestation in the Mediterranean basin are erosion of the hillsides, flooding as the waters are no longer retarded and absorbed, interference with the water supply, and siltation of lowlands and coastlands. George Perkins Marsh, who served in Constantinople, and in Rome for a period longer than any other American ambassador, understood this form of environmental deterioration well: "Vast forests have disappeared from mountain spurs and ridges; the vegetable earth accumulated beneath the trees . . . the soil of alpine pastures . . . are washed away; . . . rivers famous in history and song have shrunk to humble brooklets . . . harbors . . . are shoaled by the deposits of rivers at whose mouths they lie."[34]

Disruption of the Water Supply and Flooding Forests regulate the runoff of the precipitation they receive. Like a sponge, the plants and soil hold water, preventing floods and releasing a year-round supply to springs and streams. Ancient writers were aware of this function, as Vitruvius shows:

> Water . . . is to be most sought in mountains and northern regions, because in these parts it is found of sweeter quality, more wholesome and abundant. For such places are turned away from the sun's course, and in these especially are many forest trees; . . . nor do the sun's rays reach the earth directly and cause the moisture to evaporate. Valleys between mountains are subject to much rain, and because of the dense forest, snow stands there much longer under the shadow of the trees and the hills. Then it melts and percolates through the interstices of the earth and so reaches to the lowest spurs of the mountains, from which the product of the springs flows and bursts forth.[35]

The connection between forests and water supply was noted by other authors. Pausanias visited a place "clothed with oak woods" and remarked of it, "No town in Greece is more abundantly supplied with flowing water than Phellae."[36] Ancients also saw the effects of deforestation in light of this relationship. Pliny commented, "Often indeed devastating torrents unite when from hills has been cut away the wood that used to hold the rains and absorb them."[37] As Plato observed, the water that rushed unimpeded down mountainsides was no longer available to feed the springs. Perhaps for this reason, he portrayed his ideal Atlantis as having springs surrounded by plantations of appropriate trees. Without forests, streams that formerly flowed clear all year long became intermittent and muddy, existing only as dry courses during the summer, while hundreds of springs dried up. Due to the denudation of the Tiber watershed, Rome suffered floods that covered the lower parts of the city and backed up the sewers. The first such flood was noted in 241 B.C., and records indicate increased flooding of the river from that time onward.[38]

Erosion and Siltation   Once the land was bare of trees, the torrential rains of the wet half of the year washed away the unprotected earth. Unimpeded erosion destroyed uplands that might have grown trees again, and the silt, sand, and gravel that reddened the rivers was deposited at their mouths along the shores of the virtually tideless Mediterranean Sea. This greatly altered coastlines, in some cases pushing them many miles farther out to sea, as is the case around the mouths of the Po River. The new wetlands were unhealthy to humans because they served as a breeding ground for malarial mosquitoes, but were useful as homes for water birds and other animals and as spawning places for some species of fish.

Erosion and siltation processes around the Mediterranean in ancient times were large in scale, although the amount of soil removed from the highlands is difficult to estimate. Deposits along the coasts and in valleys and lowlands can be measured, and dated from artifacts found in them or by radiocarbon analysis of organic materials. Such studies indicate that erosion was a complicated and highly localized process.[39] Thermopylae, the famous pass between cliffs and sea near the mouth of the Spercheios River, was narrow enough in 480 B.C. to be defended by a small Greek army against a vastly superior Persian force. Today, accretion of river deposits has widened the land at least 5 miles seaward from the battle site.

As noted earlier, Plato recorded that soil erosion following the deforestation of Attica left the mountains wasted like rocky skeletons.[40] He complained about the sediments that had been deposited in lower places, obscuring the Earth's natural beauty.[41] Pausanias compared the silt deposits laid down at the mouths of two rivers: the Achelous, whose watershed was uninhabited and therefore forested, "does not wash down so much mud on the Echinadian islands as it would otherwise do," but the Maeander, whose valley had been cleared, "had turned the sea between Priene and Miletus into dry land."[42] Siltation clogged harbors at river mouths, as was true of Miletus in the case just mentioned, and Herculean labors were needed in many places to retain them. Repeated efforts to keep open Ostia, Rome's major port at the mouth of the Tiber, are described in ancient sources; those efforts are apparent in archaeological studies and evident in modern aerial photographs showing successively constructed and abandoned harbor basins.[43] Paestum declined when her anchorage filled, and much later Ravenna, the chief Roman naval port on the Adriatic coast, lost access to the sea through a similar process.

Climate Local climates, also called microclimates, change when forests are removed. Deforested tracts become more arid and windy. How far beyond the immediate area such effects might be felt is a matter for conjecture, but it seems certain that the aridification of many parts of the Mediterranean is at least in part due to human interference with regional environments. Theophrastus recorded changes in local climates that he himself observed: after the trees had been cut down around Philippi, for example, the waters dried up and the weather became warmer.[44] Such impacts were no doubt most serious in marginal areas such as the edges of the Sahara and Arabian deserts.

Malaria Malaria and other illnesses, which were debilitating and contributed to depopulation, were a secondary result of deforestation and erosion, since mosquitoes bred in the new marshes. The fact that mosquitoes were the carriers of disease was unknown to the ancients, although some of them came tantalizingly close to the truth, but they certainly knew that low, damp country had to be avoided at the peril of life and health. Opinions vary on just when malaria entered Greece (possibly in the fourth century B.C.) and Italy (perhaps the second century B.C.), and how quickly it spread, but eventually thousands of acres of land were unfit for habitation because of it. The Romans periodically embarked on ambitious programs for the draining of marshlands, destroying wildlife habitat as they did so, but many alluvial deposits were too low-lying for efficient drainage and were never completely reclaimed.

Effects on the Economy Deforestation inflated the price of wood. As abundant sources near the centers of consumption disappeared, lumber became rarer and had to be imported over longer distances. Increased prices were particularly noticeable for fine woods, but affected timber and fuel as well. Detailed price lists survive from a few periods and places, and these seem to show a pattern of rising prices.[45] Pay in kind for Athenian jurors included fuelwood, the third necessity along with bread and *opson* (fish, fruit, etc.). The shortage and high cost of building timber due to deforestation

contributed to the shift from wood to stone construction in both
Greece and Rome, and even from "brick to marble" in early imperial
Rome, since marble required no wood fuels for firing. Deforestation
also increased costs of transportation, due not only to the greater
distances merchants had to go to find wood, but also to scarcity
of timber adjacent to shipbuilding centers, which drove up the
price of ships themselves. Warships had priority over merchant
vessels in competition for materials.

Military Effects   Strategies of warfare and diplomacy were often
aimed at obtaining supplies of timber and other forest products
such as pitch, and guarding the sea-lanes and roads over which
they were transported.[46] Historians in Greece and Rome saw timber
supply as a major factor determining naval strategy in particular.
In the Punic Wars, Rome rushed ships to completion, from tree to
sea, in as little as forty to sixty days.[47] Supplies dwindled; Dionysius
of Syracuse, for instance, found all the shipbuilding material he
needed in the rich forests he controlled in Magna Graecia (southern
Italy) around 400 B.C., but Hiero, a later tyrant of the same city a
century and a half later, had to search far and wide for a suitable mast
for a large warship.[48] One way to get forests was to conquer them;
Alcibiades told the Spartans that this was one of the Athenians' major
purposes in launching the Sicilian Campaign.[49] Colonies were established as timber ports; thus Athens founded Amphipolis on the River
Strymon below heavily forested mountains in Thrace, so their
consternation when the Spartans took that city is understandable.[50]

Forest Management and Conservation

The importance of timber supply and the effects of deforestation
and erosion were evident to ancient observers, who often lamented
these effects. Therefore it is not surprising that governments as
well as private landowners exercised care in assuring a continued
supply of wood from the forests under their control. Unfortunately
such efforts were far from universal, not always effective, and
mitigated by other policies that encouraged exploitation and destruction of forests.

Private Efforts Agriculture included some forestry; Greek and Roman farmers often did not clear all their land. Cato included a woodlot as the seventh in a list of nine requirements for a good farm.[51] Some large estates contained forests that supplied timber, food (nuts, berries, and honey), and foliage for fodder. Planting of trees for timber was common both in Italy and Greece; and in addition they were planted to line roads, shelter fields, and mark boundaries. Landowners propagated trees from their own nurseries. Pliny the Younger remarked that the mountain slopes around his villa were "covered with plantations of timber."[52] Cultivated trees added so much to property value that when Crassus would not sell some large trees with his estate, Domitius refused to buy it, even though he had previously offered a princely sum.[53] Columella condemned neighbors who cut down trees near property lines, thus reducing the value of adjoining property as well as their own.[54]

Public Efforts Because timber was of great economic and military consequence, governments considered forests a proper area of their concern. The sovereign power, whether city or empire, generally asserted its ownership of all unoccupied forestland within its territory. State supervision of forests and watersheds included regulation of the forest products trade, of the timber harvest, and the construction of works to provide or control water supply, drainage, and erosion. Responsibility for these matters was regularly delegated to designated officials; in some cities the timber trade was under *agoranomoi* (overseers of commerce), while forestland in the countryside was supervised by *hyloroi* (custodians of forests) who, says Aristotle, had "guard-posts and mess-rooms for patrol duty."[55]

It was a recurrent policy of governments to encourage private exploitation of forests by leasing the right to cut trees on public land, which was a source of revenue, or by sale or grant of public forestland to private entrepreneurs or consortiums. During the Greek settlement of Cyprus, rulers "permitted anyone who wished, or was able, to cut the timber and keep the land thus cleared as his own property, and exempt from taxes."[56] Rome also granted title to cleared land. Forestland owned by the city of Rome was turned into a residential subdivision by the tribune Icilius.[57] It was Roman practice to rent tracts of woodland for development to syndicates of *equites*, citizens of second-highest rank who were usually businessmen. In the late empire, forestland belonging to the emperor was regularly sold to private owners who would pay taxes on it and provide services, either as regular obligations or as "liturgies," supposedly free gifts. These included payments in kind of lumber, charcoal, burnt lime for mortar and fertilizer, and wood for weapons.

Government policy was, fortunately, not always directed to the encouragement of deforestation. Conscious of the danger of a diminishing supply of wood, the state sometimes regulated private land so as to encourage conservation. Plato's recommendation that landowners be fined if fire spread from their property to timber on a neighbor's land doubtless represented actual Greek law.[58] Decrees of Ptolemy Euergetes, Macedonian ruler of Egypt, prohibited unauthorized cutting of wood by private individuals on their own land and required planting trees.[59] Land leases elsewhere also contained restrictions on timber cutting and stipulations for replanting.

There were public forestlands as well. Although they were often granted to individuals or communities, large tracts remained in government hands, and measures were taken, albeit sporadically, to prevent encroachment and assure their use for the good of the state. When Scipio Africanus needed fir trees to make masts for the fleet he used against Carthage in 205 B.C., he found them in "forests belonging to the state."[60] Wise administrators limited timber harvest; Theophrastus said that in Cyprus, "the kings used not to cut the trees . . . because they took great care of them and managed them." He added that later rulers of that island reaped the benefit of their predecessors' restraint; Demetrius Poliorcetes cut timber of prodigious length there for his ships.[61] Some magistrates were foresighted enough to protect public lands against greed-motivated exploitation and found political support for their efforts. When the tribune Servilius Rullus proposed that Rome sell some state forestland to raise money for other programs, Cicero was able to appeal to popular sentiment to keep the forests in the ownership of the Republic. Knowing that there were profiteers in high position behind Rullus's proposal, Cicero attacked them: "What they need now is money, money that cannot be questioned, money that can be counted. I wonder what this watchful and shrewd tribune has in mind? 'The Scantian Forest is to be sold,' he says. Did you discover the forest in the list of abandoned land holdings? . . . Would you dare to sell the Scantian Forest in my consulship? . . . Would you rob the Roman people of what gives them strength in war, and in peace a more easy life?"[62]

Tree plantations were encouraged by some governments, such as that of Ptolemaic Egypt, where the need for local wood was acute. There a nationwide tree-planting project covered wasteland, private land, royal estates, and the banks of rivers and canals.[63] Trees were started in government nurseries. Plantations were protected by laws regulating the felling of older trees, the lopping of branches, and the removal of fallen trees. Sheep and goats were excluded from areas where young trees had been planted. In addition, governments created and protected parks and sacred groves of trees (discussed in chapter 10).

Conclusion

One can hardly imagine ancient Greek and Roman civilization without wood and other forest products. As the major source of fuels, building materials, transportation, and both military and commercial supplies, trees were of critical importance to ancient peoples. It is as yet impossible to say with complete certainty just how far deforestation had proceeded by, say, the eclipse of the Roman Empire in the west in the fifth century A.D. The historian's ability to quantify many crucial developments is limited by inadequate sources, although new studies based on paleobotany and archaeology are promising. Scholars have differing views on the matter, and when more dependable information comes to light, it will undoubtedly show a pattern that is complicated, including periods of forest recovery alternating with those of destruction. But the general impression is that the extent of forest removal and consequent erosion was widespread and severe, especially in the south and east, and particularly near urban centers, though certainly not limited to those places. In mountains distant from rivers and ports, thick forests, and even a few virgin forests, managed to survive. The extent of deforestation and erosion in ancient times was certainly less than occurred in the twentieth century. Even so, it was serious enough to produce profound social and economic effects.

Shortages of wood and rising prices were among these effects, but not the most dire. Much more permanent and damaging was the devegetation of steep slopes by logging and grazing and their resultant vulnerability to rains, which are often torrential in the Mediterranean winter. Erosion swept away fertile soil, leaving rocky slopes where trees could scarcely have grown even if they had been protected. Silt, sand, and gravel from the mountains was deposited in lowlands and along the coasts, choking ports and creating poorly drained, silt-clogged marshlands. Deforestation, overgrazing, and erosion produced the most visible, far-reaching, and relatively permanent changes in the Mediterranean landscape of all those caused by human activities in ancient times.

Six

Wildlife Depletion:
Hunting, Fishing, and the Arena

An awareness of the possibility that wildlife might be totally extirpated is found in a Greek myth. According to it, the mighty hunter Orion offended Artemis, goddess of the wild, or as some versions have it, Gaia (Gê, Mother Earth) by boasting that he would kill every wild beast in the world. In retaliation, the goddess sent a giant scorpion to sting him. Before this could happen, Zeus set both the hunter and his arachnid enemy in the sky as constellations opposite one another.[1] Mythological evidence reveals some telling aspects of ancient attitudes. The recognition that wildlife might be eliminated, at least from certain areas, is apparent also in the fact that many emperors, kings, and affluent landowners set aside animal preserves where only they could hunt or provision their tables, and also in the reservation of sanctuaries where wildlife was sacred to the gods and could not be killed except under carefully prescribed conditions. Poets sang about the disappearance of wild animals: "Oh distant Nasamonian lands of the Libyans, your barren plains are no longer visited by flocks of beasts of prey, you no longer tremble at the lion's roaring in the desert; for Caesar has caught a vast number of them in nets . . . and the former lofty lairs of wild beasts are now pasturages."[2]

Human use of animals and plants began long before the historical period. As noted in chapter 3, hunting, fishing, and gathering were the major occupations of ancestral people for the majority of their existence on Earth. Eons before the classical period, the ancestors of the Greeks and Romans were hunters and fishers who lived in balance with the species on which they depended, and the attitudes of these preagricultural people survived as relics in religion and folk practices, and in doctrines such as Orphism and Pythagoreanism. In spite of this, wildlife was depleted in ancient times. Although hunting done in moderation need not reduce wildlife populations, attitudes changed, moderation was not always practiced, and other factors besides hunting were involved.

Hunting and the Gods

Writers of Greco-Roman times thought that hunting might be a purer way of life that had survived from a better time. As noted earlier, Dio Chrysostom described a family of hunters as living close to nature on Euboea, where the greed and injustice of city-dwellers had not as yet corrupted them.[3] Even later hunters whose ways were not so primitive believed that hunting was controlled by and practiced by the gods and goddesses, Artemis in particular. The gods were protectors of game species, allowing them to be taken solely when need existed and when permission had been asked and granted. Thus a wise hunter would not heedlessly slaughter prey, but took the gods into account. When a huge stag wandered across the path of the hungry Odysseus, he concluded that it had been sent by one of the gods, so he killed it in gratitude, but when his men slaughtered the sacred wild cattle of the sun-god Helios, he knew that evil would overwhelm them.[4] As an example of the survival of earlier attitudes of reverence toward animals, a sixth-century Athenian law provided that anyone who killed a wolf must pay for its public burial.[5] In antiquity, Phintias, tyrant of Acragas, had a dream warning him that Artemis would send a wild sow to kill him because he had omitted her sacrifices. He immediately promised to issue coins with the goddess's head on one side and a wild boar's head on the other.[6] Arrian, the writer of a hunters' handbook, advised his readers never to ignore the gods:

> Men interested in hunting should not neglect Artemis of the wild, or Pan, or the Nymphs, or Hermes, god of the ways and pathfinder, or any other god of the mountains. If they do neglect them, then their endeavors shall fall short of completion. Their hounds will be injured, their horses lamed, their men suffer. . . . One must . . . dedicate first-fruits of the chase.[7]

The gods and goddesses inspired respect for animal life, and enjoined practices that would make hunting less destructive, but did not forbid hunting as long as the hunters obeyed the rules that justified a human who obtained nourishment by the sacrifice of animal life. Before taking an animal, the prudent hunter would consider whether the act would offend a deity like Artemis, and would have been moved to avoid killing pregnant females and young animals, thus encouraging the reproduction of game species. Xenophon says that the good hunter would spare young hares for Artemis's sake.[8] He also dedicated the first share of his kill or catch to the goddess, and provided her with an altar on his hunting grounds.[9]

Not only did the gods protect some animals, but they appeared in their forms when it suited their purposes. Dionysos changed his shape to that of a lion or bull to frighten his enemies or drive them insane, and Zeus became a swan, an eagle, a bull, and countless other creatures including an ant, usually when it suited his amorous purposes. As noted earlier, the appearance and movements of birds in particular were held to reveal the intentions of the gods, and there were augurs skilled in interpreting them.[10] But the protection that birds and animals might receive from their close association with the gods is problematic; John Pollard remarks concerning birds whose appearances were taken as omens: "They revered them but ate them just the same."[11]

Sacred Groves as Wildlife Refuges   Protection within the *hiera temene*, lands set aside as sacred precincts of the gods, was given to the animals that lived there and enforced by laws of the local communities to which the shrines belonged. Hunters were forbidden to enter them with their dogs and weapons. On Mount Lycaeus, if a hunter saw his quarry go into the precinct of Zeus, he had to wait outside, believing that if he entered he would die within the year.[12] A cautionary tale said that the huntress Atalanta had been turned into a lioness for violating a sanctuary of Zeus.[13] In some sanctuaries there were deer or wild goats sacred to Persephone or Artemis, none of which could be hunted, although special permission might be given to capture a victim for sacrifice to the pertinent goddess. Sacrifices of wild animals were rare in Greek but not in Roman times; however, most sacrifices in both periods consisted of domestic animals.[14] As a rule, wild animals in the sanctuaries were preserved as sacred to the gods, and to kill them incurred punishment. Mythology, literature, and art are full of examples, such as Artemis's destruction of the hunter Actaeon by the horribly appropriate method of having his own hounds tear him to bits.[15] Although the usual version says this was because he saw her naked, that story is not found until late in Greek history.[16] If, as seems likely, there was an earlier version of the myth that said his offense had been to hunt a deer in the goddess's sacred demesne, then the form of his punishment truly fit the crime. He had, in any case, boasted to Artemis of his hunting prowess.[17] Bragging was also a fault of Agamemnon, the best-known literary figure to be punished for hunting in a holy place. As Sophocles says, "when taking pleasure in [Artemis's] sacred grove, he startled an antlered stag with dappled hide, shot it, and shooting made some careless boast."[18] In vengeance Artemis caused winds that prevented the sailing of the fleet against Troy until Agamemnon sacrificed his daughter "in quittance for the wild creature's life."[19] The evidence of inscriptions shows that it was not only in literature that penalties were exacted for hunting in the groves.

To provide another example of a site where animals were given the protection of a *temenos*, tortoises were preserved on a peak in Arcadia where "the men of the mountain fear to catch them, and will not allow strangers to do so either, for they hold that they are sacred to Pan."[20] Similarly, the Athenians would not let anyone harm the little owls of Athena that nested on the Acropolis, or the snake that had a den there, and to which offerings of honey-cakes were made.[21] No fishing was allowed in the waters of sacred groves, under penalty of death. In some it was lawful for priests, but the priest of Poseidon at Lepcis abstained from fish, probably because they were sacred to the sea god.[22] Artemis's eels were taboo in the spring of Arethusa, and at Pharae fish sacred to Hermes could not be caught.[23]

The Arktoi *of Brauron*   An initiation into the mysteries of humans' relationship to animals was celebrated every four years for the children of Athens. This was the Arkteia, a festival dedicated to Artemis at the rural sanctuary of Brauron. Little girls, and perhaps little boys too, were covered with symbolic bearskin robes and called "bears" (*arktoi*). Although there were bears in Attica at least as late as the first century A.D., they had become rare by the Golden Age of Athens, and saffron-dyed textile robes were substituted for the bearskins.[24] Such a festival was appropriate for Artemis, since she was believed to care for the young of both humans and animals, and myths said she sent wild animals as foster mothers to suckle infants that had been exposed.[25] Sculptures and vase paintings found at Brauron show children holding small animals such as hares and doves in poses of affection, even kissing them. These were not animals to be killed, since the sacrifice at Brauron was only a symbolic drop of the animals' blood from a small cut. Little girls performed a dance with slow, solemn steps imitating the movements of bears. Children sometimes wore bear masks.[26] The dominant idea of this initiation was the inculcation of respect and even love for wild creatures. A renewal of the festival was held in the city for young women near the age of marriage. The Arkteia shows that the worship of the gods had a positive side; Artemis might be seen as an early patron of environmental education.[27]

Kinds of Hunting

The exalted view of hunting as the pastime of the gods, under the eyes of the gods as protectors of animals, is not the only or even the most prevalent concept of hunting that can be found in the surviving evidence of the Greeks and Romans. It was also regarded as a means of obtaining food and other resources, as a form of commercial gain, as a way to prepare for and support military activities, as a safeguard for agriculture and herding, and as a sport or entertainment.

Subsistence Hunting   Although ancient civilization was founded on an agrarian base, and cultivated plants and domestic animals provided the bulk of the diet and materials for clothing, wildlife was still sought as a source of food, leather, furs, feathers, and so on. For many families, hunting was a direct means of support, or of supplementing the diet, especially in rural areas and earlier periods before many species had become rare or disappeared. Deer, boars, hares, and goats were among the mammalian species hunted for food in Homeric times and after. Turtles, frogs, and a wide variety of birds also graced the rustic table. Fishing is known from art as old as the Minoan frescoes, and seafood, including shellfish, was a major source of protein for the common people.

Commercial Hunting and Fishing   Those who did not hunt for themselves could purchase animal products from a widespread trade supplied by professional hunters, who organized game drives like those seen in North African mosaics.[28] Small-scale commercial hunters also supplied the marketplaces of towns. There one could buy wild meats such as venison and many kinds of birds, from peacocks and flamingos to small songbirds.[29] The furs of beavers and other animals from distant mountains could be had, as well as ostrich feathers and various kinds of leather.

Greek and Roman demand brought wild animal products even from beyond the Mediterranean basin. Ivory from African and Indian elephants was used in works of art ranging from huge chryselephantine statues to delicate miniatures, and was inlaid in furniture of every kind, writing tablets, desks, spoons, and other objects. Ivory in incredible quantities went into statues such as Phidias's 40-foot Parthenon sculpture of Athena and that of Zeus at Olympia, so large that it was one of the Seven Wonders. In one day's exhibit in Ptolemaic Alexandria, 600 elephant tusks were shown, indicating that at the least 300 of the mighty beasts had died.[30] Wild animal skins were worked into clothes and furnishings, and hair and feathers served as decorations on fine ladies' costumes and military uniforms.

Urban tastes supported a large fishing industry and provided work for entire villages. Fresh fish came daily to market from local fleets, and importers brought salt fish from Egypt, the Black Sea, and the Atlantic coast of Spain. Among the favorite species were red mullet, parrot wrasse, sturgeon, turbot, brill, common bass, hake, sole, and eels.[31] The Romans loved fish sauces with names such as *alec, garuum,* and *putrilago.*[32] Commercial interests not only operated fishing fleets to meet these demands, but also cultured fish in fresh and salt ponds. C. Sergius Orata ran a business on Lake Lucrina that raised fish for the elegant table.[33] Beds of shellfish, such as oysters, were carefully tended and protected against competitors. Products of the sea were collected for purposes other than food, sponges for example, or the murex mollusc that produced the famous purple dye for the robes of kings and Roman senators.

Military Uses of Wildlife   The Roman Army employed military methods in hunting to provision troops with meat. Soldiers or paid professional hunters scoured the countryside in hostile or uninhabited regions. Hunting was often regarded as a form of warfare and art portrayed humans in battle with animals. Xenophon said, "Hunting . . . is . . . excellent training in the art of war."[34] His friends the Spartans deliberately used it in this way. Perhaps this explains the strange Spartan story of the boy who was carrying a fox under his cloak. It was said he met his military trainer and stood talking to him; the fox got loose under the cloak and gnawed at the boy's abdomen, and the boy continued to stand without showing a sign of pain until he fell over dead.[35] The story was told to illustrate the ability of a young Spartan to bear pain and his willingness to die rather than admit he had stolen, but why he should have had a fox can perhaps best be explained in the context of hunting as preparation for war.

Elephants were captured, trained, and used on the battlefield, resulting in a constant drain on the wild population. At the battle of Raphia in 217 B.C., 102 Indian elephants deployed by Antiochus III of Syria defeated 73 African elephants of Ptolemy IV, collapsing the left wing of Ptolemy's battle formation, although Ptolemy managed to win the battle. Strange to say, although in modern times African elephants are known to be considerably larger than Indian elephants, the reverse was stated by every ancient author who commented on the question.[36] Perhaps this was because the African elephant then known was a smaller North African race that is now extinct. The Carthaginian elephants that invaded Italy with Hannibal in the third century B.C. came from the north slopes of the Atlas Mountains, but there are none there now.[37]

Defense of Agriculture and Herding   A reason often given by ancient writers for the destruction of wildlife was as a safeguard for agriculture and herding, and this was doubtless a major motive both for governments and the common people. Predators were killed to protect animals on farms or herds in the countryside, while birds and herbivorous mammals were persecuted because they competed for the same vegetation as domestic animals, or invaded croplands. Homer often uses the simile of lions pursued by herders in describing battle.[38] Elsewhere relentless attempts to extirpate wolves, jackals, foxes, and bear are described. These efforts promoted hunting, but the desire to protect cropland also may have had the opposite effect, bringing enactment of laws in some places against hunting on horseback.[39]

Hunting and Fishing as Sport   Hunting for its own sake as a sport, or in order to collect trophies and boast of one's own proficiency and success, is a pastime that probably developed soon after people began to live in urban conditions. Plato approved of such hunting to develop skill and courage in young men, but would have forbidden netting, trapping, and night hunting in his utopia, as well as all forms of fishing.[40]

In art and history, hunting of various animals was portrayed as a sport of kings and heroes such as Alexander the Great.[41] The emperor Hadrian loved hunting; it is said that he killed a bear at Hadrianoutherae (a name meaning "Hadrian's beasts"), a lion in

Egypt, and a boar elsewhere.[42] He, and Marcus Aurelius later, showed themselves engaged in the hunt on their coinage, a valuable propaganda image. The lion was held to be royal prey, and laws often forbade anyone other than the monarch to hunt them. Julius Alexander, a Syrian of ordinary rank, was condemned to death in A.D. 189 for usurping the emperor's privilege by slaying a lion from horseback.[43] It was not until A.D. 414 that an imperial law permitted commoners to kill lions.[44] Boar hunts were also engaged in by kings, as they had been by epic heroes.[45] Kings sometimes fished for sport: Anthony and Cleopatra did so, and the Egyptian queen tricked her lover by having one of her slaves attach a salted fish to his hook. Their conqueror, Augustus Caesar, also enjoyed angling.[46] Not everyone thought fishing was a royal sport, however. Aristotimus in Plutarch's *Whether Land or Sea Animals Are Cleverer* disparaged it as an ignoble activity.[47]

Kings and emperors often reserved hunting lands for themselves; in the case of Greek and Roman potentates, this was in part an imitation of the Persian King of Kings and his satraps, whose parks called *paradises* were as a rule "full of wild beasts" to hunt.[48] Xenophon, and later Alexander, saw many of these parks. Since many sport hunters were affluent landowners, they too created preserves for their favored activity, as Xenophon did. There were game parks, aviaries, and large fish ponds in Rome. Varro had a place near Tusculum where he fed wild boars and roe deer, but was far outdone by Quintus Hortensius, whose Laurentum estate had a game preserve of fifty *jugera* (35 acres) surrounded by a wall. At feeding time, Hortensius had a horn blown to attract the animals, and an actor dressed like Orpheus who played a lyre as if his song were enchanting the wild beasts.[49] He gave his preserve the Greek name *therotrophion*, but there were others called in Latin *roboraria*, *vivaria*, and *leporaria*. These precincts preserved many animals, since common hunters were excluded, there were defenses against poachers, and the owners wanted to have large numbers to show off to their guests.

A series of ancient handbooks, some of which have survived, purported to give advice to sport hunters. These are usually entitled *Cynegetica*, from Greek words meaning "to lead dogs," since hunters often used packs of dogs in pursuing game. Authors of these treatises include three Greeks: Socrates' friend Xenophon and Epictetus's disciple Arrian, both of whom were avid hunters, and Oppian, who probably was not. The Latin writer Nemesianus of Carthage is represented by fragmentary works on hunting and bird catching. The sport of fishing also has its literature, the *Halieutica* of the famous Latin poet Ovid, which actually contains little about fishing, and a similarly titled work by Oppian. Ausonius, writing in Gaul, devoted much of one of his poems to fishes and fishing.[50] All these works portray hunting or fishing as sports of the well-bred gentleman, and they sometimes advise him to limit his catch, spare certain animals, and avoid unworthy methods for sportsman-like reasons.

Wildlife Used as Entertainment: The Arena

Wildlife served to entertain large numbers of people in several ways. An animal or bird that was rare, exotic, or beautiful might simply be exhibited. Animals were tamed and taught tricks, as bears and lions commonly were. Small, popular shows where one animal fought another, such as cockfights or dogfights, usually involved domestic species, although sometimes wild birds or beasts were baited to combat or to devour each other. Fights were staged between partridges or quails. In a strange game called "quail-tapping," popular in Athens, a quail was put in a ring and the owner offered bets that it would stay there even if knocked on the head.[51] But for sheer spectacle, exploitation of animals and spectators, and waste of life, nothing could surpass the Roman arena.

The shows put on for popular amusement first in Roman circuses, and later in amphitheaters, exhausted the ingenuity of their producers. Sometimes these were pageants or plays in which animals played a part, often involving violence or sexual perversion in addition to acrobatics. Even the rarer animals, at first exhibited as curiosities, were afterward mutilated and killed. From at least the middle years of the Roman Republic, criminals were executed by being exposed to wild beasts that had been starved or were goaded into attacking them. *Venationes*, or mock hunts, in which armed men on foot or horseback chased and killed animals, constituted a major part of the shows. The arena, so called because it had a floor covered with sand, became soaked in blood. These contests were the subject of many mosaics and paintings.

The first *venatio* in Rome apparently was held in 186 B.C. by Marcus Fulvius Nobilior, conqueror of Aetolia.[52] For whatever reason, a law forbade the use of African beasts for this purpose, but Cnaeus Aufidius allowed exemptions in 170.[53] In the following year, the aediles (the magistrates responsible for the shows) exhibited sixty-three leopards, forty bears, and some elephants. Elephants had been seen for the first time in Rome in 275 B.C., when Manius Curius displayed at his triumph a number he had captured from Pyrrhus of Epirus, who had brought them to Italy for his military campaign. Romans jokingly called them "Lucanian cows," after the province where they had fought Pyrrhus. Elephants were first "hunted" in the circus in 99 B.C., and were pitted against bulls twenty years later.

In the late Roman Republic, the variety of wild animals and the number killed increased dramatically. Scaurus, in 58 B.C., brought crocodiles and hippopotami from the Nile. Soon afterward, Pompey had 20 elephants and 600 lions killed by armed Gaetulians. Caesar at various times showed a lynx from Gaul, 40 elephants, and a giraffe he had received as a present from Cleopatra. Numbers continued to rise as the early emperors attempted to gain popularity by entertaining the people. Augustus held twenty-six *venationes* in which 3,500 animals were killed, including tigers from India.[54] Claudius was another emperor who enjoyed watching the beast fights. Nero, in addition to his more infamous shows, flooded an arena and displayed polar bears catching seals. At the dedication of the Colosseum under Titus, 9,000 animals were destroyed in 100 days, and Trajan's conquest over Dacia in A.D. 107 was celebrated by the slaughter of 11,000 wild animals. To these hecatombs in the city of Rome must be added the numerous *venationes* held in other towns throughout the empire.[55]

The "hunters" in these sadistic spectacles were called *bestiarii*, and were trained in schools like that of Domitian on the Caelian

Hill.[56] Sometimes they used dogs or horses in the arena. Many of them were proud of their skill, and there were families who followed the occupation through generations. A technology of death supported them; for example, cages were constructed under amphitheaters, complete with elevators and ramps to bring the beasts up to the arena without endangering the attendants too much.

The demand for a constant supply of animals was enormous, supported by an organized business for their capture and transportation. Many found employment in this enterprise. It was far from easy, since the beasts had to be kept in good condition in pits, nets, cages, or boxes, and carried or led from place to place until they were delivered. For the most part it was a private business on which the government levied an import tax of 2.5 percent.[57] Roman officials and the military amply assisted the trade, however, and soldiers were dispatched to round up the animals. Those transporting animals destined for the emperor's shows could requisition food and accommodations from towns through which they passed. This was no small expense for towns on the usual routes, considering the size and number of the animals, and late imperial edicts limited the time they could stay in one city to seven days.[58] Those destined for Rome landed at wharves in the Campus Martius and were held temporarily in the enclosure for wild animals outside the Praenestine Gate.[59] There were extensive imperial menageries, including one for the elephant herd at Ardea under the care of an officer titled the *procurator ad elephantos*. A large proportion of the creatures collected for this trade must have died along the way.

Romans of every social level from emperor to common people attended the games, and most Romans who wrote about them approved. There were few protests against the bloody "sport" of the *venationes*, which is perhaps not surprising in light of the fact that objections to the killing of humans in the gladiatorial exhibitions were also rare. In 55 B.C., the elephants in Pompey's show at the dedication of his theater gained the crowd's sympathy when, wounded by javelins, they defended themselves by snatching the shields of their attackers, attempting to break out of their enclosure, and trumpeted piteously. Cicero protested at this incident, "What pleasure can it possibly be to a man of culture, when . . . a splendid beast is transfixed with a hunting-spear . . . the result was a certain compassion and a kind of feeling that the huge beast has a fellowship with the human race."[60] When he governed Cilicia, Cicero refused to make his provincials collect leopards for the games; by the way, this proves the existence of the species in Asia Minor as late as the first century B.C. Marcus Aurelius, the Roman "philosopher-king," also disliked the cruelty of the games. In earlier times, a few writers voiced opposition to hunting of any kind; this was a teaching of the Pythagoreans, who refused to have anything to do with hunters, butchers, or priests who sacrificed animals. Varro also was antihunting: "There you go, chasing wild boars on the mountains with your spears, or stags, which never did any harm to you, with your javelin. What a 'splendid' art!"[61] Even a confirmed hunter such as Arrian said one should not take pleasure in the sight of the kill.[62]

The Technology of Hunting and Fishing

Achilles outran deer, said Pindar, and caught them with his bare hands.[63] This simplest form of hunting is not unknown among primal people, but Greeks and Romans generally used assistance. Sometimes other animals were pressed into service, such as the hunting dogs that are known from Mycenaean times, and whose domestication for this purpose probably goes back to the Paleolithic era.[64] Various breeds were trained for the work; a fresco from Tiryns shows hunters with a huge hound. Hunting from horseback is not as ancient as with dogs, but certainly dates from pre-Homeric times. It was widespread in classical days, described by Xenophon and Perses.[65] Falconry, regarded as a sport of Persians and other barbarians, was practiced among the Greeks, according to Aristotle, and became popular with the last of the Roman aristocrats.[66] The use of prey animals as bait, such as tethering goats to catch lions in a pitfall, was a common technique.[67] But sporting hunters like Xenophon denounced the use of a female animal's own young to trap her: for example, tying up a fawn to decoy a doe.[68] A repertoire of hunting implements developed.

The idea that hunting and warfare are similar and use the same weapons is found before the classical period; a dagger from Bronze Age Mycenae shows shield-bearing warriors attacking lions with their spears, and a ring of the same period bears the design of an archer shooting a stag from a chariot.[69] Spears and javelins are often mentioned in the literature of hunting, and were redesigned for use against specific prey such as boars.

Nets have been used from time immemorial; a wild bull caught in a net can be seen on one of the Vapheio cups dated to Mycenaean times. In Greece and Rome, nets of strong linen ropes were preferred. Deer and boar, as well as many other animals, were taken in nets of various designs.[70] Xenophon lists three types: purse, road, and long nets, but there were doubtless others. A purse net was a large bag with a mouth that could be closed by a noose, a road net was a rectangular one used to block game trails, and a long net was crescent-shaped with a belly and was usually set up in a forest where it could be hidden. Footsnares, devices that combined hidden nooses with wooden or iron spikes set in plaited circles of twigs, often over small pits, were also common.[71]

Birds were caught in nets, snares, cages, and on rods or branches smeared with sticky birdlime. They were decoyed, called by clever imitators, attracted by mirrors, or lured with food. As an instance of the latter, a small pit was dug, filled with berries, and two potsherds were balanced over it by a peg; when the bird dislodged the peg, the potsherds covered the hole and trapped the bird.[72] Birds were also brought down with small arrows. A huge bird like the ostrich was a considerable exception; Arabian ostriches were chased on horseback.[73]

Fishing technology is a subject unto itself. Nets and spears were utilized; as Homer says of the cannibalistic Laestrygonians, "Like folk spearing fishes they bore home their hideous meal."[74] Not only hand-lines, but poles of cane or light elastic woods, often 6 to 8 feet long, were known.[75] These had fixed lines made of horsehair, flax, or a fiber called *sparton* taken from the stems of the *genista* shrub, a plant common on Mediterranean hills. Floats were carved of cork. Hooks were fashioned of iron or bronze, and baited with real insects or with feathers and other materials to make an artificial fly.[76] Poisonous vegetable substances such as cyclamen root were used to kill fish in small bodies of water, a practice condemned by Plato.[77] Commercial fishermen erected towers on shore to sight schools of tunny and other large fishes. At night, torches were carried on fishing boats to attract the catch.[78] Finally, it is reported that skates and other fish were attracted by music and dancing.[79]

The Ownership of Wildlife

The ownership of game and fish in enclosures or ponds was vested in those with title to the land; outside private places, it was considered to rest in the sovereign authorities, or in those to whom they delegated it, as was the case also with unoccupied, virgin, or abandoned land.[80] Rivers, and the fish in them, were considered public property in Roman law.[81] But poaching by common people happened constantly, whether on public, private, or sacred land. The prevailing attitude was that wild animals belonged to "no one" until they were caught, and then they belonged to those who caught them. The state asserted its interest only in exceptional cases, as in protecting the animals inside a sacred *temenos*, but generally its policy was to encourage agriculture, grazing, and the reduction of the number of wild animals.

Depletion and Extinction

The surviving evidence gives the impression of declining populations of wildlife, and the gradual extinction of certain species in one area after another. Writers often remark that animals are no longer to be found where they were once abundant. Lion bones have been unearthed in archaeological sites such as the Mycenaean palace of Tiryns.[82] Herodotus reports that when the Persians invaded Greece, lions came down from the mountains to attack the camels in their baggage trains.[83] Aristotle also notes their presence in his homeland, but lions were gone by the first century B.C.[84] Leopards and hyenas also disappeared from Greece, and lynxes, wolves, and jackals were limited to the mountains, where they

105

hold out today in small numbers. Bears could be found in the Peloponnesus up to A.D. 100, and probably much later; a few still exist in mountainous northern Greece.[85] Hunting reduced wild cattle, sheep, and goats to remnant herds, and eliminated them from some islands in classical times. This was only one of a series of extinctions of island fauna, following the earlier disappearance between 6000 B.C. and 2000 B.C. of dwarf forms of elephants, hippopotami, antelopes, and deer; giant forms of shrews, hedgehogs, and dormice; and still other endemics.[86]

Procurement of animals for the Roman arena cleared larger mammals, reptiles, and birds from the areas most accessible to professional hunters and trappers. They exhausted the hunting grounds of North Africa, where elephant, rhinoceros, and zebra became extinct. The hippopotamus and crocodile were banished from the lower Nile to upper Nubia. By the fourth century A.D., a writer could lament that there were no elephants left in Libya, no lions in Thessaly, and no hippopotami in the Nile. Lions had been extirpated from western Asia Minor, although the king of beasts persisted in Syria, where the emperor Julian hunted them, and in the Taurus Mountains; in both these areas a few could be found as late as the nineteenth century. In the Atlas Mountains their numbers were reduced in antiquity; a few lions remain there today.[87] Distant areas felt the Roman demands; tigers disappeared from Armenia, and from Hyrcania in northern Iran, the closest sources to Rome.[88] Collection of animals for the games was not the only cause of disappearance; all these creatures were hunted and killed for other reasons as well. Among the causes of the extinction of the North African form of the elephant, for example, were the use of the animal in warfare and, more important, the ivory trade. The Romans were persistent, efficient, could pay well, and came to dominate the commerce in animals and animal products throughout the Mediterranean basin, so the major responsibility for extinctions was theirs.

Bird populations also diminished. The former richness of Mediterranean bird life can be sensed today in such relatively undisturbed areas as the French Camargue near the mouth of the Rhone River, with its flocks of flamingos; or Coto Doñana in Las Marismas on the lower Guadalquivir River in Spain. But these are the precious exceptions. The birds in Aristophanes' play berate humans for persecuting them, for setting snares and lime twigs for them even on temples.[89] Ancient people devoured avian species that seem to have had too little meat to make the effort worthwhile, but so do some modern Greeks and Italians.

There were complaints of the depletion of fisheries in antiquity. It has been suggested that the disappearance of mosquito-eating fish from Italian marshes aided the spread of malaria in the second century B.C. and subsequently.[90] Increasing prices for fish on the Roman market may indicate that there were fewer left to catch than before. The finest rare fish might have sold for their weight in gold; three mullets once brought 30,000 sesterces at Rome, and Pliny says this species rarely exceeded 2 pounds in weight.[91] As seas go, the Mediterranean was not particularly rich in fish, so the parts of it most accessible to the fishing fleets could have been impoverished fairly early.

Introduction of domestic species that compete with wild ones must have happened countless times, particularly on islands. The devastating effects of goats, rats, and opportunistic birds like pigeons have been observed in newly discovered lands since the fifteenth century A.D.; there can be no doubt that it happened in isolated places as they were visited by ships or settled by new groups of people in Greek and Roman times.

The process with the most damaging effect on all forms of wildlife was, as it still is, habitat destruction. The clearing of forests, the spread of agriculture, the introduction of weeds and other exotic plant species, the overgrazing of grasslands, and the draining of lakes and wetlands all affected wildlife even more seriously than hunting. Two areas that were the objects of persistent attempts at drainage throughout antiquity may serve as examples: Lake Copais in Boeotia and the Pomptine Marshes near Rome. Although neither of these large wetlands was completely drained in antiquity, many thousands of acres of irrigable tillage land were recovered by the construction of canals and tunnels, with consequent effects on birds, fish, and other wildlife.[92] Many lakes and marshes in the Mediterranean basin were drained; in the prevailing limestone country, natural underground channels often existed that could be cleared or widened.

The Study of Animals

Observation of animals in the wild or captivity helped philosophers to gain knowledge of the natural world. Aristotle, the greatest ancient commentator on animal anatomy and behavior, believed in the importance of direct observation, and some of his comments have been vindicated in modern times. For example, he recorded that the male catfish guards the eggs that he has fertilized, as well as the young up to forty or fifty days old. This was disbelieved by early nineteenth-century European biologists, since the catfish they knew did not behave in this way, but it was subsequently noticed that Greece has a species (*Parasilurus aristotelis*) that does so, which was undoubtedly known to Aristotle or his informants. Aristotle also reports facts that could have been discovered only by means of dissection.[93] On the other hand, many of his statements are simply wrong and could have been corrected by observation.

The Peripatetic School of philosophy strongly shaped the Museum of Alexandria, a research institute founded by Ptolemy I Soter and Ptolemy II Philadelphus with the aid of Demetrius of Phalerum and Strato of Lampsacus, both followers of Aristotle and Theophrastus. This unique institution continued Aristotle's interest in observation of animals by maintaining a large zoo. Among the many animals and birds exhibited were elephants, Saiga antelope from north of the Black Sea, oryxes, hartebeests, ostriches, camels, parrots, leopards, cheetahs, and a chimpanzee. In addition, during the reign of Ptolemy II alone, there were "twenty-four great lions, leopards, lynxes and other cats, Indian and African buffaloes, wild asses from Moab, a python forty-five feet long, a giraffe, a rhinoceros, and a polar bear (whose journey south must have been exciting), together with parrots, peacocks, guinea-fowl, pheasants, and many African birds."[94] To collect such animals for study, the Greco-Macedonian rulers of Egypt sent out far-ranging expeditions, some of which penetrated into Ethiopia by way of the Red Sea. Numerous animals from India were brought to Mediterranean cities by Indian or Greek merchants and ambassadors. An Indian delegation, with wild animals including tigers, tortoises, and a python, was welcomed by the emperor Augustus on Samos in 21 B.C.[95] Augustus "took especial delight in 'untold numbers and unknown shapes of beasts.' "[96] One can imagine his delight in capturing the Ptolemaic menagerie when he conquered Egypt; doubtless many of the animals killed in the excessive *venationes* at his celebrations came from that source. Thus did scientific curiosity yield to bloodthirsty prurience, but the two kept company in Rome. The medical writer Galen says that physicians assembled at dissections of elephants, and presumably other animals killed in the games, to gain anatomical knowledge.[97]

Pets and the Love of Animals

The bond between humans and domestic animals is well known in classical literature from Homer onward; Achilles' horses wept for Patroclus, their driver, and Odysseus could not suppress a tear when his old hound Argos recognized him after so many years.[98] The cat came to Greece from Egypt, where it had been domesticated for more than a thousand years. But wild animals, too, were sometimes loved and respected. Arion was not the only individual said to have been rescued from drowning by dolphins, who were believed to be especially fond of children. Pythagoras is said to have had a bear that kept him company, and an eagle that would fly down and perch on his shoulder. These stories may or may not have been true, but it is certain that the Greeks and Romans captured and tamed an amazing variety of wild animals and kept them on their land or in their homes. Only emperors could own elephants or lions, but in Republican times at least one private citizen had impressed his friends by riding an elephant when he came to dinner at their homes.[99] Among the mammals and reptiles attested in private households or collections are Barbary apes, monkeys, ferrets, hedgehogs, deer, giraffes, gazelles, captive wild goats, and harmless "house" snakes. Many birds including peacocks, various pheasants, parrots, cranes, storks, flamingos, rails, crows, starlings, magpies, thrushes, and nightingales were kept individually or in aviaries; some were valued for their song, and others because they could be taught to talk.[100] Captive animals, especially smaller ones, could have escaped and established wild populations in areas where they had not existed before, but there seems to be no record of this.

An ancient animal rights movement, if so one might term it, existed among writers, mostly of Pythagorean bent, who honored the sanctity of all forms of life and maintained that animals possess rational souls. Ovid made Pythagoras himself a character in the *Metamorphoses* and had him advise King Numa against animal food, since it was through eating the flesh of living creatures that the Golden Age came to an end, and against animal sacrifice as making the gods into partners of mortals in wickedness.[101]

Plutarch also spoke on behalf of animals. In the dialogue *Whether Land or Sea Animals Are Cleverer*, set as a learned debate among cultured huntsmen, he argues that animals possess a degree of reason. Human beings, he adds, also have reason only to a degree; if what we wish to demonstrate is "true reason and wisdom, not even man may be said to exercise it."[102] But since animals are rational, we are unjust if we kill them when they have not injured us. Plutarch does not go as far as the Pythagoreans, however; he would permit killing animals "in pity and sorrow," as well as eating meat as an unfortunate necessity.[103] But Plutarch's most entertaining comments on this subject are contained in a brief dialogue between Odysseus, Gryllus, and Circe. With her magic arts, Circe had changed many men into various species of animals. Odysseus won the right to have his sailors retransformed and furthermore asked Circe to do the same for the other Greeks. Circe agreed on the condition that Odysseus convince a spokesman for the beasts that it was better to be a human than an animal. Chosen to speak for the beasts was Gryllus, a hog granted the power of speech by Circe. He refused the chance to return to human form because animals, he maintained, are superior to mankind in every virtue: courage, temperance, and intelligence. Besides, animal virtues are natural; humans must cultivate theirs. Odysseus, in spite of his fame as a persuasive speaker, lost the contest. Driven to use the argument that beasts cannot be rational because they have no inborn knowledge of God, he left himself open to Gryllus's riposte that Odysseus's father was Sisyphus, a notorious atheist.[104] That the dialogue was not a mere set piece is clear from Plutarch's serious objections elsewhere to hunting, animal slaughter, and the excesses of the arena. Rejecting the proposition of Hesiod and the Stoics that "human beings have no compact of justice with irrational animals," Plutarch exhibited admiration and sympathy for the myriad forms of living things and was an early defender of animal rights.[105] Unfortunately, neither in his case nor in any other known from ancient times does it seem that such ideas resulted in practical programs to help wildlife.

Conclusion

The major problem of wildlife in the ancient world was its depletion and disappearance in many areas. The combined evidence of literature, archaeology, and distribution of fauna in more recent times indicates that some species became extinct, while the ranges of others were restricted due to habitat alteration and to killing for various purposes. The process of wildlife depletion was not uniform, however. Due primarily to the lower human population in ancient as compared to modern times, refuges existed where habitats had not been altered and hunting pressure was low. Also, as the palynological evidence indicates that deforestation occurred in cycles with periods of recovery, so it must also be true that wild species rebuilt their numbers during intervals when human demands and environmental impacts relented. Fluctuations in numbers of animal species occur even without human intervention, as ecological interactions occur among species and with environmental changes. Still, some of the effects of Greek and Roman exploitation of wildlife were irreversible, as when species were made totally extinct, or extirpated from islands or other areas where their natural reintroduction was impossible. On the other hand, the introduction of domestic and feral species such as goats and cats to formerly isolated places initiated predation and competition with native species and the destruction of the vegetation on which they depended. The result of all these factors was depletion and extinction of wildlife and an impoverishment of ecosystems.

Seven

Industrial Technology
and Environmental Damage

T hat human technology can damage the earth is not just a modern idea. The elder Pliny remarked, "Mountains were made by nature herself to serve as a kind of framework for holding together the inner parts of the earth. . . . We quarry them and haul them away for a mere whim."[1] He also noted the human failure to restore and reclaim: "But least of all do we search for means of healing [the wounds caused by mines in Mother Earth], for how few in their digging are inspired by the desire to cure!"[2] Ancient technology was capable of creating works of remarkable size, but it also inflicted scars on the landscape that can still be seen, from the quarries of Pentelicus in Greece to the mining pits of Spain, and more widespread erosion resulting from the removal of vegetation to supply charcoal burners. There was other damage less easy to assess today but noticed by ancient writers, the pollution of air and water by poisons released in extractive activities and industrial processes. In addition to the ritual and moral meaning mentioned in chapter 4, pollution was also given something like its modern sense of contaminating water, air, and earth with the waste products of human activities, including industrial processes.[3]

Technological Capacity

Prometheus originated technology by bringing fire from the sun, according to Greek myth, and instructing mortals in its use. That the stolen gift was a dangerous one may be symbolized by the wrath of Zeus, who punished Prometheus by chaining him to a crag in the Caucasus Mountains and causing him to be tortured daily.[4] Greek and Roman thought remained ambivalent about technology, both proud of the great works of humankind and sure that these works marred the earth, challenged the gods, and called forth divine retribution.

The extent of damage done by technology to the environment depends in large part on the efficiency of the machines used and also on the nature and magnitude of the sources of energy that are available. In general, more powerful technologies produce effects that are deeper and more widespread, effects produced directly and indirectly through demand for resources such as fuel. In the ancient world, the sources of energy available to industry consisted of human and animal labor, wood and charcoal fires, water power, and (for transportation) wind power. Of these, human labor either directly or by means of machines undoubtedly accomplished the most. Oxen were used for pulling; and horses, mules, and donkeys for carrying and pulling. Small size and the lack of an efficient harness reduced the efficiency of equines, particularly horses. Wood and its partially oxidized product, charcoal, was by far the most common fuel, although other vegetable substances were also burned. Coal was known, but rarely used, and petroleum was regarded as a curiosity. Water power was harnessed by wheels, and wind power by sails. The steam engine and windmill, known to the Greeks of Alexandria, received no common practical use.

The mechanical engineering devices invented by the Greeks and Romans or adopted by them from older civilizations or from the so-called barbarian peoples beyond their frontiers increased in number and sophistication as the centuries passed. Technological improvement, however, was not rapid or steady, and there were retreats as well as advances. The simplest machines, known from much earlier times, were the lever, the wedge, and the wheel and axle. The Syracusan engineering scientist Archimedes, who boasted concerning the lever, "Give me a place to stand and I will move the Earth," was not the only one to develop applications of simple machines.[5] Winches (horizontal drums around which ropes or chains wound) were used to move cranes and hoists and to drag heavy objects such as blocks of stone or ships. For lifting column sections and other architectural members, cranes were used from 515 B.C. onward; before that, levers and rocking cradles had sufficed.[6] A crane used to lower an actor onto the stage in the Greek theater, the "machine" of the *deus ex machina*, was powered by a man using his weight to revolve a *carchesion*, or cage wheel. The pulley, which provides mechanical advantage in lifting, was known in Assyria in the eighth century B.C., and was adopted in Greece not long afterward. Multiple pulleys appeared by the fifth century. The screw principle, an innovation of the third century B.C., was used in Archimedes' pump, a device widely used in irrigation and mining that raised water by revolving a tight-fitting, broad-threaded screw inside an inclined tube. At the same time, the two-cylinder piston pump was described by Ctesibius of Alexandria; it was cast by the lost wax technique in Roman times, and twenty-one examples of it have been uncovered by archaeologists.[7] Gears were developed with sophisticated ratios and arrangements; the most noteworthy example is the Anticythera Machine, an astronomical and calendrical computer of the first century B.C. that was probably made in Alexandria. The waterwheel was described by Vitruvius in the same century in its undershot form: that is, one in which the water revolves the wheel by passing underneath it.[8] The overshot wheel appeared a century or two later. Both forms were widely used to power grinding wheels and saws, and a wheel turned by animal or human power, or by water power, was used to raise water in mines and in irrigation.

It is evident from the list just given that technological innovation occurred at various times during the period under consideration. Not all of the machines invented were widely adopted. An intriguing example of an unproductive invention was the prototype steam engine described by Hero of Alexandria (fl. A.D. 62).[9] Hero mounted a free-spinning, hollow sphere on a pipe and bracket on the lid of a vessel in which water was boiled. Steam rose through the pipe into the sphere and escaped through open pipes, bent at right angles, on the surface of the sphere, causing it to rotate. While this engine was adapted to no practical use, Hero does describe other elements of machinery such as pistons and valves that conceivably could have been combined with the steam principle he had discovered to produce a useful steam engine. It is interesting to speculate why the steam engine was not developed further, and also why Hero's windmill, which he used to work the water pump of a musical organ, was not adapted in ancient times to the more prevalent uses it received during the medieval period.[10]

Technological innovation depends on a body of knowledge and experience leading up to a new application, a need for the new device, its efficiency and therefore economic viability, and social receptivity to it.[11] The first two certainly existed for the steam engine and windmill. The windmill, but possibly not the steam engine, could have been made efficient at the time. Why the Romans should not have been receptive is a puzzle. It has often been said that their use of slaves inhibited technological advance, and there are stories about the rejection of specific inventions. For example, the emperor Tiberius is said to have heard that an unbreakable, flexible glass had been invented, and promptly to have ordered the invention suppressed and the inventor's workshop destroyed because he feared the substance would be more valuable than gold and would depress the monetary system. The story is recorded by Pliny the Elder, who doubts its truth himself. Vespasian, a later emperor, is reported to have rejected a new column-moving machine on the grounds that it would do the work of many men and produce unemployment.[12] Yet efficient cranes were in common use in Roman construction, and the existence of slavery did not prevent the acceptance of many new machines and industrial processes, some of which were operated by slave labor. Of course the adoption of these machines would have increased the impacts on the environment, thus exacerbating problems.

The sheer magnitude of the ability of ancient technology to alter the landscape may be illustrated by the dimensions of Roman roads. These were constructed not only as straight as possible, but permanently and deeply, almost like buried walls, as Plutarch aptly described them: "The roads were driven through the countryside, exactly in a straight line, partly paved with hewn stone, and partly laid with impacted gravel. Gullies were filled in, intersecting torrents and ravines were bridged, so that the layout of the road on both sides was the same, and the whole work looked level and beautiful."[13]

The labor and materials expended on road construction and the extent of changes made in the countryside were, in fact, greater than might have been required for an adequate system. In order to lessen a grade south of Rome, a road was cut 117 feet deep through solid rock, and another, the Via Cassia, has one roadcut 4,875 feet long, 66 feet deep, and 20 feet wide. The total length of the Roman road network at the end of the second century A.D. has been estimated at 56,000 miles of major highways, more than enough to circle the world twice, and 200,000 miles of smaller roads, giving a total distance long enough to reach the moon.[14]

Extractive Industries

The industries that involve direct removal of materials from the earth include mining, quarrying, and digging of various substances that are the raw materials for pottery, glass, bricks, concrete and mortar, fertilizer, and the like. These human activities have a definite impact on the earth, producing pits, tunnels, and underground cavelike chambers. Such scars in turn expose the landscape to erosion and allow leaching of chemicals into water at a rate much faster than would occur under natural conditions. In addition, these industries and their associated processing industries such as metallurgy and ceramics place demands on forests for wood for construction, and wood and charcoal for fuel.

Mining   The Greek playwright Aeschylus put into Prometheus's mouth the claim to have given to mortals the knowledge of metals and mining: "Next the treasures of the earth, / The bronze, iron, silver, gold hidden deep down—who else / But I can claim to have found them first?"[15] But according to Lucretius, humans discovered metals when they set forest fires and found them melted, oozing out of veins in the earth. They experimented with the stuff and found they could fashion it into tools and weapons.[16] The Greeks and Romans inherited from earlier civilizations the knowledge of a variety of metals and continued to exploit them, developing new methods as they did so. The most important metals and the ores from which they extracted them were gold, from auriferous quartz; silver, from argentiferous galena; copper, from chalcopyrite and chalcocite; tin, from cassiterite; lead, from galena; iron, from pyrites and hematite; zinc, from calamine; and mercury, from cinnabar.[17] The methods used for extraction of the ores were placer mining (washing the material from alluvial sand and gravel), open-pit mining, and tunneling into veins deep below the earth. To these, the Romans added hydraulic mining, in which forceful flows of water were directed on ores to wash them down to places where they could be recovered.

Mining extended to virtually every area of the ancient Mediterranean basin. The Athenians inherited the works of their Mycenaean ancestors, who had mined silver at Laurium since before 1500 B.C. The silver mines on the island of Thasos had been worked by the Phoenicians before the Greeks.[18] The Spartans had an iron mine, the source of fine weapons, in southern Laconia. Deceleia, a foothill suburb of Athens whose capture by the Spartans helped them win the Peloponnesian war, was particularly valuable because of its mines. Philip of Macedon conquered Chalcidice chiefly so he could exploit the placer gold of Mount Pangaeus. Alexander the Great took a *metalleutes* (mining engineer and prospector) named Gorgus with him to India, where he found salt, silver, and gold.[19] Like the Greeks, the Romans looked down on mining as degrading labor, though they were willing to profit by it. Italy was dotted with mines that had been worked by the skilled Etruscans and other pre-Roman peoples. They found iron on Elba, tin in Gaul, and copper at Tres Minas and elsewhere in Spain, a province whose exploitation for metals by the Romans became famous. The First Book of Maccabees, for example, remarks, "Now Judas had heard what the Romans had done in the country of Spain for the winning of the silver and the gold which is there."[20] Tin, used in bronze manufacture, was taken from mine tunnels in Cornwall.²¹ The conqueror of Dacia, Trajan, enriched his imperial treasury with gold from mines there. Roman mines were scattered from northern Britain to the eastern desert ranges of Egypt. The mines mentioned here are by no means all that existed, but they indicate the number and variety of those worked in ancient times.

Many of these mines were of respectable size even by modern standards. At Laurium, more than 2,000 vertical shafts gave access to more than 87 miles of tunnels.²² Some Roman silver mines in Spain were about 800 feet deep. The Rio Tinto mines had eight levels of galleries, about 25 feet apart. Spanish silver mines produced 9 million denarii per year at the height of their productivity, and those near Carthago Nova alone employed 40,000 men in 179 B.C.²³ Six mines in southern England during the second century A.D. produced 550 metric tons of iron per year.²⁴

Since in theory natural resources such as metallic ores belonged to the sovereign power, their exploitation was supervised by the state. When a new ore body of gold or silver came to light, a "gold rush" may have ensued as miners flocked to enrich themselves, but the officials were not far behind with their rules and contracts. Such a scene occurred, for example, at Ivrea (Eporedia) in the foothills of the Pennine Alps around 150 B.C. Since coinage was predominantly in gold and silver, the mines of precious metals increasingly became property of state treasuries. Laurium belonged to the city government of Athens and was administered by a democratically chosen board. The Roman emperor Tiberius began the practice of acquiring all gold and silver mines for the imperial fiscus, and by the time of Vespasian the process was complete.²⁵ Hadrian and his successors controlled the mines, leasing them to contractors. Sometimes the operation of mines was directed by public officials, but more commonly state-owned mines were leased to syndicates of private entrepreneurs who often employed slave labor. Slaves were hired from contractors at an agreed wage that was paid to the contractor, not the slave.²⁶

Greek and Roman miners accomplished work on an amazing scale considering the level of their technology. Their tools are similar to those that continued in use until recently. Picks of horn, antler, and stone were employed in early times. Copper and bronze are softer and more brittle than many kinds of stone, so that iron was later used extensively for mining tools. Iron picks dating to around 500 B.C. were found in a mine on the island of Siphnos.[27] A pick with a curved blade, about 8.5 inches long, was typical at Laurium. Stone hammers persisted in some places until the fourth century A.D. along with iron ones. A hammer was used to drive the gad, called *xois* in Greek, a spike used to break rock or ore. Roman gads often had an eyelet fitted with a wooden handle to reduce the chances of the miner hitting his hand with the hammer. Where there was room and a vein rich enough to justify the effort, battering rams of up to 150 pounds were used to break the matrix. To move broken ore, there were rakes with wooden handles and flat or spoon-shaped short-handled wooden spades. Archaeology has revealed many other types of tools, including wedges, crowbars, hoes, and metal saws. To carry ore along the tunnels there were baskets, or leather bags with shoulder straps like backpacks. These could be attached to ropes and wound to the surface by cranes, capstans (vertical cylinders rotated manually, used for hoisting weights by winding in a cable), winches, or animal power. Otherwise miners could climb on ladders, sometimes made of notched tree trunks.

Another method of breaking rocks, safer in an open-cut mine than in a tunnel but used in both, was to heat the rock with fire to a high temperature and then pour vinegar on it; the sudden cooling would contract and crack it. It is not known why wine or vinegar was considered superior to water for this purpose. Hannibal used the method to open a road for his elephants through the Alps.[28] As shafts and tunnels lengthened, dangerous sections might be lined or supported with timbers. Bodies of ore could be undermined and deliberately collapsed by removing stone or wooden supports.[29]

Working in shafts and tunnels requires artificial light, and in ancient times this meant burning something such as wood, a torch made of splinters of softwood or skin soaked in fat, or a lamp consisting of a shallow stone or ceramic dish filled with oil and supplied with a wick. This, combined with the use of fire in quarrying, created a need for ventilation. Shafts were opened and air encouraged to move through them by waving fans or linen flaps.[30] The air leaving the mine was inevitably polluted.

Another constant problem in mines was drainage; this, along with the need for air supply, limited the depth to which shafts and tunnels could be sunk. Where topography permitted, tunnels could be dug at a downward incline to the surface to divert underground rivers. One such drainage tunnel a mile and a quarter long exists in a mine at Coto Fortuna in Spain. Elsewhere, water had to be raised by bailing with buckets or baskets, or by some more sophisticated means such as the Archimedean screw (Greek *cochlias;* Latin *cochlea*) described earlier, piston pumps, or waterwheels. A "nest" of eight waterwheels in series was found in another Spanish Roman mine at Rio Tinto, for instance.[31] In hydraulic mining, favored by the Romans, the initial problem was to bring a sufficient flow of rapidly moving water to the ore, then to provide for the recovery of valuable material and, finally, drainage. Using a strong current of water brought from high altitudes for torrential flow and conducted through canals or aqueducts that often consisted of troughs of timber, they brought the river to the ore and then to settling tanks for separation. This meant the redirection of streams from their natural channels, and their pollution with many substances, some poisonous. Not all impurities could be precipitated in settling tanks, since some of them were soluble.

Quarrying   Quarrying presents most of the same problems and uses technology similar to that of mining. Its aim is to remove large, potentially useful blocks of various kinds of stone. To permit this, most ancient quarries were of open-pit type, but in certain places where strata of useful stone led underground, tunnels and galleries were excavated. This was the case in the quarry of fine crystalline marble on the Greek island of Paros, and also in part of the infamous limestone quarry at Syracuse where Athenian soldiers were interned after their defeat in the Sicilian Campaign. In the latter, there is one quarry face 88 feet high and 6,560 feet long. More than 112 million tons of stone were removed from this single quarry during its period of use.[32]

Evidence of ancient quarrying methods can still be seen on Mount Pentelicus, the source of the white marble used in the Parthenon and other public buildings. Blocks of stone were freed from the matrix by vertical cuts made with bronze saws; the softness of bronze was compensated for by the use of abrasives such as powdered quartz. The horizontal break below the block was made by cutting notches with picks into the rock along a line, driving wooden wedges into the notches, and then soaking the wedges with water so as to swell them until the block split loose along the line. The rough blocks had wooden sledges built around them, and slid down the mountainside along tracks on their runners or on rollers, the speed of descent controlled by ropes looped around posts set in holes cut in the rock. When it was necessary to go uphill, they were pulled up inclined planes by capstans. At the base of the mountain, the blocks were loaded onto carts and pulled into the city by oxen. Further shaping of the block happened at the building site, with final details of carving done after it was put in place.

Roman quarrying was similar to Greek.[33] Tools found in archaeological sites include pickaxes with broad edges, iron wedges, and saws.[34] During the fourth century A.D., saws in quarries were sometimes driven by watermills such as the one found near Trier.[35] The Romans stockpiled ready-cut blocks, often near rivers so they could be shipped as needed to Rome, where the Marble Wharf was ready to receive them.[36] The finest marble quarry was located at Carrara, near Luna by the sea, and began production as early as 100 B.C.[37] The massive amount of fine stone incorporated in the growing city is indicated by Seneca's famous dictum that the emperor Augustus found Rome a city of brick and left it a city of marble.[38] Roman taste in stone buildings ran to huge size; the 80-ton blocks of Carrara marble that stand in Trajan's column are dwarfed by one block cut in the reign of Antoninus Pius for the Temple of Bacchus at Baalbek which measures 68 by 14 by 14 feet and weighs 1,500 tons.[39]

Quarries of special types must be mentioned. Good millstones were highly valued, and the Romans shipped them by the Rhine from a quarry at Niedermendig. Emery, a fine abrasive, took its name from a quarry at Cape Emeri on the island of Naxos; Pliny the Elder calls the substance *naxium*. There were salt mines, but most salt was evaporated from the water of the Mediterranean, which is saltier than the larger oceans, or from salt springs or lakes such as the Dead Sea and Lake Tatta in Asia Minor.[40] Clays for ceramics are relatively common in the Mediterranean basin, but particularly fine ones, high in calcium, were sought out by potters.[41] Glass is manufactured from sand, a common material, but certain sands of special purity and color were prized. For example, the soft, white sand of the River Volturnus was much used because it produced colorless glass.[42] A great weight and volume of substance removed from the earth was required for the production of concrete and mortar. Mortar was known as early as Minoan times in Greece.[43] Concrete construction, called *opus caementicum*, was invented by the Romans before the early second century B.C. Concrete consisted of aggregate, that is, pebbles or broken stone (*caementa*) from quarries, mixed together and bonded with mortar made from lime and *pozzuolana*, a volcanic ash found in central Italy, especially around Vesuvius. The mix was blended with water and poured into forms made of wood, brick, or hewn stones. Water caused the mixture to harden, and it was discovered that mortar hardened well under water, so that concrete could be used in bridges and harbor construction.[44] Such works were immense, and required shipping vast amounts of the volcanic material all over the Mediterranean basin and beyond.

Environmental Effects of Mining and Quarrying   The impacts of mining and quarrying on the ancient landscape were widespread and noticeable. A mine called Scaptê Hylê, or "excavated forest," on the island of Thasos is mentioned by Herodotus, who says "a whole mountain there has been turned upside down in the search for gold."[45] As the name indicates, a forest was removed by the digging, and undoubtedly more trees were cut for timber and fuel. The mines at Laurium inflicted "a great scar upon the Attic landscape," and "by the time of Strabo the wooded surface of the region had been completely bared to provide timber for the mines and charcoal for the smelting of the ore."[46] Pliny the Elder provides a description of the effect of the deliberate caving in of a gallery in a Roman mine: "The fractured mountain falls asunder in a wide gap, with a crash which it is impossible for human imagination to conceive, and likewise with an incredibly violent blast of air. The miners gaze as conquerors upon the collapse of nature."[47] Scars left by ancient quarries such as those at Pentelicus and Syracuse are visible today, although some are being obliterated, along with the archaeological information they contain, by modern projects much larger than the ancient ones. In addition to the direct effects of the excavations, erosion of the hillsides was triggered by the removal of protective cover. Some people were aware of these processes, and wished that something could be done to repair the damage, as the quotations from Pliny at the beginning of this chapter indicate. But land restoration or replanting after mining was not a Greek or Roman practice.

Another effect of mining was the diversion of large amounts of water, much of it near the headwaters in the mountains, which had "portentous consequences for the face of the Earth."[48] For example, a gold-mining project of the Salassi in the second century B.C. diverted most of the flow of the Durias River and deprived the farmers in the lower valley of water that they had used for irrigation. When the Romans conquered the Salassi, this diversion continued under the publicans who held the mining contracts.[49]

Not only were streams redirected and their channels dried, but ground and surface waters were polluted. Poisons such as lead, mercury, and arsenic got into the water used in hydraulic mining, or leached out of mines through drainage. Even long after a mine was abandoned, pollution continued, and metallic salts were carried down from higher elevations to places where the contaminated water was used for drinking or irrigation.

Air pollution also was a problem noted by ancient authors. Mine workers suffered the worst effects of this kind of pollution. Lucretius gives a description: "What stenches [the mine at] Scaptensula breathes out underground! And what poison gold mines may exhale! How strange they make men's faces, how they change their color! Have you not seen or heard how they are wont to die in a short time and how the powers of life fail those whom the strong force of necessity imprisons in such work? All these effluences, then, Earth sends steaming forth, and breathes them out into the open and the clear spaces of heaven."[50] Vitruvius recommended testing air in mines with lighted lamps.[51] This may sound dangerous, but methane, the most common explosive gas, seldom occurs in metalliferous ores. Impure air came not only from gases trapped in the earth, but also from the poisonous fumes of fires used for lighting the tunnels and breaking rocks. "The miners meet with flinty rocks which they break up by heating them and pouring vinegar on them . . . steam and smoke make the air in the galleries unbearable."[52]

Conditions in the workplace environment were truly horrid. Workers often lived underground, coming up to the open air once a week.[53] They crawled along low, narrow passageways; at Laurium, these average 3 feet high and just over 2 feet wide. Roman tunnels are a bit higher, but 4 feet is common. Skeletons provide evidence of cave-ins and suffocation. Miners were often slaves or condemned criminals, but there is occasional evidence of concern for safety and health; a bronze miner's helmet similar to modern style was found in a Spanish lead mine.[54] The "Good Emperors" of the second century A.D. provided baths near mines and other benefactions.

Technology permitted ancient miners to utilize only rich ores lying relatively near the surface, and accessible deposits eventually were exhausted. Gold mines were often worked out and abandoned. Copper mining ceased on the Greek mainland before classical times, so ores on Euboea and Cyprus were more heavily exploited. On Euboea, they gave out in the first century B.C. During the late Republic, the Senate forbade mining in Italy, but it is unknown whether this was intended to preserve local supplies for emergencies, to aid contractors in Spain, or to prevent concentrations of mine slaves who were prone to revolt.[55] In any case, there was an ever-widening search for raw materials. Trajan conquered Dacia partly in order to exploit its mines. The tin mines of Spain gave out in the middle of the third century A.D., and the Romans had to develop reserves in distant Britain. At the same time, a shortage of precious metals created a crisis that threatened the

monetary system. In the following century, the imperial government created officials with titles such as *Comes metallorum per
Illyricum* to oversee the location of mines and the supply of metals.
Eventually, the Romans worked out most rich surface deposits in
the empire.

Metallurgy, Ceramics, and Allied Industries

After they were mined, ores were processed to separate the useful
metals: gold, silver, copper, iron, lead, tin, zinc, and mercury.
Furnaces were temporary structures of clay and stone. Paintings
of them on ceramic objects show them to be tall and narrow;
sometimes they were provided with chimneys. Others were excavated in the earth in the form of bowls or shafts. Most smelting
techniques required high temperatures and therefore large
amounts of fuel. Some of them also employed salts or other metals
such as lead or mercury; the utility of acids was little known. That
some Roman processes were more efficient than Greek may be
gathered from comments like that of Strabo on the refineries at
Laurium: "The silver mines in Attica were originally valuable, but
now they have failed. Moreover, those who worked them, when
the mining yielded only meager returns, remelted the old refuse,
or dross, and were still able to extract from it pure silver, since the
workmen of earlier times had been unskillful in heating the ore in
furnaces."[56] Modern technology allowed resmelting of ancient slags
to begin at Laurium in 1864.

After the metal was isolated, the smith, "Athena's servant,"
worked it into jewelry, utensils, tools, weapons, or armor.[57] This
required more fuel and produced additional pollution. Coinage
generated pressure for precious metals. During the first century
B.C., the Roman mint consumed 50 metric tons of silver a year;
many coins were then 94 percent pure. Each ton of silver required
removing about 100,000 tons of rock from the mines. The demand
for gold and silver increased in subsequent centuries, as large
amounts were spent for luxuries from beyond the eastern frontiers,
for which there were few exports to offer in exchange. Caches of
Roman coins have been excavated in India and Southeast Asia.[58]

125

The importance of the ceramics industry in Greece and Rome may be judged by the vast number of *ostraca* (shards of pottery) found in archaeological sites. The factories required tremendous amounts of fuel that was burned in cupola-shaped kilns. Shortage of fuel in Italy during the late Roman Empire may be a reason for the shift of the "Samian" pottery industry to provincial manufacturers. Bricks and tiles were produced in huge kilns. One tile kiln near the Temple of Heracles at Nemea in Greece measured 15 feet in each direction, and yet made only 140 of the huge tiles required for that structure.[59] Bricks were staples of Roman construction. It is said that Domitia Lucilla, mother of Marcus Aurelius, made a fortune fabricating them for the great villa of Hadrian at Tivoli. Anyone who has seen the immense brick ruins there can well believe in the profitability of that concession. Glass-blowers and glaziers had busy establishments in Roman times, with additional fuel needs.

A major industry throughout ancient times was limestone kilning for fertilizer, plaster, and mortar, which used not only limestone from quarries, but especially in times of war and social upheaval, buildings and statues as well. To provision one lime kiln for one burn in the highlands of Greece required a thousand donkey loads of juniper wood, and fifty kilns required 6,000 metric tons of wood yearly.[60] Roman kilns for this purpose have been found at Tretau in Gaul, at Iversheim on the Rhine, and elsewhere.[61]

Environmental Effects of Metallurgy and Related Industries   The major fuel required for industrial processes was charcoal, produced by the partial combustion of wood in an oxygen-poor atmosphere, although wood itself was utilized as well. In Greece, the import and sale of charcoal and wood were controlled by *agoranomoi* (superintendents of the market).[62] Charcoal made from various woods was valued for different purposes.[63] Combined with use in cooking and heating, industry produced a demand for wood that contributed to widespread deforestation. In the Mediterranean basin, at least 70–90 million tons of slag from the Greco-Roman period are known, representing the divestiture of 50–70 million acres of trees. The smelting of one ton of silver required 10,000 tons of wood, but also produced 400 tons of lead.[64] Faced with demands like these on sylvan resources, Rome turned more and more to forest-rich northern Europe for metals and glass, areas such as the Vosges, the Forest of Dean, and even beyond the frontiers in Slupia Nova, Poland. "A widening ripple of cut forests" spread outward.[65] There were complaints of wood shortage even in Gaul. Coal was used only where no wood was available. Pliny reports that coal was burned in Campania to make bronze because of the wood shortage there; in Britain it was shipped by canal to the treeless fenland.[66]

Iron used less fuel than copper in smelting, which helps to account for the preference for the black metal over bronze.[67] The Romans found other fuel-saving strategies. The depletion of forests on the iron-rich island of Elba explains why only the first stage of smelting was done there; the bloom was shipped to Populonia, where wood and charcoal from the Ligurian Mountains was available.[68]

Air pollution resulted not only from wood and charcoal smoke, but also from the fumes of various noxious substances that were heated or burned. Speaking of metallurgists in Spain, Strabo observes, "They build their silver-smelting furnaces with high chimneys, so that the gas from the ore may be carried high into the air, for it is heavy and deadly."[69] The poison there was lead, often a major component of silver ore. Vitruvius noticed its effect on those whose jobs kept them in contact with it: "We can take example by the workers in lead who have complexions affected by pallor. For when, in casting, the lead receives the current of air, the fumes from it occupy the members of the body, and burning them thereupon, rob the limbs of the virtues of the blood."[70] That air pollution from smelting was not minor or merely local may be indicated by the fact that measurements of the lead content of arctic snow preserved in glaciers in Greenland show a marked increase in concentration at the time when the Romans began more efficient smelting in the second century B.C.[71]

Vitruvius also worried about lead in the water supply; some industrial activities were known to pollute streams.[72] Lead in pipes and the joints of aqueducts could have contaminated water that was acidic, although much of the water in the Mediterranean area flows through limestone and is charged with calcium carbonate, a material that can be deposited as travertine inside aqueduct channels and pipes, and consequently can isolate the water from lead. The Greeks and Romans were in greater danger of lead in their food, particularly acidic food prepared and served in lead and silver vessels. There has been speculation about the effect of lead poisoning on segments of the ancient population, since its effects include infertility and impaired nerve activity in the brain and elsewhere. Tests of bones from burials have shown elevated levels of lead.[73] Mercury poisoning may also have presented a problem, at least for workers who smelted the metal from cinnabar, or who worked in gold, where mercury was used to make amalgam in a process that vaporized some of the mercury.

Conclusion

Industrial technology was by no means as important a segment of the total economy in Greek and Roman times as it is in the modern world, but it advanced in size and techniques and was able to make many changes in the ancient landscape. Among its most important environmental impacts were exhaustion of accessible ores, scarring of the land and deforestation with consequent erosion, diversion and pollution of water, air pollution, and exposure of workers to injurious materials. All these were noted by ancient writers, and a few of them were countered by measures to protect the health of workers; for example, chimneys were built to disperse air pollution from smelters. Due to the relatively small size of ancient industries when compared with modern, the total effect of most of these problems was not as great, but there were exceptions. Perhaps the most significant effect was deforestation. Because wood and charcoal were the usual fuels, and fossil fuels were almost unknown, forests suffered proportionately more from ancient industry than they were to do in the Industrial Revolution. It has been estimated that one operation, the Roman iron smelting center at Populonia, used as much wood annually as is produced by one million acres of Mediterranean coppice forest.[74] Of course, forests are renewable resources, but chapter 5 explained why their yield was not always sustained. The impairments inflicted by ancient industry on the natural environment, although scattered, seldom entirely healed over with a mantle of soil and vegetation, and many of the scars are visible today.

Eight

Agricultural Decline

That agriculture has an impact on the environment was well known to the ancients. In the play *Antigone*, Sophocles' chorus sang that man does many things, "And she, the greatest of gods, Earth— / ageless she is, and unwearied—he wears her away / as the ploughs go up and down from year to year / and his mules turn up the soil."[1] The results of all this labor were neither predictable nor always rewarding. The complaint that Earth was not producing as well as she once did was voiced by many writers. Hesiod sketched a history of the world as a series of steps declining from the Golden Age, when mortals found that "the fruitful field unforced bare them fruit abundantly and without stint," to the Age of Iron, his own time, when to get their daily bread humans could "never rest from labor and sorrow by day."[2] Lucretius also complained of lessening harvests, comparing the people among whom he lived to their happier ancestors:

> But the same Earth who nourishes them now
> Once brought them forth, and gave them, to their joy,
> Vineyards and shining harvests, pastures, arbors,
> And all this now our very utmost toil
> Can hardly care for, we wear down our strength

Whether in oxen or in men, we dull
The edges of our ploughshares, and in return
Our fields turn mean and stingy, underfed,
And so today the farmer shakes his head,
More and more often sighing that his work,
The labor of his hands, has come to naught.
When he compares the present to the past,
The past was better, infinitely so.[3]

Both Hesiod and Lucretius subscribed to the antithesis of the idea of history as progress. But that does not mean that the increasing infertility of which they complained was a mere rhetorical device. They were not isolated voices. Agricultural writers, too, spoke of a decline in productivity, resulting either from the senescence of Earth or from the failure of mankind to care for her. There is evidence of lower yields, farmers leaving land that can no longer support them, and deserted fields, not only in literature, but also in laws enacted to counter these trends. Failure of the soil to support the people, whether through declining productivity or local increases in population, led to land hunger that was expressed in emigration and conquest of new territories. Large cities found it necessary to import grain from distant shores to feed their people.[4] Agricultural decline was not constant; there were periods of improvement. Nor did it follow the same course everywhere; Egypt, with the annual gift of fertile silt deposited by the Nile flood, was an exception. Still, it is hard to avoid the impression that agriculture in major parts of the ancient world faltered, and that the situation was particularly bad during the late Roman Empire.

This problem was of the greatest seriousness, since agriculture was the basic and most widespread economic activity, and had the greatest effect on the natural environment. All ancient civilizations were agrarian. Other industries were less developed, making up a much smaller segment of the total economy than in modern times. Agriculture was by far the paramount sphere of employment and investment. The fortunes of agriculture affected all other activities, and would therefore constitute an excellent indicator of the degree to which the Greeks and Romans maintained or failed to maintain a healthy relationship to the natural environment. While for those living at the subsistence level, agriculture was a way of life, for many of the affluent it was also a business engaged in for profit. Before considering the environmental problems connected with that way of life and that business, let us review the nature of Mediterranean agriculture.

Mediterranean Agriculture

Greco-Roman agriculture was adapted to soils and climate that presented the farmer with challenges.[5] Rich soils well suited to cultivation do not cover the majority of Mediterranean lands; Greece is less than one-fifth arable due to prevalent mountain ranges, and although Italy is better favored, the Apennine chain, often steep and formidable, runs the length of the peninsula. Pliny says the predominant soil, *terra rossa* (see chapter 2), is difficult to work and weighs down hoes and plowshares with enormous clods.[6] When it dries, it forms a crust. All this augurs hard work for the farmer.

The Mediterranean climate, so deceptively pleasant, presents a dilemma to the native cultivator. As quoted earlier, Hesiod said that the climate of Ascra, his home, was "bad in winter, sultry in summer, and good at no time," that is, not good for farming.[7] The rains, not overly abundant in most of the basin, come mainly in the colder months between October and April, when heat and light energy for growth is least available. Fortunately temperatures rarely drop below freezing, except in the mountains, so that winter crops are possible. The summer is hot and dry, making irrigation necessary for almost anything that matures in that season. There are critical tasks for the farmer in virtually every month.

Crops Grain, grapes, and olives comprise the "Mediterranean triad" of agriculture. Grain, the source of bread, was the chief dietary staple. The crops were mainly barley and wheat, with some millet and panic grass; oats and rye do not do well in the dry conditions of Greece and Italy. Barley was commoner than wheat, cheaper, and not preferred, although the fact that sacrificial cakes for religious rites were made of barley indicates its traditional predominance. Winter wheat was planted in early fall and harvested in May or June, its success depending on winter rains. Spring wheat, harvested in fall and requiring irrigation, was less often grown. All grains preferred relatively flat, rich lowland soil.[8]

Legumes consisted in part of pulse crops such as lupines, vetch, kidney beans, peas, broad beans, lentils, and chickpeas. These were sown annually in spring and watered when in bloom. They provided food for animals as well as humans. Farmers also planted fodder crops such as alfalfa and clovers, which thrive best if irrigated.[9] Other common crops included sesame, rape turnips, and hemp.

Vineyards "Wine does of a truth 'moisten the soul' and lulls our griefs to sleep," said Socrates.[10] It was the drink most often served in Greece and Rome, so a major portion of the agricultural landscape was occupied by vineyards. The grapevine is a perennial; it can be pruned so as to support itself, or trained on stakes, trellises, or trees. Trees were popular props, so that all three major food plants could grow in the same field: vines climbing up olive trees, with grain sown between the rows.[11] The vine prefers well-drained rocky soil, and could be planted on fairly steep hills. Grapevines had to be protected against such pests as caterpillars and mice.[12] Foxes, with their fabulous love for grapes, were often trapped.[13] Cato the Elder says a vineyard of 100 *jugera* (63 acres) required two oxen, three asses, an overseer, his wife, and sixteen slaves.[14] The vintage came in September in Italy and Greece, when bunches of grapes were cut and placed in baskets; then they were trodden by workers who had carefully washed their feet and wore clothes that absorbed sweat.[15] The must (juice) was put in pottery vats for fermenting. Most wine was consumed within three or four years and mixed with water before drinking. Drinking water was often flavored, and purified to some extent, with sour wine.

Orchards "Is not Italy so covered with trees that it looks like one great orchard?" asked Varro.[16] Of the many fruit trees that grew there, and in other Mediterranean lands, the most prevalent was the olive. The fruit was sometimes treated and eaten, but more usually pressed for oil, a staple in cooking and the most important source of fat in the diet. As the major export, olive oil was the economic mainstay of Athens. The trees require well-drained sites, but can thrive in a variety of soils, so many groves are sited on hillsides. Since trees had to be spaced between 25 and 60 feet apart, and it took about fifteen years for a new plantation to produce well, they were more likely to be planted by landowners with capital and large holdings. So valuable were producing trees that Athens enacted a law against uprooting more than two per year by any landholder.[17] Irrigation was often necessary, and pruning was essential. The fruit ripened in October, when harvesters spread cloths under the trees and beat the branches with long, slender poles.[18]

Among fruit trees, figs were favored. Caprification, the fertilization of the fruit by attaching male branches of wild figs containing gall wasps to domestic trees, was practiced.[19] Similarly, the role of pollen in getting date palms to set fruit was known. Other orchard trees included apple, pear, plum, apricot, pomegranate, carob, lemon, and citron. Some varieties were introduced from abroad: in 73 B.C. Lucullus introduced the cherry from Cerasus in Pontus.[20] The peach reached Asia Minor from China in the second century B.C. by way of Persia, hence its Latin name, *malum Persicum*.[21] Nuts such as almonds, walnuts, and pistachios were also planted.

Agricultural Specialties Market gardens, whose fresh produce was intended for timely sale, grew up close to large cities. Among their products were cabbage, asparagus, artichokes, cucumbers, garlic, onions, and leeks. Flax, the source of linen, was a prevalent winter crop in Egypt, where the Greeks encountered it. Greece was generally too dry for flax, but it was sown as a spring crop in the Po valley, moist parts of Spain, and the Black Sea coast.[22]

Animals in Agriculture Almost every Mediterranean farm had domestic animals. Cattle were important for plowing and pulling carts; cows' milk was not much used. Adapted to meadows and forests, cows ate not only grass, but also the leaves of low tree branches, giving pastures a parklike appearance. Horses were more useful in the military, chariot races, and transportation than in agriculture. To be able to afford horses conferred social dignity; one of the higher classes in Athens was called *hippeis* and a similar one at Rome the *equites*, both meaning "horse-owners." At home on moist plains, horses did not do well in mountainous areas like most of Greece. The iron horseshoe was invented in the second century B.C.; before that horses went unshod, or with leather shoes.[23] More often seen carrying loads on the farm were asses or their vigorous hybrid offspring, mules.

Sheep and goats were sources of milk, cheese, wool, hair, skins, and meat. They might be allowed to graze on crops before they flowered, in order to keep them from going too much to leaf and to encourage seed development. Also, farmers sometimes grazed sheep in orchards to keep down surface growth and manure the ground, but goats were kept out of orchards due to their penchant for eating tree leaves and bark.[24] Sheep were sheared twice a year, in spring and fall.[25] Swine completed the mammalian component of the farm menagerie. Pork was the favorite meat of the Romans; there are fifty recipes for it in Pliny's cookbook. Pigs are forest animals that enjoyed roaming in the woods to consume beechnuts, acorns, and chestnuts. There were many breeds of each farm species; especially prized varieties were widely imported.

Farmers often cultured eels and other fish in lakes or ponds. Beekeeping was much practiced (the art was regulated by Solon in 594 B.C.), since honey was virtually the only sweetener known and wax was useful. Rough silk was made from native worms; Chinese silkworms were not introduced to the Mediterranean until the sixth century A.D. Among farm birds, geese, ducks and pigeons were common from early times. Peacocks, guinea fowl, and pheasants were sometimes kept.[26] Chickens are first mentioned in the sixth century B.C., having made a long journey from South Asia as domesticated birds.[27] Cockfighting soon became popular, and Themistocles included it in a festival at Athens after the Persian War.[28]

Agricultural Technology

Greek and Roman agricultural implements and machines were relatively simple, and many of them, or ones much like them, had been used for thousands of years. Technological innovation was not unknown, but came slowly and met with resistance grounded in tradition. Typical of tools used in agriculture were the spade, hoe, mattocks, and picks.[29] The plow never entirely replaced them, since crops were often interplanted with trees and vines, and cultivation had to take care of the roots. Vines were pruned, and the bunches of grapes cut, with special knives and billhooks. The simple wooden plow, even with an iron share, broke the soil without turning it over, so a field had to be plowed at least twice. This helped to make cultivation labor-intensive. Horses were small, and the horse-collar, which enabled a horse or mule to pull without choking itself, had not been invented, so plowing was usually done with oxen under a yoke. Seed was sown by broadcasting and plowed under. Harvesting was done with iron sickles. Grain was loosened from chaff by having animals tread on it, or by a threshing sledge, a heavy board with flints embedded in the underside. Later, small wheels sometimes replaced flints (a Carthaginian invention). After threshing, the grains were separated by winnowing, either throwing it into the wind with a pronged shovel, allowing the chaff to blow away, or by tossing it in a fan or basket.

Mills for crushing grain and grinding it into flour showed technological advance.[30] The earliest devices were the mortar and pestle and the saddle quern (a stationary stone over which another is pushed forth by hand). The rotary quern, with a round upper stone revolving on a lower one, appeared around 600 B.C. The donkey-driven mill, used to crush silver ore at Laurium, was adapted to grind grain by 300 B.C. It had a hollow, waisted stone looking like two cones joined at a common, open vertex, which revolved on a lower conical stone. Grain thrown into the top would emerge as flour at the bottom.[31] The first Greek watermill had a vertical axle with the millstone mounted directly on it, so that the wheel had to turn horizontally. Later the undershot waterwheel (where the water flows beneath the wheel), was connected to a millstone by gears. The great mill at Barbegal, Provence, in the fourth century A.D., had sixteen overshot wheels (with the water falling on the wheels from above), and could meet the needs of 80,000 people.[32] Presses operated by wedge, beam, or screw were used for grapes and olives.

While ancient agricultural techniques persisted for centuries with some degree of success, technology failed to advance production sufficiently. Varro advised "a degree of experimentation" in agricultural methods, but innovation was rare, if not absent, in Greece and Rome.[33] The *vallus*, an animal-drawn reaping machine from northern Gaul, is mentioned by Roman writers from the first century A.D. onward, but was not adopted to any major extent on Mediterranean croplands.[34] Other technical improvements of the northern barbarians, such as the wheeled plow, did not catch on because they were not suited to light southern soils.[35]

Environmental Problems of Agriculture

There were several possible reasons for the declining yields about which so many ancient authors complained. Plant growth, on which animal and human subsistence depends, is governed by a number of ecological factors. These include such variables as solar energy; air supply and temperature; water supply; availability of mineral and organic plant foods; the action of other organisms that consume, compete, or cooperate; the presence or absence of toxic substances; depth and other physical properties of the soil; and the genetic qualities of the seed. Unfavorability in any one of these may produce temporary or permanent agricultural decline, and some of them presented problems to the Greeks and Romans.

Climate   The Mediterranean climate has abundant sunshine and comparatively equable temperatures. The most limiting factor is the light rainfall, coupled with a high rate of evaporation that prevails over much of the basin in summer. Precipitation is extremely variable from year to year, which makes dry farming a chancy enterprise. Weather is a factor over which human beings had almost no control, other than choosing to plant at times and

137

in places that were likely to be favorable (changes in climate are discussed in chapter 11). The climate in the period covered here differed little from the early twentieth century A.D., so that it seems unlikely that climatic change is the major explanation of Greek and Roman agricultural decline. Some of the desertification along the margins of the Sahara in North Africa toward the end of the Roman period may have been exacerbated by climatic change, although human disturbance of the natural environment, particularly deforestation, seems the primary cause.

Soil Exhaustion   Plants absorb nutrients from the soil; if these are not replaced, yields will diminish from year to year. Apparently this was the case in large parts of the Mediterranean area, and it increased through the centuries. Many Latin writers connected the deteriorating situation in their own days with the exhaustion of the soil.[36] Columella remarked that no one alive in his day could recall when the grain harvest produced as much as four times the seed that had been sown.[37] Why was this? Were farmers unaware of methods that could be used to restore depleted soil? On the contrary, a reading of the Greek and Roman books on agriculture shows that the authors had a thorough understanding of intensive agriculture and knew how to keep soil productive. And this was not just theoretical learning, but represented the accumulated experience of peasants and landowners. When they were not hindered by economic or environmental crises, Greek and Roman farmers were probably as productive as any before the nineteenth century.

Columella attacked the idea, held by Lucretius and others, that Earth produces less and less because she is growing old. Unlike that of an aging woman, the fertility of Earth, he holds, can be restored by proper agricultural practices that any farmer should know.[38] The use of fertilizers was one of these. "Sowing must not take place except on ground that has been manured," maintained Pliny the Elder.[39] Farmers knew the value of animal manure and compared that of different species. Sheep and goats, it was said, produced richer dung than that of cattle or horses. Pigeon droppings were especially prized, and keepers of the temple on Delos made a tidy income by selling the droppings of the sacred birds in their dovecote.[40] Human wastes were also used; Athens piped city sewage out through the Dipylon Gate to a reservoir and then by brick-lined canals to fields on the nearby plain. Human wastes were also removed by workers under the supervision of a town official, the *coprologos*, and then spread on local fields.[41] Composting was recommended by the best writers.[42] Such soil-enriching crops as lupine, bean, and vetch could be plowed under as green manure. Broken or powdered limestone or chalk was applied as mineral fertilizer. Marble was burnt to make fertilizer, a process that consumed excessive amounts of wood and charcoal and sometimes destroyed works of art. Marl (a loamy mixture of clay, shells, and lime) was mined and applied to the land. On Aegina, burrows excavated to remove marl were adapted for underground homes by the people, who were called Myrmidons ("ants").[43]

One of the oldest methods of restoring soil fertility was fallowing, combined with repeated plowing to bury weeds. Hesiod said that fallowing is "the guardian against death and ruin."[44] More economical is crop rotation, where soil-restoring legumes are planted in alternate years with other crops. The ancients observed that legumes enrich the soil, although the reason for this was unknown.[45] Various rotational schemes are given by ancient authors, but their use in the Mediterranean was limited by the small size of farms and the necessity of planting each species only where soil and exposure would favor it.[46]

Seed selection was another way to improve yields. The best varieties were favored and fresh seed was saved from plants in their prime.[47] Hybridization occurred, although it was not understood. Theophrastus's observation that changes that "take away from the nature of the plant" are noticed in the third year after the seed of annuals is planted in a new environment may reflect the fact that, in hybrid crosses, it is the third generation that exhibits variation.[48]

Land Ethics   It should be evident from this sampling of the vast store of Greco-Roman agricultural knowledge that ancient farmers knew how to treat the soil. Xenophon enunciated a basis for agricultural land ethics when he commented, "Earth willingly teaches righteousness to those who can learn; for the better she is treated, the more good things she gives in return."[49] Only because he possessed the agricultural competence to restore exhausted land did he offer this advice to those who wanted to gain honestly in land speculation: buy mistreated land, improve it through proper methods, and sell it at a profit.[50] Cicero voiced a similar idea, saying "the farmer keeps an open account with the Earth."[51]

When the ancient farmer was able to carry out the principles he understood, the fertility of the soil was maintained. He was often able to do so, because farms were generally small. In Athens, for example, they varied from 6 to 125 acres, and Alcibiades' 70 acres was considered large.[52] The share of each colonist at the Greek colony of Metapontum in southern Italy was 15 acres. Allotments for Romans in the Gracchan land reforms were 19, and Julius Caesar's veterans received just over 40 acres. It may well be that on smaller subsistence farms where traditional peasant wisdom was applied, productivity held up better than it did on the huge Roman ranches (*latifundia*) under the stresses of monoculture and overgrazing.

That in spite of agricultural knowledge, there was decline, particularly in the late Roman Empire, indicates that other factors, economic, political, or military, prevented maintenance or regeneration of the land base. As Mikhail Rostovtzeff remarked,

> If . . . there was exhaustion of the soil in Italy and in the provinces in the centuries after the great crisis of the third century, this must be ascribed to man, not to nature. Men failed to support nature, though they knew as well as we do, or as the Japanese and the Chinese, how it should be done. It is very probable that, in the late Roman Empire, exhaustion of the soil in some parts was a real calamity.[53]

Erosion Control   The intervention of nonagricultural factors may be seen clearly in the case of erosion control. Certainly erosion, the physical removal of the soil by water or wind, is the most radical form of soil exhaustion and the least amenable to restoration. It was a problem well known to Greek and Roman landowners and they took measures such as ditching and terracing to control it in hilly terrain. Terracing was commonly used in the Greek islands and mountains, parts of Italy such as the slopes of Vesuvius, Etna, and the Apennines, and in Roman provinces.[54] It survives today with its original purpose. I recall arriving in terraced vineyard country just east of Delphi in central Greece on the morning after a violent thunderstorm; I watched a farmer recovering soil that had washed down off a terrace by shoveling it into baskets, loading them two at a time onto the pack saddle of a single donkey, leading the animal back up to the top of the terrace, and emptying the baskets there. The same scene, including replacement of stones in terrace walls, must have been repeated countless times by that farmer's predecessors. Such countererosional works are very labor-intensive.[55] If anything interrupts the labor, walls collapse, ditches are choked, and a tremendous amount of erosion takes place in a short time. Erosion due to lack of maintenance was surely some-times the fault of absentee landlords who failed to keep watch over what was happening on their land. But the effects of war were more widespread. Warfare could prevent maintenance by making a territory unsafe, by conscripting farmers, or by killing them. Rural populations were the manpower resource of ancient armies. Study of underwater siltation at the mouths of Mediterranean rivers indicates that erosion was more rapid during periods when a particular drainage basin was the seat of warfare.[56]

Water Supply: Problems Related to Irrigation   How necessary it was to supplement rainfall with irrigation has already been mentioned. Water was taken from springs, streams, and rivers, and diverted into fields, pastures, orchards, vineyards, and market gardens. It was time-honored practice: Homer mentions it.[57] And there is a germ of truth in the myth that Danaus first brought irrigation to Argos from Egypt.[58] Plato provided for its regulation in his ideal state.[59] History records that governments were active in regulating water use. Themistocles, as water commissioner in Athens, dedi-cated a statue of a water-bearing maiden from the fines paid by people who had stolen from the public supply to irrigate their own farms.[60] The laws of Justinian defined irrigation rights, allowing for the use of all the water in a stream.[61]

Cisterns, dams, and reservoirs were constructed to save winter flow for use in the dry season. Water was conducted through aqueducts and canals to the farms. Channels were of varying diameter; inscriptions survive that tell how long owners could let water run into their holdings.[62] The Aqua Crabra, an aqueduct near Rome, was used for irrigation. Roman irrigation works in North Africa were impressive in size and extent, including aqueducts and masonry dams to control and divert the waters of rivers that today almost never carry a usable flow, due to deforestation and desertification.[63]

Water could be raised from channels by several devices. The shaduf, a pivoted, counterbalanced pole with a bucket, was known in early Egypt and continues in present use. Pumps such as the spiral Archimedean screw and the two-cylinder Ctesibian force-pump were employed from Hellenistic times into the Roman Empire. A number of waterwheels like those described for mining and milling were also adapted for irrigation.[64]

A troublesome problem of irrigation is salinization. It can be avoided by good drainage, but in poorly drained basins, salt can concentrate in the soil to the point where plant growth suffers. Coastal marshes and river deltas where the flushing action of fresh water is impeded suffered salinization from encroaching sea water.

Agricultural Policy

Governments in ancient times were concerned with agricultural production and undertook major works of irrigation and drainage. The state's motivation was not only the need to feed the people, but also to secure resources for its activities.

Taxation   Taxes bore heavily on the agricultural sector because it was by far the predominant source of production. Government administration and the army depended on these taxes for salaries, equipment, and supplies. As long as agriculture was productive and flourishing, the state was strong, but when productivity was low, the tax base would shrink, and then even a relatively light tax would seem oppressive to farmers.[65] From the early third century A.D. onward, the Roman government collected in kind an annual tax, the *annona militaris*, which did not vary with the yield of the harvest. Such a tax encouraged the depletion of the land while depriving farmers of the means to restore it; much marginal land must have gone out of production as a result. Contributing to the decline of the Roman Empire in the west was the fact that primary producers were unable to uphold their essential part in the economy because they were subjected to repeated increases in taxation, which they could not pay due to low productivity. The dwindling of population in the late Roman Empire resulted from the inability of rural families, after paying rent, taxes, and other exactions, to rear enough children to offset the high death rate.[66]

The Impact of the Military Greek and Roman governments expected agriculture to provide resources for the military. This meant that unsupportable pressure was placed on the agrarian segment of society with the result that agriculture failed even where, with proper care, the soil could have produced adequate harvests. To this must be added the devastation of warfare itself. Ancient armies lived off the land. Deliberate environmental warfare like that waged by the Spartans in Attica during the Peloponnesian War, when they burned farms and chopped down olive orchards, was not rare in Greece.[67] The destruction caused by war in the Roman Empire was particularly acute during the third century A.D., when almost constant military campaigns of rival claimants for the imperial throne devastated the countryside.

Expansion of Agriculture into New Territories Ancient governments encouraged farmers to open new land. If the total acreage in production could be enlarged, the tax base would increase, and the effects of declining productivity might be countered, at least in part. Removal of forests or draining of marshes opened new, undepleted soil for planting, although crops would visibly decline after a few years, as Columella noted. A study of lowland deposits near Rome showed that in the second century B.C., a period when new lands were being opened to cultivation by urban settlers, the rate of erosion was ten times that before the disturbance.[68] That there would be further bad results of removing the wilderness, with the disappearance of fish and wildfowl that depended on the lakes and marshes, hardly came to the notice of ancient writers. Lucretius saw one aspect of what was going on:

> The opulence of the Earth
> Led folk to clear its wealth, convert the woods
> To open harvest-fields, kill the wild beasts, . . .
> [Woodcutters] made the woods climb higher up the mountains,
> Yielding the foothills to be tilled and tended.[69]

On disturbed land, introduced cultigens and weeds replaced native species, while many plants disappeared. Sometimes these had been valuable, as in the case of wild silphium, a gum-producing plant, which had been the mainstay of the trade economy of Cyrene until it was extirpated by excessive collection.[70]

Governments and speculators drained lakes and marshes through tunnels and ditches to open acreage to agriculture.[71] The Spartans drained marshes in the Eurotas valley, but the greatest achievement of the kind was the draining of Lake Copais in the Hellenistic period.[72] Theophrastus noted that the draining of country in Thessaly and Thrace produced marked changes in local weather.[73] Roman projects of the middle to late Republic and early empire are too numerous to list. Many were successful, but some failed despite repeated attempts. For example, the Pomptine Marshes in Italy were said to have been drained by Appius Claudius (312 B.C.), Cornelius Cethegus (182 B.C.), Julius Caesar, Augustus, Nerva, Trajan, and finally by Theodoric the Ostrogoth (sixth century A.D.). The lack of success of this and other projects has been attributed to inadequate technical knowledge, incompetent or fraudulent workmanship, and failure to appreciate the magnitude of the problems.[74]

Abandonment of the Land   A major problem faced by the ancients, the Romans in particular, was that of abandoned fields (*agri deserti*). Livy observed that deserted areas in Italy were formerly thickly populated.[75] In Campania alone under Theodosius, there were 528,000 *jugera* (330,000 acres) that had lapsed from cultivation.[76] Parts of North Africa, now desert, once had extensive groves of olives, as olive presses found in archaeological sites there testify. It may seem strange to discuss this problem when the expansion of agriculture into new lands was just mentioned. But the two processes often went on at the same time. It is understandable that farmers abandoned land that had become unproductive due to erosion and other forms of soil exhaustion, and moved to lands recently cleared or drained, whose fertility had not yet been sapped. As was noted, deforested land will produce good crops for a few years before it becomes exhausted. As Vladimir Simkhovitch remarked, "What happens when the fields fail to reward labor and are abandoned? If the highlands are not capable of covering themselves readily with vegetation, the top soil is washed away and a desert is left, while the deserted lowlands with clogged-up drainage are bound to turn swampy and unhealthful."[77] Governments tried their best to keep land under cultivation. Ownership of unclaimed or abandoned land was offered at times to anyone who would occupy and cultivate it.[78] If the land in question was deeply eroded, no one could have made it productive without expending large amounts of capital, and such incentives would have been ineffective; but in cases where damage to the land was not severe, a number of years of fallow, even without plowing, may have served to restore fertility.

Replacement of Cultivation by Stock Raising   A process similar to abandonment in some of its effects was the conversion of large areas from cropland to pasture. In many cases it may be difficult to distinguish one from the other, since owners of extensive *latifundia* devoted to ranching often acquired abandoned cropland for their holdings, and forced smallholders off the land in order to take control of it. Latin writers comment on this change in land use, which began when rich Romans appropriated public land. Pliny complained, "The large estates are ruining Rome as well as its provinces."[79] Seneca asked the owner of a *latifundium*, "How far will you extend the boundaries of your possessions? An estate which formerly held a whole nation is now too narrow for a single lord."[80] The trend had been viewed as a problem ever since the end of the war with Hannibal, which had depopulated much of rural Italy. The preference of large landowners for livestock over cultivation is epitomized in the comment attributed by Cicero to the first Roman agricultural writer: "Cato, when asked what is the most profitable thing in the management of one's estate, answered: 'Good pasturage.' 'What is the next best?' 'Fairly good pasturage.' 'What is the third best?' 'Bad pasturage.' 'What is the fourth best?' 'Tilling the soil.' "[81] Livestock ranches could be run profitably with a few trained slaves, much less labor than that required for crops. But Varro differed, holding that huge estates given over to stock raising were harmful, since they deprived arable land of the services of animals in controlling vegetation and providing manure. The conversion of arable land into pasturage was punishable by Roman law, but the law proved ineffective; it was opposed by the wealthiest Roman citizens. Declining Italian grain production was made up by imports from the provinces. From the late Republic on, Rome brought in countless shiploads of grain to feed the urban population, and it is estimated that these imports supplied three-fourths of the city's food.[82] The distribution of cheap grain in Rome helped to ruin grain production in central Italy and reinforced the tendency to convert from crop production to grazing.

Declining Population   The inevitable results of chronic agricultural decline were food shortages, famines, and depopulation. During most periods, and certainly after the second century A.D., most of the Roman Empire had a declining population and agricultural work force, resulting in lowered food production. Falling population aroused concern, particularly in regard to Roman citizens, and laws were passed encouraging marriage and childbearing. Augustus provided an award of 1,000 sesterces to every head of family who produced a child.[83] The legal rights of childless citizens were curtailed. Charitable institutions such as alimentary foundations to feed orphans and other needy children were established by conscientious emperors from Nerva to Constantine.[84] Diocletian tried to counter the effect of a declining number of children raised to maturity by means of his Edict of Occupations, which required bureaucrats and military men to provide sons who would fill their official positions when they retired or died. But this measure did not touch the root of the problem, which lay in the inability of the land, as it was treated by the Romans, to allow an increasing population.

Conclusion

The environmental sustainability of agriculture in the Mediterranean basin can scarcely be doubted, as long as the limitations of the Mediterranean ecosystem are recognized. This means that measures must be taken to prevent erosion; to maintain the biotic community that is fertile soil; to preserve and restore the forests, wetlands, and water resources whose interaction with agricultural areas is necessary to sustain them; and to limit population growth. It might appear that ancient societies never reached the capacity of the Mediterranean basin to sustain agriculture, since the area today supports a higher population than existed there in ancient times. But one may ask whether the present energy budget of Mediterranean agriculture is sustainable, with its high inputs of chemical fertilizers and insecticides and high outputs of air, water, and soil pollution.

Ancient agriculture may offer a model of sustainability in the typical small farm described by such writers as Xenophon, Varro, and Columella. That farm was a complex ecological unit. A wide variety of annual and perennial plants, shrubs, and trees were grown, each in the portion of the land best suited for it by soil, topography, and exposure. Sections of forest, whether original or replanted, were used as woodlots, and trees were planted to shelter fields and buildings from wind and sun. Animals grazed on fallow or among the trees to control vegetative growth and enriched the soil with their manure. The topography of the zone is generally more congenial to small farms of the kind that native peasantry developed than to vast stretches given over to one crop in monoculture that is vulnerable to pests and diseases. Agriculture balanced with nature is a state of affairs that can be upset by a tax structure that makes unreasonable economic demands. It requires peace and is disordered by war. It also requires a willingness to try new methods carefully, to recognize error, and in short, to listen to

Earth and to be taught by her. As an ancient writer said, "It is thus that the Earth conceives and yields her harvest so that food is provided for all the creatures, if winds and rains are neither unseasonable nor excessive; but if anything goes amiss in the matter, it is not deity we should charge with the fault, but humanity, who have not ordered their life aright."[85]

Nine

Urban Problems

The impact of ancient cities on the natural environment, on the land and its resources, on air and water, and on animal and plant populations, produced environmental problems prefiguring many of those familiar in modern settings, such as air and water pollution, traffic and noise, and difficult decisions regarding land use and urban planning. The urban environment received graphic criticism in ancient times. The most vocal complaints were directed against the defects of Rome, then the world's largest city, by its own poets. "The smoke, the wealth, the noise of Rome" repelled Horace, who also objected to suburban encroachment on fertile farmlands.[1] Martial inveighed against the noise pollution that disturbed his sleep, cataloging its many sources including predawn traffic, busy bakers, metal-workers' incessant hammers, and loud schoolteachers.[2] Juvenal expanded the list of urban ills, decrying traffic congestion, fires, public works projects that destroyed natural beauty, chamber pots emptied out upper-story windows, and ever-increasing crime and vandalism. "Where have we ever seen a place so dismal and lonely," he groaned, "We'd not be better off there than afraid, as we are here, of fires, / Roofs caving in, and the thousand risks of this terrible city?"[3] Though complained about most by Romans, urban environmental problems were also known elsewhere. Athens, Alexandria, and scores of others also suffered from crowding; noise; air and water pollution; accumulation of wastes; plagues; and additional dangers to life and limb. Impacts of cities on the natural environment were not limited to their immediate neighborhood, since each city made demands upon the resources of a hinterland of considerable extent, even in many cases overseas.

City Planning

Ancient cities have two major forms: those that grew organically but planlessly, usually around a defensible height; and those that reflect the imposition of a rational structure on a natural site. Earlier Greek poleis exemplified the former image; streets in Athens were a jumble of narrow passageways around the fortified Acropolis, giving way only to the Sacred Way, a large ceremonial road, or to the open space of the Agora, where there were facilities for trade and city government. Rome was also an unplanned city and remained so in spite of many attempts by consuls and emperors to provide order to a situation that was not so much chaos as an adjustment of human habitation and movement to the shape of the natural site, with its topography and drainage, and to the structures that had been established in the historical past.

City planning found its sphere in the establishment of new colonies, the expansion of ports, and the restoration of centers damaged by war. In the case of a new town, a site had to be selected, traditionally by divination.[4] The founder of a city, called *oikistes* (Greek) or *conditor* (Latin), was expected to receive a sign of divine favor that would direct him to the proper site. Alexander the Great was directed by a figure in a dream to the place where his greatest foundation, Alexandria in Egypt, would be built.[5] The god Apollo, through his oracle at Delphi, took a particular interest in the location of Greek colonies. Doubtless his priests had gained some knowledge of environmental conditions at likely sites. For example, they sent people from Thera to found a city in Libya, and would not accept the attempt to colonize an island off the Libyan coast as a fulfillment of the oracle.[6]

Philosophers were more "scientific" about choosing locations for new cities. But Plato retained some of the old belief in divination, teaching that, in addition to the physical characteristics of a site, a city founder should take account of the spirit of the place. "Some localities have a more marked tendency than others to produce better or worse people, and we are not to legislate in the face of the facts," he remarked, implying that *nomos*, human culture, must be altered to accord with the natural environment in a particular *topos*, or locale. "Some places, I conceive, owe their propitious or ill-omened character to variations in wind and sunshine, others to the waters, and yet others to the products of the soil, which not only provide the body with better or worse sustenance, but equally affect the mind for good or ill. Most markedly conspicuous of all, again, will be localities which are the homes of some supernatural influences, or the haunts of spirits who give a gracious or ungracious reception to successive bodies of settlers. A sagacious legislator will give these facts all the considerations a person can, and do the best to adapt legislation to them."[7]

The Hippocratic work *Airs, Waters, Places* maintained that the health of the people living in a city is determined by its position in relationship to solar exposure, prevailing winds, and the quality of its climate and water supply.[8] This doctrine has obvious application to the siting of a new town. Hippocrates believed that an eastward aspect is healthiest for a city, and Aristotle agreed.[9] Vitruvius advised taking the direction of prevailing winds into account when planning the orientation of streets and placement of buildings.[10]

Rectilinear Plans City planning, the conscious creation of an artificial environment in which to live, is of great antiquity and began with the rise of city-states in Mesopotamia. Many Greek cities were deliberately planned; for instance, an inscription from Colophon in Ionia shows that citizens appointed a planning committee of ten who hired an architect.[11] The earliest name of a city planner that has been preserved is Hippodamus of Miletus, a "metrologist" who "discovered the method of dividing cities."[12] He applied principles he observed in celestial phenomena to urban design.[13] Hippodamus believed that 10,000 citizens would be the ideal size for a city.[14] But he is chiefly associated with the "Hippodamian" plan, in which regularly spaced straight streets cross one another at right angles to make rectangular blocks, some of which are designated as locations of public buildings and the marketplace. He observed, and perhaps participated in, the rebuilding of his home city after the Persian Wars. He created a new plan for Athens' port, Piraeus, and another for Thurii, Pericles' panhellenic colony in Italy, in 443 B.C. It is not impossible that he planned a new Rhodes in 408, though he would have been an elder statesman by that time.[15] The Hippodamian rectilinear plan was much copied, as at Olynthus in 432 B.C. and Priene in Asia Minor in 350, and in colonies in Magna Graecia, such as Agrigentum and Metapontum; but some new towns, such as Elis (471), Megalopolis (371), and Mantinea, had irregular plans.[16]

Radial Plans   Meton, another Greek urban planner, also based his designs on celestial phenomena.[17] He is caricatured by Aristophanes in the *Birds* as the would-be architect of Cloudcuckooland, and the plan suggested there is radial: "In its center will be the marketplace, into which all the straight streets will lead, converging to this center like a star."[18] Plato described Atlantis as a perfectly radial city with alternating circles of land and water, and the geometrically regular model city in his *Laws* had twelve equal quarters centered on the acropolis.[19] He advised against a city wall: "No, if men must have a wall of sorts, they should construct their dwellings from the outset in such a fashion that the whole town forms one unbroken wall, every dwelling house being readily defensible by the uniformity and regularity with which all face the streets. Such a town, with its resemblance to one great house, would be no unpleasing spectacle."[20] Vitruvius designed an ideal city with eight sides and radial symmetry, a formal rational conception that was never built. Indeed, wheel-like cities were almost nonexistent in practice. Rhodes and Halicarnassus were compared to theaters, but this referred to the topography of their sites, not a circular arrangement of streets.[21] The modern Greek architect Konstantinos Doxiadis detected a radial arrangement in ancient monumental centers such as acropolises, sacred enclosures, and agoras, when viewed from their ceremonial entrances.[22]

Hellenistic and Roman Plans Alexander and his successors, busy founders of cities, used variations of the Hippodamian plan. Their standard arrangement consisted of lines of uniform rectangular blocks, each approximately twice as long as broad, set at right angles.[23] For example, Dura-Europos in Syria was founded in rectilinear style by Nicanor about 300 B.C.[24] Hippodamian streets had been narrow, but many Hellenistic cities, especially great capitals like Alexandria and Antioch, were planned with wide boulevards lined with colonnades, statuary, and trees. Public buildings were placed at the ends of fine vistas. Alexandria was designed by Deinocrates with wide avenues and canals, dominant positions for major structures, and walls integrated into the total plan. Pergamum, whose steep site prevented straight streets, was reconstructed as a magnificent terraced crescent intended to impress the beholder with the might of the Attalid kings who commissioned it. Such lavish constructions accelerated the demand for stone, metal, and timber.

When the Romans founded towns on open sites, they revealed a conception of standardized environmental order. Everywhere from the Sahara margins to the British Isles, one finds a plan based on that of the military camp. This is nearly square in outline, with fortified walls pierced by four gates, one on each side. Two main roads connected the gates on opposite sides and met each other at right angles in the enclosed space. These roads were termed by the land-surveyors (*agrimensores*) the *cardo*, from a word for "hinge" or "axis," and the *decumanus*.[25] Examples of cities on this plan include Aosta, Italy, founded 2 B.C., and Thamugadi, Algeria, around A.D. 100.

The city of Rome, home of the orderly Romans, lacked the neat planning visible in the colonies, and violated the principles set forth by Vitruvius. Crooked streets wandered among and over the famous seven hills and extended out past the irregular courses of successive walls. Rome lay beside the Tiber in a "pestilential region," as Roman writers admitted.[26] The Forum originally had been marsh. Projects for drainage and sanitation were undertaken, but the dampness of the site remained a problem. Sections of the city might be realigned after fires, as done by Nero, and other emperors built supplementary forums alongside the old one, but due to the city's size, a thorough replanning was impossible.

Urban-Centered Organization of Land   A city is more than just the built-up area. It should be viewed as an ecosystem, including the surrounding lands upon which it depends for food and other resources. In the Mediterranean city-state, town and country were a unit, or so writers thought.[27] Aristotle says that Hippodamus "divided the land into three parts: one sacred, one public, the third private: the first was set apart to maintain the customary worship of the gods, the second was to support the warriors, the third was the property of the husbandmen."[28] Plato, in describing his model city, turned as a necessary preliminary to an examination of natural features such as the sea, mountains, and forests.[29] An ideal for the philosophers was that a city should be self-sufficient, finding all the natural resources it needed in its own territory. In fact, this never occurred.

The Greeks and Romans distinguished landscapes according to the ways in which they were used, or not used, by human beings. First was the area within the wall, if there was one, and including built-up suburbs. This was the city proper (Greek *polis*, Latin *urbs*), the land occupied by and most altered by human inhabitants. Within this area were the fortress (*acropolis* or *asty*, *arx*) with temples, treasuries, and other official buildings; the marketplace (*agora, forum*), with governmental and commercial structures; and residential quarters.

The productive rural area where the results of human labor were evident was divided into three distinct categories, mixed as they might be in the actual countryside.[30] Cultivated land (*aroura, ager*) consisted of cropland, gardens, and orchards. Next was grazing land (*nomos, saltus*), with its herds of animals. This is separate from the preceding category; the farmer and cowherd may not have been friends. The third category was woodland (*hyle, silva*), forests used as sources of fuel, timber, fodder, and other products.[31]

Beyond these lands lay the uninhabited landscape, wilderness (*eremos* or *eremia; deserta, solitudo,* or *vastitas*). These words all refer to the emptiness of the land: its lack of people. One might be tempted to exclude this category of land from consideration as part of the urban ecosystem, were it not that the city government universally asserted sovereign ownership of wilderness within its own territory. It contained resources such as wildlife that could be hunted or ores that could be mined, and its living and nonliving components interacted with other parts of the urban ecosystem.

One category of land use remains: sacred space (*temenos, templum*), areas set aside for worship and dedicated to gods and goddesses. *Temene* could be located physically within any of the other categories, but theoretically sacred space is even more untouched than wilderness because economic activities including hunting and wood gathering were nominally forbidden.

Population

A small, independent, self-sufficient city was the classical Greek ideal. Most poleis were of modest size and, in spite of the development of manufacturing and commerce, basically agrarian. There must have been hundreds like Priene, with only 4,000 inhabitants, and few like Athens and Syracuse with populations in the hundreds of thousands. Plato designed the *Republic* for a citizen body numbering 8,000, but later in the *Laws* provided space for only 5,040.[32] Of course the total population of these utopias would have been larger, allowing for wives, children, and slaves, although Plato did not envision a large number of resident foreigners such as lived in Athens.

The Hellenistic Age was a period of rapid urbanization in which large, splendid capitals arose with heterogeneous populations. The artificial environment of these great centers was pervasive enough to make nostalgia for country life and rural scenes a major theme in the literature of the age. Theocritus, former inhabitant of rustic Cos, created the genre of pastoral poetry in urbane Alexandria. An estimate from 60 B.C. gives the size of the free population of Alexandria as 300,000 and states that it was then the largest city in the world, which suggests a total size of about a million, including slaves and foreign residents.[33]

Rome grew to become the most urban of Mediterranean cities, claiming as many as 1,200,000 residents by the middle of the second century A.D.[34] Long before that, Vitruvius spoke of an immense number of citizens needing countless places to live.[35] Over the centuries there was a large extension of the area covered by the city. Roman writers commented on the suburban sprawl, with villas of the rich occupying the nearby hills; as Horace said, "Rich men's luxurious buildings leave few acres for the plow."[36] Still the city was not huge by modern measures; in the fourth century A.D., Rome covered just under 7 square miles.

Environmental Problems of the City

Crowding, Traffic, and Noise Pollution   Ancient cities did not approach the area of modern ones, and none had the population of several millions that is now common in megalopolises, but they did crowd their people into small areas with narrow, usually unpaved streets. This was true of Athens, where perhaps 100,000 inhabitants occupied a city whose walls were nowhere further than a mile from the Acropolis. Except for those who could afford villas on the hills outside the walls, Athenians had little space.[37] No wonder Socrates sought the tree-shaded banks of a small river outside the city for his conversation with Phaedrus.[38] Some of the planned Hellenistic cities with their wide avenues may have been less congested; Strabo makes Alexandria sound so, although he says the ancient buildings had been neglected in his own first century A.D.[39] Even there, one suspects many parts of the city had a bustling Middle Eastern ambience.

The figures available for Rome indicate a high density of occupation, particularly when one allows an area for parks, public buildings, and the ample dwellings of the rich. The "main population of the city . . . lived in cramped, noisy, airless, foul-smelling, infected quarters, paying extortionate rents to merciless landlords, undergoing daily indignities and terrors that coarsened and brutalized them."[40] Cicero and Martial complained of poor streets that were narrow, muddy, dusty, slippery, and unlighted.[41] In Rome, only major streets were paved, and all were filled with crowds. Subura, the most densely inhabited quarter, seethed with people.[42]

Traffic crawled slowly but nonetheless dangerously. Getting through the streets was a struggle.[43] Pedestrians, wagons, and the well-to-do in sedan chairs, disputed the right-of-way with overloaded marble carts.[44] To alleviate the congestion that threatened to strangle the city, Julius Caesar's law, the *Lex Iulia Municipalis*, prohibited wheeled traffic in the city between sunrise and two hours before sunset, except for sacred chariots and vehicles performing essential public services.[45] No doubt there was a rush hour between roughly 4:00 and 6:00 P.M., especially since the streets were not lighted at night. Thus modern efforts to close parts of Rome to cars have an ancient precedent. This law was strictly enforced at first, and extended to other cities by later emperors, but fell into disuse in the chaotic third century.[46] Caesar's law did little to lessen noise pollution, but shifted much of it to night hours when it would disturb the sleep of urban dwellers whose walls were thin and whose windows were open. Noise came not only from traffic but also other sources such as industry, trade, building and demolition, and the numerous baths. Writers complained of the "din" to which they were subjected.[47]

Housing The characteristic Mediterranean house was built of brick or stone, with a wooden roof covered with tiles. Whenever space and resources permitted, it was centered around an inner courtyard, and rooms opened into this rather than outward, an arrangement well suited to the climate. This plan was found inside towns as well as outside; in Pompeii (a resort town) houses were comfortable, only one or two stories high, facing inward and insulated from the street, with pools and gardens in open peristyles. But demands on space limited this plan's use in more congested cities. There, as in Ostia, the port of Rome, buildings rose several stories, and families lived in small apartments.

In Rome the houses of the wealthy were spacious, but the majority of people lived in uncomfortable apartments in *insulae*, structures whose heights must sometimes have exceeded seven stories, since Augustus set a limit of 70 feet, which Trajan later lowered to 60.[48] The reason for these restrictions was the danger of collapse, since *insulae* were often too tall for their foundations and supports.[49] There was no running water in these tenements; the tenants had to use a public fountain down the street, and also the public latrines, or a commode. No glass or screens kept insects out, and dust, dirt, and rubbish tended to accumulate. Since no fireplaces or chimneys were provided, charcoal braziers had to be used for heating and cooking, and oil-burning lamps for light; the smoke was supposed to blow out the window. In spite of danger and discomfort, more and more apartment buildings were constructed; by A.D. 350 there were 46,602 of them in Rome.[50]

Fire   Since floors and roofs were of wood, and lamps and charcoal fires common, the peril of fire was ever-present. Fires in buildings happened often and were not easy to extinguish once they took hold in the crowded city. A vivid picture is given by a second-century A.D. resident of Rome: "We catch sight of a certain apartment house, many stories in height, enveloped in flames and the whole neighborhood burning in a huge conflagration."[51] Due to the danger of fire and the absence of fire escapes, the uppermost floors in *insulae* had the least expensive apartments. Crassus profiteered by buying collapsed or damaged buildings at bargain prices, some of them while they were still burning.[52] Augustus formed a brigade of 7,000 freedmen firefighters, but it was only partly effective.[53] He also built a wall around his forum as a firebreak.[54] The famous fire of Nero was only one in a series of conflagrations that destroyed sections of the city. One of Nero's edicts was a fire safety building code promulgated after that disaster.[55]

Water Supply   Water was at first provided from nearby rivers, or from springs and wells within the city, such as the fountain of Peirene at Corinth.[56] As cities grew, local water supplies were exhausted. Solon encouraged well-digging in Athens, and dozens have been discovered in the Agora excavations.[57] Wells were dug by hand; they were circular and lined with wood, stone, or brick. Vitruvius provides methods of locating underground water and likely sites for wells, such as observing water evaporation, burying a bronze or lead vessel or lamp and looking for condensation, and judging the soil, topography, and types of plants.[58] But wells, too, became inadequate for growing cities.

Rivers often carried pollutants and varied greatly in volume, while local sources of water proved inadequate or dried up as cities grew, so governments reached out to more distant supplies through aqueducts. These ran at ground level as covered canals or were raised or buried to maintain a working grade. About 530 B.C., the people of the island of Samos excavated a tunnel to bring water through a mountain to the city.[59] This remarkable work, which still exists, was designed by Eupalinus of Megara, and is about 3,300 feet long and 6 feet square in cross section. It was bored from both sides of a hill at once, and the two sections came very close to meeting at the halfway point, but before joining, one bore swerved as if the engineer were searching for the other one. Also, the slope of the tunnel was not sufficiently steep to let water flow rapidly, so a second tunnel with a steeper gradient was bored underneath the first. The engineer Theagenes devised an underground aqueduct from Mount Pentelicus to Athens which was provided with a vertical airshaft every 50 feet.[60] Meton built another aqueduct to Piraeus. "At Olynthus a very fine [aqueduct] has been found, designed to bring water to a city fountain from hills several miles to the north, and showing a knowledge of engineering which few would have attributed to the Greeks before Hellenistic times," remarks Wycherley.[61] As an example of Hellenistic engineering, the inverted siphon may be mentioned. The principle was described by Hero of Alexandria in his *Pneumatics* in about A.D. 65, but it had been used for centuries.[62] Eumenes II of Pergamum, 180 B.C., had commissioned a closed-pipe inverted siphon system that had a pressure of 260 pounds per square inch at the lowest point.[63]

Roman aqueducts are surviving wonders of the ancient world, even in a nonfunctioning condition. Frontinus boasted, "With such an array of indispensable structures carrying so many waters, compare, if you will, the idle Pyramids or the useless, though famous, works of the Greeks!"[64] By gathering water from springs, lakes, and streams over a large part of the countryside, hydraulic engineers made a major impact on the environment. The water that aqueducts carried away was no longer available to vegetation, wildlife, and agriculture. When all the aqueducts of Rome were fully operating, they carried a flow at least one-third greater than the average flow of the Tiber.[65] The first, the Aqua Appia built in 312 B.C. by Appius Claudius, ran entirely underground for 10 miles. The Anio Vetus, 270 B.C., crossed ravines on small bridges, and was 40 miles long. Later aqueducts were even longer, and were partly raised on high arcades that give the visual impression most modern people have of Roman aqueducts. The Aqua Claudia, built in A.D. 47, had an arcaded section of 8 miles. Romans constructed aqueducts for cities other than Rome; Augustus ordered one for Alexandria, the Flumen Augusti.[66] Hadrian built many aqueducts all over the empire.

The height of arches in raised sections was limited by the stonework's strength to 70 feet, so greater heights were achieved by adding additional tiers. The Pont du Gard in Provence has three tiers and reaches 180 feet. The Romans made pipes of wood, ceramic with leaded joints, or lead. Lead pipe sections were made by folding rectangular sheets into triangular or circular shapes, and would take pressure only up to 50 pounds per square inch without extraordinary measures such as setting them in stone or concrete.[67] The slope of an aqueduct had to be calculated carefully to keep the flow at optimum volume, but at the same time to prevent overflow, and hydraulic engineers responded well to the challenge. Vitruvius recommended that the slope be not less than 1/200, but the aqueduct of Nemausus, which crossed atop the Pont du Gard, actually varies between 1/1,500 and 1/14,285, slopes that appear level to the eye.[68]

On entering the city, most water from aqueducts was conducted into tanks where sediment settled out, guaranteeing cleaner water. The tanks were built in pairs so that while one was being cleaned, the other continued to operate. Then the water traveled in pipes to points of use. Distribution in Rome was recorded in three categories: public supplies such as fountains, cisterns, the military, and official buildings, 44.3 percent; baths, 17.1 percent; and private houses, 38.6 percent. In the fourth century A.D., Rome had 11 public baths, 856 private baths, and 1,352 fountains and cisterns.[69] The public was supplied through fountain houses such as the Enneakrounos (Fountain of Nine Spouts) in Athens, or the lavish Nymphaeum at Miletus.[70] Cisterns stored water for times of need; one of the largest was Justinian's underground "Hall of 1001 Columns" in Constantinople, built in A.D. 528, which is 463 by 240 feet in size, and actually has 420 columns.[71]

City governments carefully supervised water supply, and the office of water commissioner was an important one. In Athens, the Superintendent of the Fountains was elected by show of hands.[72] This places the office in the category of those who, like generals, needed special skills and therefore could not be selected by lot. Water theft, a fairly common offense, was punished by fines.[73] Rome had officers called *Aquarii* in charge of supply and maintenance. Augustus appointed a board of *curatores* controlled by an Imperial *Procurator Aquarum*. The latter was given entire responsibility by Claudius.[74] Sextus Julius Frontinus, the author of a valuable book on aqueducts, filled this office during A.D. 97–104. Measures to obtain and safeguard the water supply were characteristic of the Romans wherever they went, and were one of the keys to the success of their legions. Without clean water, soldiers and colonists would have been decimated.

Water Pollution Ancient physicians and hydrologists stressed the need for pure water.[75] Vitruvius noted that sunlight causes the purest particles of water to evaporate, concentrating the pollutants ("heavy, coarse, and unhealthy parts") in what is left. He advised testing water for purity by methods such as evaporation, sedimentation, boiling, and the addition of wine, a powerful antiseptic, in small quantities.[76] To purify water, ancient authors say, one can expose it to the sun and air; filter it through tufa, lampwicks, or wool; allow it to percolate through clean sand; or boil it.[77] Athenaeus of Attaleia wrote "On the Purification of Water," discussing filtration and percolation, but it survives only in short citations in Oribasius. Sources of water varied greatly in purity. The quality of that from the Roman Aqua Virgo and Aqua Marcia was so fine that even settling was not needed. On the other hand, water from the Aqua Alsietina was undrinkable, and used only for mills, ornamental fountains, and sewer flushing.[78] The channels of aqueducts were generally covered with stone slabs to prevent pollution.

Vitruvius knew that lead pipes could be dangerous. "Water . . . is made injurious by lead, because white lead is produced by it; and this is said to be harmful to the human body." He then described symptoms of lead poisoning in workers exposed to it, and concluded, "Therefore it seems that water should not be brought in lead pipes if we desire to have it wholesome."[79] Lead pipes will contaminate acidic water, and certain bacteria found in water systems may provide the acidity necessary to put the lead into solution. But fresh water in the Mediterranean area is often charged with calcium carbonate from limestone, which buffers acidity and can deposit travertine in pipes and channels. These deposits are sometimes many inches thick in aqueducts, and would have kept the lead in channel joints from leaching into the water.[80] In addition, the insides of aqueducts were waterproofed with *maltha* concrete, a pinkish mixture including lime, pork fat, and the milk of unripe figs.[81]

Waste Disposal   Garbage and sewage presented a considerable problem for ancient cities, as a result of the tendency of people to deposit refuse in any convenient spot, or simply to throw it out a window, although care was advisable since one could be sued for damages. Laws at Athens and elsewhere directed that waste matter be carried outside the walls for a certain distance before it was dumped.[82] Street cleaning is mentioned in many Roman laws, and in inscriptions at Pergamum and other places in the eastern Mediterranean. Julius Caesar required every citizen to keep the street in front of his or her residence swept clean.[83] Drainage sewers were often covered, and excess water in the city supply used to keep them flushed out. As noted in chapter 8, Athens had a sewer that provided fertilizer for her own fields.[84] But not every Athenian house was connected to the sewer; many had their own cesspools.

Because of its huge size, Rome generated more waste, and had the potential to do more damage to the environment than other ancient cities. But Rome also took more measures to protect public health. The Cloaca Maxima was Rome's main drain. About 15 by 11 feet in cross section in some places, it could be maintained by workmen from within.[85] Under ordinary conditions, much of Rome's waste matter was flushed out through sewers and into the Tiber, which, it was hoped, would carry it past Ostia into the sea. There was no way to treat sewage. Often during floods, the Tiber backed up through the sewers and inundated lower sections of the city. It is reported that the drain in the floor of the Pantheon looked like a fountain at such times.[86] During the empire, there were spacious public latrines in Rome, richly decorated with marble and mosaics and seemingly designed for conversation as well as their primary purpose. Vespasian met with criticism when he taxed public conveniences, creating history's first pay toilets.[87] The sewers drained the latrines, and some large private houses, but not usually the *insulae*. People dumped every imaginable form of refuse into the river including stale grain and bodies that had been denied burial.[88] The level of odor pollution can scarcely be imagined. It is no wonder that there is only one mention of drinking from the Tiber in all Roman history.[89] Swimming in it, which is mentioned, must have taken place upstream off the Campus Martius.[90] To deal with the accumulated mess, conscientious emperors dredged the river; Augustus "widened the bed of the Tiber and cleaned it out, filled as it had been for some time with rubbish and narrowed with projecting buildings," and much later Aurelian followed his example.[91] Augustus appointed *curatores alvei et riparum Tiberis* (supervisors of the river bed and banks of the Tiber), and Trajan added the sewers to their jurisdiction.[92]

Air Pollution Countless cooking and baking fires, smoky lamps, charcoal fires to heat rooms, the smoke pouring from furnaces in the baths, from metal working, and from kilns for firing of pottery, not to mention the ubiquitous dust, meant that a city could be seen a long way off because of its polluted air. To Homer, smoke was the first sign of human habitation.[93] Horace remarked on the thousands of wood-burning fires in Rome.[94] Many people are surprised to discover these ancient references to air pollution, but it should be remembered that in the nineteenth and twentieth centuries as well, in large nonindustrial cities with few cars, fires and the dust of human activities produced a heavy pall. Temperature inversions, which are natural occurrences as common in ancient times as they are in the Mediterranean basin today, held smoke and dust in suspension over cities. Air pollution was familiar to the Romans, who termed it *gravioris caeli* ("heavy heaven") or *infamis aer* ("infamous air").[95] A trip out to the country, in the right direction, offered welcome relief. But Martial commented that the sun was so obscured by the smoke and dust in the city that people coming back from the countryside would lose their tans after a few days.[96] There was a "brown cloud" over ancient Rome, just as in many modern metropolises. The difference lies in the chemical nature of the pollutants and their amounts.

Vermin and Disease   Humans have always been accompanied by a number of opportunistic organisms that share their habitations, flourishing in the conditions created by people and threatening human health. The laws of ecology are not repealed when a city is founded, and they do not always operate to the benefit of its human inhabitants. A number of these organisms are vectors of disease: rats, mice, lice, bedbugs, fleas, flies, gnats, and mosquitoes are among those found almost everywhere. With the inefficient ancient methods of waste disposal, rats had plentiful sources of food, and sewers were accessible for their movement and breeding. Domestic cats, dogs, and weasels helped to control their numbers to some extent. Large cities were especially vulnerable to contagious diseases. There were several altars to the goddess Febris (Fever) at Rome, with good reason.[97] The periodic pandemics of plague that spread across the Mediterranean basin attacked the cities with particular severity.[98]

Burial   Treatment of the dead was a concern of ancient cities, and obviously connected with the subject just discussed. The Greeks and Romans often buried the deceased rather than cremating them.[99] Corpses were a potential source of disease, so a virtually universal law forbade burial within city walls. Outside every Greek and Roman city, therefore, tombs lined the roads. At Athens, the

Ceramicus cemetery lies just outside the Dipylon Gate and contains interments from every century of the city's ancient history. Near Pompeii, Rome, and dozens of cities, funeral monuments can be seen strung out along the roads. Catacombs are found widely in the Mediterranean area. Outside Rome, they were excavated in tufa, a soft volcanic rock that also served as building material. During the Roman Republic, burial was not permitted inside the official city limits, but as time passed the inhabited area spread beyond these. Bodies of paupers and others were thrown into charnel pits. At the time of Augustus, efforts were made to end these practices. Cremation became more common, and the worst of the charnel pits were covered and planted with a garden.[100]

Roads

Roads are a city's means of reaching outward to tap the natural resources of the countryside and other cities through trade and exploitation. Understandably, they were maintained by the cities. While classical Greeks often preferred to travel by sea, they sometimes constructed respectable roadways, as their Mycenaean ancestors did in the Argolid, perhaps the very "well-drained roads" of which Homer speaks.[101] The road used to bring marble from Mount Pentelicus to Athens was paved with limestone slabs. Sacred roads, such as those from Athens to Eleusis, Elis to Olympia, and the approach to Delphi, were partly paved. Some roads had artificial ruts to keep carts from slipping. Lines of trees were planted to shade roads; one near the Isthmus of Corinth was lined with pines, and another along the Alpheus River had myrtles and other trees.[102] Amyntas II and Philip II of Macedonia built many roads. But Strabo complains that Greek roads were bad, poorly drained, and often steep.[103] In Hellenistic times, Greeks copied the admirable Persian roads, as well as the system of mounted messengers with post houses. In Ptolemaic and Roman Egypt, mail went by "camel express" as an alternative to shipping on the river.[104]

The deservedly famous Roman roads stretched beyond the city gates in every direction. They are some of the most notable marks the Romans left on the landscapes of Europe, Asia, and Africa.

They had Etruscan road building as a model, but improved on it, adopting lime mortar from the Greeks in southern Italy about 300 B.C., and realizing the usefulness of *pozzuolana* cement a century and a half later.[105] Roman highways are major works of construction; built with foundations secure enough to have supported a wall, they were paved with stone and concrete. Vitruvius describes a four-layer base, three to four times as deep as under a modern road.[106] They followed lines as straight as possible, crossing marshes on causeways of pilings and rivers on magnificent bridges, many still existing. The roads did not lie lightly on the countryside, nor were they engineered to follow contours and avoid erosion, although they were well-drained. Engineers responded brilliantly to the challenges of narrow gorges and difficult mountain passes. Roads were wide; Augustus decreed a width of forty feet. The labor of road building was performed by the army or by contractors hired by central or provincial authorities.[107] So extensive was the system that its maintenance was a serious drain on public budgets. In road building, as in much else, the Roman attitude to the natural world was that of the conquest of nature and confidence in human power. Roads secured the extent of Roman domination and made land transportation more rapid, economical, and competitive with sea transport. They encouraged the development of agriculture, mining, and industry farther from metropolitan centers by providing access to distant areas. Because of the network of roads, more forests were felled and more plants and animals were transported, with the result that they were introduced to new lands or extirpated in their original ranges. Roads increased human mobility and reduced the inaccessibility of marginal territories, amplifying the impact of the Romans on the natural environment.

Rural Nostalgia

City-dwellers developed a yearning for rural scenes as they considered the discomforts of urban life. The larger the city, the stronger was this feeling. The polarity between city and country was a major theme in Greek and Latin literature, and the comparison was almost always favorable to the country. This strain first became prominent in the crowded city of Alexandria, where pastoral school writers centered around Theocritus adopted a romantic style of nature description, celebrating the beauties of the countryside [108]

Horace, Martial, Juvenal, and others maintained country retreats and extolled the virtues of the rustic life (see chapter 4). But how long busy urbanites could stay in their rustic retreats was problematic; some "seceded," abandoning Rome, while others found a hundred things to do in town, and even when they managed to escape to the country, friends and business associates hounded them and dragged them back.[109] Some compromised by buying villas in the suburbs, spending vacations at seaside resorts, or creating and enjoying parks and gardens.[110]

Conclusion

Perhaps the most informative way in which a city can be viewed is as an ecosystem; that is, as a series of ecological relationships.[111] This is not simply to say, as many urban sociologists have said, that there is an interrelationship of various social and economic groups within the structure of a city, and that such ecological concepts as succession, distribution, and competition can be used to study their spatial arrangement and history.[112] Such a mode of study does not show the city as a genuine ecosystem; it adopts ecology as a metaphor, not a description, and creates an ideal structure that is hierarchical, not ecological. A city must not be studied in artificial isolation from its hinterland. A city is not a truncated phenomenon, but exists in a natural context.

Greek and Roman cities had an overwhelming effect on the environment where they were located. This is true both in the built-up area and in the immediate vicinity with various categories of land use. Cities are, after all, habitats constructed by humans for human occupation. Many problems found in modern cities are not new; ancient cities knew them to a greater or lesser extent. But the impacts of urbanism were by no means limited to the area covered by dwellings and fields, or even to the greater territory over which a city exercised political authority. Each city exploited the resources of the land it could dominate along its frontiers, and tentacles of trade and economic power might reach outward beyond them to draw valued materials of many kinds from lands located at great distances overseas or across mountain and desert barriers. The deforestation of isolated places occurred in response to the demands of distant cities, so that the cedars of Lebanon were sacrificed to form the fleets of Antioch and Alexandria, or to adorn the palaces of Roman emperors. Nowhere is this far-reaching economic influence of cities more evident than in the lengths to which they were willing to go to obtain grain for their hungry populations. Greece reached into the lands around the Black Sea, Rome imported from North Africa, and grain ships visited Egypt from the furthest Mediterranean cities.

The failure of ancient cities to adapt their economies to natural systems in harmonious ways is a basic cause of their decline, and a reason why so many of them exist today as ruins within eroded and desiccated landscapes. Cities placed too great a demand on available resources, depleted them within their sphere, and then went as far as they could to gain access to additional resources, until this effort also failed. They declined because they failed to maintain the balance with their own environment that is necessary to the long-term survival of any human community. Nature was treated as an apparently inexhaustible mine rather than as a living system, as an exploitable empire rather than as part of an organic whole that included them as well. Ecological disharmony interacted with social, political, and economic forces to assure that many Greek and Roman cities would disappear or be altered beyond recognition in a fragmentation of the ancient world that represented in most places a disastrous decline in the level of civilization. Environmental impacts were so great as to be self-destructive. The same forces are at work in analogous ways in the modern world, and societies are unfortunately relying on attitudes derived from ancient antecedents that have already demonstrated their failure.

Ten

Groves and Gardens,
Parks and Paradises

S etting aside special areas for trees, other plants, animals, and natural features, is not a new idea. The Greeks and Romans had long preserved sections of the natural environment as sanctuaries sacred to gods and goddesses, or as hunting and pleasuring grounds for rulers or the people. Gardens or planted parks in private or public ownership also provided environmental amenities. These represent a positive influence of human culture on nature, saving certain areas from some forms of the damage that has been noted in the foregoing chapters.

Sacred Enclosures

The Greek and Roman landscape was dotted like a leopard skin with hundreds of places that were held to be sacred space. As noted in chapter 9, this was one of the major categories of land use. A sacred precinct (*hieron temenos* in Greek and *templum* in Latin) was an area set aside and often walled to mark the boundary between holy and ordinary space. These usually contained groves of trees and springs of water, though often mountaintops or other prominent features were so treated. Within them the environment was preserved, as a rule, in its natural state. The motive for this conservation was religious reverence, the idea that such places were inhabited by the gods. The presence of deity was recognized in the quality of the environment itself. As Seneca remarked, "If you come upon a grove of old trees that have lifted up their crowns above the common height and shut out the light of the sky by the darkness of their interlacing boughs, you feel that there is a spirit in the place, so lofty is the wood, so lone the spot, so wondrous the thick unbroken shade."[1] Or Ovid, "Here stands a silent grove black with the shade of oaks; at the sight of it, anyone could say, 'there is a spirit here!' "[2] Virgil had his character Evander remark that when they saw the old tree-covered Capitoline Hill, the rural folk who lived around it exclaimed, "Some god has this grove for dwelling!"[3] This primal attitude long persisted in popular feeling, as Pliny the Elder indicated: "Trees were the first temples of the gods, and even now simple country people dedicate a tree of exceptional height to a god with the ritual of olden times, and we . . . worship forests and the very silences they contain."[4]

Worship took place in an outdoor setting; originally the temple was identical to the reserved natural site. The buildings later erected in the sanctuaries were at first simply protective shelters for the images of the gods, while the altars remained outside under trees and sky. The intent was to keep the area as primeval as possible. In archaic times many of these reserves were sections of virgin forest; although not all were groves, the special association of trees with sacred places is unmistakable, so that even treeless sanctuaries were called groves.[5] Virgil noted that the gods favor wild trees "unsown by mortal hand."[6] Sacred enclosures were wilderness areas in the sense of being preserved from changes wrought by humans, but they were not wilderness in the sense of regions that lack human beings. They were in use for worship, supervised by local authorities, and priests or guards sometimes lived in them. Management policies were developed and as time went on, many took on the aspect of parks, with planted and cultivated trees. Pausanias described a *temenos* at Gryneum: "Apollo has a most beautiful grove of cultivated trees and of all trees which, without bearing fruit, are pleasant to smell or see."[7] On Lesbos was a grove of apple trees dedicated to Aphrodite, to whom, as the recipient of the golden apple awarded by Paris, the apple was sacred. Temples never lost their connection with trees; it was felt that every temple needed to have trees around it, and if there were none, they were planted. When the Athenians built the Parthenon on the barren limestone outcropping called the Acropolis, they excavated two rows of pits in the rock, filled them with soil, and planted cypresses in them. Similar holes are found beside other temples such as the Hephaesteum above the Athenian Agora.

The Extent of Sacred Precincts   Sacred enclosures varied in size. Some were small plots with a temple and a few trees; from a distance these must have resembled the walled cemeteries filled with cypresses and other trees beside Orthodox churches in modern Greece. Apuleius spoke of travelers praying under the trees on "a little sacred hill fenced all around."[8] But the grove of Daphne was 10 miles in circumference; the sacred land of Crisa, near Delphi, was a plain reserved from cultivation that covered many square miles; and a grove near Lerna stretched all the way down a mountainside to the sea.[9] Pausanias described the grove of Asclepius at Epidaurus as "surrounded by mountains on every side," implying that it was extensive.[10] Alexander the Great found an entire island dedicated to a goddess identified as Artemis, covered with dense forests filled with deer.[11] Since sacred groves numbered many hundreds, the total area included in them was considerable, so that protection was extended to a significant fraction of the ancient landscape.

Because the groves were strictly protected, the trees in them often grew to remarkable dimensions. It was believed that large, notable trees were uniquely cherished by the gods and served as dwelling places for tree spirits, or dryads. Such trees were allowed to live until wind, fire, or rot brought them down. The plane trees at Pharae were hollow with age and big enough to sleep or picnic inside.[12] One hollow tree in Lycia, which must have been in a sacred grove, was 81 feet in circumference, and provided Lucius Mucianus space for a banquet for eighteen.[13] Pausanias saw examples of arboreal gigantism at Psophis, cypress trees called the

171

"Maidens" that "overshadowed a mountain," although he did not mention the size of the mountain. "These cypresses," he added, "they deem sacred to Alcmaeon, and will not fell them."[14]

Regulation of the Sacred Places　The rules protecting land reserved for the gods were strict and numerous, and followed a consistent pattern although specific laws varied from place to place and in different periods. The underlying principle was that the groves were property of the gods and ought not be damaged in any way. First was a definition of the boundary of the sacred area and a prohibition against trespass. To step over the line, however it was marked, was to pass from ordinary ground to holy ground, and was allowed only for those who were prepared and would not pollute it. In Virgil's *Aeneid,* it is a sacred grove from which unworthy mortals were excluded by the sonorous words, *Procul o procul este profani* ("Keep out, profane ones!").[15] In Pellene was "a grove surrounded by a wall, sacred to Artemis the Savior . . . no man [was] allowed to enter it except the priests."[16] This is an exception; usually ordinary persons could enter if they were ritually clean, that is, not guilty of serious unabsolved crimes such as bloodshed. They might be excluded if they were carrying iron or weapons of any sort, or accompanied by hunting dogs. Women were excluded during menses and during and for a time after childbirth. One had to be careful to know about unmarked boundaries where one went, because penalties both religious and civil applied even if the transgressors were unaware they had strayed onto consecrated ground.

A basic law found everywhere forbade felling trees or cutting branches. "Men call them the holy places of the immortals, and never mortal lops them with the axe."[17] Even removal of fallen dead timber or leaves was prohibited. In the grove of Hyrnetho, "of the olives and all the trees that grew there, no man might take home the broken boughs, or use them for any purpose whatsoever, but they leave the branches where they lie, because they are sacred."[18] If a tree was felled, it was believed that its spirit, the dryad, died, and the god might leave the sanctuary. As noted in chapter

172

6, all living denizens of the groves were protected, and hunting, fishing, and bird catching were strictly forbidden.[19]

Wild animals were granted haven but domestic ones were excluded. Penalties were set for herders who allowed cattle, sheep, goats, swine, or horses to graze in the precincts, nor were animal-drawn vehicles allowed to enter.[20] Those who observed any infractions of the rules governing sacred places were required to report them, under penalty of law.[21] Other common rules prevented plowing, sowing, and the erection of unauthorized buildings.[22] The Third Sacred War (355–347 B.C.) was fought over the issue of illegal cultivation of Apollo's sacred ground at Crisa. Setting fire to a sacred grove was the most heinous of crimes, even in wartime, although it did happen. People, including slaves, who sought shelter in a grove were granted sanctuary, and punishment was visited upon anyone who violated that right, even to retrieve slaves. Cleomenes, who burned 5,000 Argives to death in a god's forest, was driven mad by the thought of divine retribution.[23]

Civil regulations governing sacred groves are recorded in many inscriptions, often on stones in the precincts themselves. The local magistrates with jurisdiction over sanctuaries were generally those who administered religious matters; there was no separation of church and state in ancient times. In Athens and Chios, the officer was called "king" (*basileus*), not the head of state but the democratic appointee who retained the old royal title for religious purposes.[24] The priests who guarded the groves, as well as everyone else, were required to report acts of injury to officials who could prosecute the miscreants. Penalties were severe. Fines in amounts ranging from fifty to a thousand drachmas were exacted for cutting down a tree or carrying away leaves. Since an average workman was paid one-third to one drachma per day, the fines were high enough to discourage attempts to profit by theft from the precincts. Expensive mandatory sacrifices could also be assessed. Slaves were whipped or imprisoned for the same offenses. To these heavy punishments, ritual curses were joined. Ancient polytheists believed that the gods heard such curses and tradition was full of examples of divine retribution for infractions, stories that the common people took seriously. When Erysichthon ignored the protest of a dryad and cut down her tree, he was stricken with hunger that could never be satisfied.[25] Hunger seems an appropriate punishment for a crime against the land. Others were driven mad or were changed into trees, fish, or other creatures.

Exceptions   Certain exceptions were made to the protective regulations. These were not common enough to destroy the groves, but did allow a kind of "multiple use." Most of the exceptions were intended to ensure religious use of the sanctuaries' resources. As much wood could be taken as was necessary for sacrifices, and worshippers might bear branches and wear crowns made from holy trees. Animals in the precincts, such as wild goats and deer, could sometimes be captured and offered to the deity. Furthermore, the trees in a grove could be used in building a temple. Although classical temples were mostly of stone, their roofs required long timber roof poles and rafters. Since large trees survived in groves when they had been cut elsewhere, it is understandable that temple builders looked to the very resources they supervised, and beyond them to other sacred groves. The magistrates of Carpathos ordered a tall cypress to be felled in the precinct of Apollo and sent to Athens for use in rebuilding a temple of Athena.[26] The Athenians, in raising an inscription of thanks to their benefactors, recognized that such use of a consecrated tree was appropriate. Wood from sacred trees was believed to keep magical powers when fashioned into objects. It was therefore used to make statues of gods; staffs for augurs, speakers, and generals; military standards; scepters of office; heralds' wands; policemen's nightsticks; divining rods; and lot-tokens for oracles.

Management   With so many uses for wood from sacred groves, foresters were needed to oversee their management. Mythology gave Aristaeus the title of "caretaker of groves" (*cultor nemorum*), but there is historical evidence as well.[27] The municipal guild of woodmen (*dendrophoroi*) in Athens were charged to locate, cut, and bring to the city each year the sacred tree of the Great Mother. At Olympia there was an official woodman on the staff of the sanctuary of Zeus. "His duty is to supply states and private persons with wood for sacrifices at a fixed price."[28] This priestly forester also superintended sacrifices. Thus wood cut in the groves was selected by experienced personnel.

Since cutting sacred trees involved formal violation of the groves, special sacrifices had to be held to obtain forgiveness. Each year the Arval Brethren, a Roman priesthood who had care of a large forest dedicated to Dea Dia near the city, "offered two young pigs in order to expiate the unavoidable desecration of the sacred grove by the use of the axe in pruning and felling it . . . whenever iron was brought into the grove, as for . . . the lopping and felling of the trees . . . there were sacrifices *ob ferrum illatum* ["for the bringing in of iron"], and, when the work was done, *ob ferrum elatum* ["for the taking out of iron"]."[29] More openly mercenary, Cato the Elder provided an all-purpose prayer to be used with the sacrifice of a pig to obtain permission from a god or goddess to cut wood or till the earth in a sacred grove.[30] If such a prayer were used often, it would erode the protection offered by sanctuaries. The rules of the Arval Brethren, however, also illustrate the principle that every tree that was cut had to be replaced by planting another. Customarily, "when the trees fell from decay, or, worse still, were struck by lightning, and when replanting was undertaken, still more solemn sacrifices (*suovetaurilia maiora*) [the sacrifice together of a ram, an ox, and a pig] were offered on the spot."[31] Since trees were protected, and selected with care when cut, and since there was a firm obligation to replace every tree that fell for whatever reason, the sacred groves tended to survive the general deforestation.

The groves were used for many purposes other than timber. In spite of the rules against grazing, art and literature abound in pictures of cattle, sheep, and goats foraging in sacred groves.[32] Virgil says that sheep graze where "a grove / Black with thick holm-oaks broods with holy shade."[33] Ovid reports that at the festival of Parilia, shepherds offered expiation to the gods for entering sacred groves, sitting in the shadows of hallowed trees, and lopping leafy branches for their animals to eat.[34] There would have been no use for such a ceremony unless herders often, deliberately or inadvertently, resorted to the groves. In addition to temples, other buildings of quasi-religious and public character were erected in consecrated precincts: baths, stadiums, gymnasiums, schools, old people's homes, and the ancient equivalents of hospitals.[35] Public meetings and elections sometimes were held there. These could hardly have enhanced the sylvan qualities of the groves.

Leasing and Reforestation   Sacred land was sometimes privately owned, and could in some circumstances be rented. Xenophon mentioned as a well-known fact that people lease "enclosures and sanctuaries" (*temenê kai hiera*).[36] Much later, Juvenal complained that groves around Rome were being rented out to foreigners.[37] One purpose of leasing was for the removal and sale of wood and other forest products. Legal documents survive for leases. On the island of Chios, a family called the Clytidae rented out a sacred grove on their land, and the terms were recorded in an inscription.[38] They required the tenants to reforest the grove by planting young trees.[39] This indicates a similarity between the practice of replanting in the groves that were managed by priesthoods and those in private hands. Since some of the same people also managed forests outside the consecrated lands, they undoubtedly saw the advantages of replanting and assuring sustained yield of resources. Thus the sacred groves could have served in an unintended way as experimental forests where conservation practices were demonstrated.

Limitation of Sacred Space   The practice of setting physical boundaries for sacred spaces consecrated and protected what was within, but by implication unhallowed the land outside. Beyond the bounds, the gods no longer protected the earth, and people were free to use it as they saw fit. Inside the *temenos* there might be glimpsed a holy light, but outside shone only the ordinary light of day. Thus an enormous step had been taken toward desacralizing nature.[40] Pausanias, writing in the first century A.D., gives the impression that over much of Greece, sacred groves were isolated islands of forest in a generally denuded landscape. Strabo provides similar descriptions for most of the Roman Empire, and further points out that even some sanctuaries had lost their trees: "But the poets embellish things, calling all sacred precincts 'sacred groves,' even if they are bare of trees."[41]

Paradises, Parks, and Gardens

Royal Preserves   Parks and gardens for secular purposes, public or private, were also created. Some were preserved as the property of rulers, and used for hunting or enjoyment. The legendary King Alcinous of Scheria, visited by Odysseus, had a large garden with trees and fountains near his palace.[42] Parks with groves of trees in them, either natural or planted, were called "paradises," a word derived from the Persian *pairi-daêza*, "enclosure," because they represented a tradition perpetuated by Persian kings and satraps and adopted by other monarchs. Soon after the Persian Wars, Gelon, ruler of Syracuse in Sicily, planted a superb royal park containing fruit trees and flower beds.[43] Theophrastus remarked that paradises in Syria protected fine large Lebanon cedars.[44] Exotic trees imported and planted in these arboretums were more than curiosities; Apollonius advised Zeno to plant 300 fir trees in the paradise at Philadelphia, "for the tree has a striking appearance and will be of service to the king."[45] By service, he undoubtedly meant that they would eventually be felled for timber. Nero imitated the Persian paradises by planting many acres of landscaped gardens, meadows, and trees around his Domus Aurea (Golden House) in central Rome.[46] Hadrian's extensive gardens at Tivoli, 16 miles outside the city, were deservedly famous.

Private Reservations   Wealthier landowners imitated royalty and limited forest clearance by enclosing tracts of woodland as private reserves. Quintus Hortensius built a wall around more than 50 *jugera* (33 acres) of his land and treated it as a park.[47] Others planted trees of many species together in studied disorder to make an artificial wilderness (perhaps like the gardens of China, where art exhausted itself in an attempt to be indistinguishable from nature).[48] Still others made collections of exotic trees.

177

Urban Parks and Gardens   Smaller parks and gardens existed in the cities, relieving the urban environment and offering open space and greenery. Private gardens, provided with flowing water and planted with trees, flowers, and shrubs, were often seen near opulent mansions, even relatively simple homes. A large house might enclose a sizable garden in a peristyle. Cimon of Athens made himself popular by throwing his own garden open to the people, turning it in effect into a public park.[49] Theophrastus planted a garden with specimens of imported plants and trees near the Lyceum and used it as a teaching arboretum for his students. Epicurus met with his disciples in a private garden, and his school was thenceforth known as the Garden School. The greenbelt that virtually encircled the city of Rome, composed of villas and semi-agricultural lands was, on the other hand, an unintended benefit of the desires of rich owners for quiet rural surroundings and the semblance of the farm life of their ancestors.

Parks developed by governments and open to the public provided amenities in every city. Many of these, like the Academy in Athens, originally were sacred groves and temple grounds, but statesmen added walks, plantings, fountains, and places for recreation and exercise. Some Hellenistic cities were graced with parks as part of their original plans, located so as to give a spacious impression to public areas. Seleucus Nicator had the boulevards of his capital city, Antioch, ornamented with flower beds, and Ptolemaic Alexandria had fine gardens along its avenues.[50] The Romans created an impressive series of private and public gardens to improve the quality of life in the cities of their empire. In Rome itself, Pompey provided a vast enclosed park containing trees, fountains, and statues.[51] Public gardens surrounded by colonnades eventually stretched across the Campus Martius and other sections of the city. Maecenas bought a large piece of land that had been used as a charnel pit for paupers, planted it with trees and flowers, and made it a public park, while the mausoleum of his powerful friend Augustus was surrounded by gardens containing cypresses.[52] Later, Vespasian expanded the green space in the most congested part of Rome by opening one large tree-shaded park near the Temple of Pax, and another around the Temple of the

Deified Claudius.[53] Roman gardens were formal, with geometric lawns and flower beds, polygonal pools of water, symmetrical fountains and waterfalls, and trees and hedges clipped into fantastic shapes by topiary art.[54] They constitute a major attempt to make nature conform to the patterns of the human mind.

Conclusion

The Greeks and Romans appreciated the amenities of open space and greenery, whether they were found in carefully tended gardens or natural tracts that had been preserved in something like their original state. The motives for demarcation and protection were largely religious; that is, the areas were considered to be the precincts of the gods. It was not the act of setting them aside or surrounding them with walls that consecrated them; rather, the act of dedication recognized an original sacred character of the places. The reservation of sacred groves was probably the greatest single means of conservation in the ancient world; as Greek and Roman writers note, plants and animals survived within them when they had disappeared from surrounding areas.

Other tracts of wild land were claimed and protected by sovereigns for purposes of hunting, pleasure, or the provision of timber. Gardens and parks, whether created by city governments or by private individuals, lessened the encroachment of buildings and urban crowding, demonstrating at the same time the love of the people for green open space. The motives responsible for these positive environmental developments were esthetic appreciation on the one hand, and economic self-interest on the other. It is possible that some of the preserved areas served as resource pools providing natural resources on a sustainable basis, as in the case of groves managed for timber or to supply sacrifices.

Human greed made the protection of these reserves difficult, because although the gods were believed to want to keep them inviolate, there was no doubt that humans desired to use them in many ways. While penalties exacted by governments and threatened by divine sanctions were fairly effective, religion and the state also allowed exceptions from the regulations, permitting use of the resources they were intended to preserve, the construction of buildings, and even at times the alienation of land. Finally, the increasing dominance of Christianity at the end of the Roman Empire reversed the religious motive, adding a desire to destroy pagan shrines to already existing economic motives which urged that the reserved resources be used immediately for profit. Many sacred groves were then either adopted by churches and monasteries, which still protect a few of them, or they were destroyed. Public and private parks and gardens survived where peace and stability permitted.

Eleven

Environmental Problems as Factors in the Decline of the Greek and Roman Civilizations

The downfall of civilization, the Roman philosopher Seneca maintained, is inevitable: "The entire human race, both present and future, is condemned to death. All the cities that have ever held dominion or have been the splendid jewels of empires belonging to others—some day men will ask where they were. And they will be swept away by various kinds of destruction: some will be ruined by wars, others will be destroyed by idleness and a peace that ends in sloth, or by luxury, the bane of those of great wealth. All these fertile plains will be blotted out of sight by a sudden overflowing of the sea, or the subsiding of the land will sweep them away suddenly into the abyss."[1]

When discussing environmental reasons for the decline of ancient civilizations, we need to establish the extent to which they are anthropogenic (produced by human activities) or not. The causes of catastrophe listed by Seneca may be divided into two categories: those caused by human failings, such as war, idleness, and luxury, and those visited upon humankind by such external disasters as tidal waves and earth movements. These two classes can be distinguished among the causes that operated in the natural environment. The evidence examined in this book leads to the conclusion that environmental factors were significant causes of the decay of Greco-Roman economy and society, though not the only causes, and that the most important of these factors were anthropogenic. The ancients were unable to adapt their economies to the environment in harmonious ways, placed too great a demand on the available natural resources, and depleted them. Thus they failed to maintain a balance with nature that is necessary to the prosperity of any human community.

The result of the process of environmental deterioration is evident in the landscape. "Even to the untrained observer of the present day who views the environment of the semi-arid regions of [North Africa], there is an apparent contrast between the extensive and impressive ruins of the Roman period, both cities and large rural villas, and the desolation of the countryside about them."[2] But what were the causes of the ruination of city and countryside?

Nonanthropogenic Factors

The major factors contributing to the decline of ancient civilization that impinged on humankind from the environment were climatic change and epidemic diseases.

Climatic Change   Some Greek and Roman writers were aware of the problem of climatic change and reflected on it. A character in one of Plato's dialogues asks a rhetorical question, "Can we suppose there have not been, all over the world, . . . multifarious climatic revolutions which presumably lead to many modifications of living organisms?"[3] Plato connected these changes to the risings and fallings of states and institutions. Aristotle astutely observed that climatic changes generally escape human observation because they take place by slow degrees over long periods of time.[4] Claudius Ptolemy kept a weather journal, with the expectation that rainfall and the frequency of storms would vary from year to year. Incidentally, he mentions Roman bridges over Arabian watercourses that are now dry. Columella recalled that "many authorities now worthy of remembrance were convinced that with the long wasting of the ages, weather and climate undergo a change." One of these authorities, Saserna, supported this conclusion with the observation that in the north, less severe winters had allowed olive and grape harvests where formerly these plants would not grow.[5]

Changes of climate in historical times are undeniable. The round of seasons is never exactly the same in two different years, and periods of unusual heat, cold, drought, or flood have always been remarked. Though shorter fluctuations of rainfall and temperature are more easily noticed, long-term changes of averages occur over periods of centuries and millennia. It is not yet possible to give a complete account of the climatic changes that occurred in the ancient period. As three scholars working on this problem reported in 1981, "Prior to about A.D. 500 the data allow only the broadest of generalisations to be made: time resolution is relatively poor and only scattered sites are represented, often in locations far from civilizations contemporary with the data."[6] Research in historical climatology continues, however, and it is to be hoped that the general account that follows may be improved in the next few years.

The climate during the centuries when Greece and Rome flourished was, roughly speaking, similar to prevailing conditions in the early twentieth century. It was, after all, a Mediterranean climate then as now. But changes have occurred in average temperatures and rainfall amounts and patterns over large zones, and even more markedly in smaller areas where altering weather patterns may have been exacerbated by changes in the distribution of land and water, removal of vegetation, and so on. There is evidence of changing sea level, glacial advances and retreats, a varying treeline in the high mountains, and changes in the ability of farmers to raise specific crops in certain areas.

To understand the changes experienced in the Greek and Roman world, it is well to begin with the prehistoric background of the ancient Mediterranean climate. The latest climatic changes of great magnitude occurred with the end of the most recent Ice Age, the Würm Glaciation. Temperatures during the reign of ice were on the average about 13 degrees Fahrenheit colder than at present. The northern half of Europe was covered with ice, and the higher mountain ranges of the Mediterranean bore a mantle of glaciers that descended as much as 5,000 feet below the elevation of present Alpine glaciers. Since so much of the world's water was locked up in ice, the sea level was perhaps 330 feet lower than now. The vegetation belts, and the animals adapted to them, were further south. The Sahara had forests, rivers, and lakes. A warming trend interrupted by fluctuations began around 15,000 B.C., and Europe emerged from the grip of the ice by 10,000 or 9000 B.C.[7]

Further warming brought temperatures as much as 3.6 degrees warmer than today's in a period called the Hypsithermal (Climatic Optimum), from 6000 to 3100 B.C. Melting ice brought the sea upward 7 to 10 feet above its present level. The Mediterranean climatic regime turned drier, and the Sahara went through a long unsteady desiccation that brought it close to its modern state. Following the Hypsithermal came a cooling period of approximately 300 years (3100–2800 B.C. or perhaps a bit earlier) termed the Piora Oscillation. Glaciers advanced slightly and warmth-loving trees declined in Europe.[8]

A varied period known as the sub-Boreal followed, punctuated by the great eruption of the Thera volcano in the Aegean Sea close to 1625 B.C., which must have produced a brief cold spell. By this time the Minoan Civilization was flourishing on Crete and neighboring islands. In Mycenaean times and later, perhaps from 1500 to 300 B.C., average temperatures were lower, at times as much as 5 to 7 degrees below the present range. Of course, there were large deviations during that long period, and the 1200s may have been warm. Rhys Carpenter suggested that the end of Mycenaean civilization was caused by a serious drought in the Peloponnesus between 1200 and 750 B.C., but little evidence has been found to support his theory.[9] In Greek Archaic times, 700 to 500 B.C., average temperatures were possibly 3.6 degrees cooler than now. Of course, all average figures such as these must be understood to be estimates and generalizations. There were many seasonal and annual variations and abnormal spells, in all periods. Still, the impression persists that in the Golden Age, Greece was a little colder than it is now. Greek buildings had gabled roofs, and the people supplied themselves with warm mantles. In Rome at the same time, authors noted snow, a Tiber that could freeze in the winter, and the presence of beeches (cold-tolerating trees) in the city.[10]

During the Hellenistic and Roman periods between 300 B.C. and A.D. 400, conditions were warmer than in the preceding centuries and remarkably like the present. Agricultural writers reported that vines and olives could be cultivated further north than previously. The sea level may not have been as high as now, and the average temperature lower, since a majority of Roman port facilities around the Mediterranean are now under water. At the moment there is little agreement about the magnitude and timing of changes in the eustatic sea level, and measurements are difficult to make in the Mediterranean, whose earthquake-prone shores are subject to geological rise and fall.[11] The fact that the climate in Augustus's time was much like today's should not lead anyone to the conclusion that it was not different before or after then, however.

In and after the fourth century A.D., the climate seems to have turned warmer and drier for a time. But it would be venturing beyond the evidence to attribute the fall of Rome to this scantily documented fact. Drought may have been a factor in halting the caravan trade with China, but this might actually have helped Rome by reducing the drain of gold to the East to pay for luxury items. Drought in Asia may have sent nomadic peoples outward in waves that eventually broke on the frontiers of the Roman Empire. One of the arguments in favor of the hypothesis that drought destroyed Rome is the existence of abandoned Roman waterworks in the North African desert. But a student of that area, Brent Shaw, argues persuasively that there was no major climatic deterioration in North Africa, so that the environmental ruin visible there can be attributed more convincingly to effects of human occupation. Many Roman wells and cisterns are still in use, he observes; the failures of aqueducts and other large water control structures are due to neglect, damage, and disrepair.[12]

The present state of knowledge about climatic change in the ancient historical period does not permit firm conclusions about

185

its effects, but although it may have been a contributing cause in the decline of civilization, it does not appear to have been a major one. Whatever climatic changes occurred, it seems that agricultural deterioration was chiefly the result of human mismanagement and neglect.

That human activities may change climate might seem a modern idea, but Aristotle's discerning student, Theophrastus, observed it in several instances. Drainage and deforestation, he thought, affected regional weather. He reported that in "the country around Larisa in Thessaly, where formerly, when there was much standing water and the plain was a lake, the air was thicker and the country warmer; but now that the water has been drained away and prevented from collecting, the country has become colder and freezing more common. In proof the fact is cited that formerly there were fine olive trees in the city itself and elsewhere in the country, whereas now they are found nowhere, and that the vines were never frozen before but often freeze now."[13] In Crete, the mountain forests had been cut down, permitting the winds to blow without any obstacle, with the result that agriculture became impossible, presumably because the sheltering effect of the trees had been lost and much soil was blown away.[14] Both deforestation and drainage had occurred near Philippi in northern Greece, but in this case the effect was less freezing, possibly due to the fact that trees had trapped the cold air in low-lying hollows, and there was more wind after they were removed.[15] Thus the effects of human agency on climatic conditions were recognized as early as the fourth century B.C.

Epidemics   Severe outbreaks of communicable disease were sometimes attributed to gods. The *Iliad* says that Apollo sent a pestilence upon Agamemnon's army in retribution for an insult to his priest.[16] Apollo was given the epithet *hekebolos* ("he who strikes from afar") because he sent plagues, and significantly was also god of rats and mice. But he was called *epicurus* ("helper") too, because he could deliver countries from disease, as he saved Bassae in Arcadia.[17] The god Pan revealed a remedy for plague to the magistrates of Troezen in dreams.[18] Aesculapius, god of healing, was introduced at Rome to avert a pestilence in 293 B.C.

Without methods of inoculation, ancient populations could develop immunities to communicable diseases only at great cost in human life. Even immunities could not protect populations from new outbreaks of pestilence caused by mutated organisms, however. Hippocrates describes cases whose symptoms sound like bubonic plague to modern readers.[19] But because diseases can change through time, it is not always possible to adduce a modern diagnosis for an ancient epidemic. Pandemics seem to have increased in frequency when Alexander's conquests and Roman trade made contact with population centers in the Orient, bringing exotic strains home to add to native Mediterranean pathogens.

There is no doubt that epidemics affected the course of ancient history. The Great Plague that weakened Athens in the Peloponnesian War is said to have spread to the port of Piraeus from Egypt. Ironically, the Athenian blockade of the shipping of their Spartan enemies was effective enough to prevent the spread of contagion to them. Although Thucydides gives a clinical description of the symptoms of this plague, it has proved impossible to identify it convincingly.[20] The Carthaginian siege of Syracuse in 396 B.C. ended when the attackers were decimated by a plague. Had they succeeded, Rome might have been in a much more perilous situation in the First Punic War.[21] Many epidemics occurred during the Roman Republic; Livy mentions a dozen or more, including one in 461 when cattle as well as people died, and corpses too numerous for burial were thrown into the Tiber.[22] After Augustus's reign there were plagues of increasing severity, not surprisingly, since Roman merchants then journeyed regularly to India, and even reached the court of the Han Emperor in China.[23] A plague during Nero's reign killed 30,000.[24] Worst of all was the plague that came during the reign of Marcus Aurelius, the symptoms of which were described by Galen.[25] It was brought to Rome in A.D. 164 by troops that had served on the Euphrates, and killed as much as one-third of the population; 2,000 deaths a day in Rome are reported at its height. Not all plagues were bad for Rome; invasions of the Huns and Vandals were blunted by plague.[26] Bubonic plague swept the known world in A.D. 540–565 under Justinian.[27] It entered the Mediterranean through the port of Pelusium in Egypt, may have come there from India, and is said to have halved the population of the Roman Empire.[28]

The effects of epidemics on the decline of Greek and Roman civilizations must have been significant. Human numbers tend to build up after attacks of pathogens because the survivors are resistant, and birth rates rise as if to replace lost numbers. But if wars and other diseases intervene, losses may not be repaired for decades, if at all. Further, there is a connection of plague with famine and lessening of agricultural productivity, since farmers not only die from the disease, but also may flee from the districts it attacks.

Malaria is different from the plagues just described, since it is chronic, endemic to certain areas, and produces debilitation over a long period as well as death. Skeletal evidence shows that it was present in the eastern Mediterranean basin as early as Mesolithic times.[29] It has not been detected in Greece until the fifth century B.C., and was not common there until the fourth, but by then it was the most prevalent disease. Empedocles is said to have delivered the town of Selinus from fever by draining a river marsh; this would have been a reasonable way to deal with malaria, which is carried by mosquitoes, a fact the ancients did not know. In the fourth century, malaria spread into lowlands near Rome, especially the Pomptine Marshes. Dea Febris (the Fever Goddess) became an important object of worship, and after the Second Punic War, Roman soldiers were more commonly drawn from mountain districts free of malaria. Malaria was associated with the "bad air" of wetlands. Varro came near the truth about malaria's vector when he advised anyone establishing a farm that "precautions must . . . be taken in the neighborhood of swamps, . . . because there are bred certain minute creatures which cannot be seen by the eyes, which float in the air and enter the body through the mouth and the nose and there cause serious diseases."[30] From this imprecise passage, it is hard to know whether to credit him with coming close to the germ theory or to the realization that mosquitoes carry malaria. But there is no doubt that the ancients associated mosquitoes with swamps and disease. Columella says that marshland "breeds insects armed with annoying stings, which attack us in dense swarms," and other things, "from which are often contracted mysterious diseases."[31]

The effects of malaria exacerbated many of the problems that led to the fall of ancient civilization. Farmers deserted rich alluvial soil that might otherwise have produced good crops, and many moved to cities where they swelled the numbers of the urban poor, following the affluent who had been the first to depart. The result was falling productivity, not only because land was abandoned, but also because those who initially survived malaria were weak, discovered that exertion brought on renewed attacks, and therefore avoided work. There was a loss of energy and work time for the population in general.[32] Malaria is not just something that impinges on human populations from the environment, however. Its spread is facilitated by human interference in the landscape through actions such as deforestation, with the erosion and deposition that follows.

Anthropogenic Factors

The activities of *Homo sapiens* have changed the natural environment since the species arose; this fact was necessary to human survival. But some changes do not damage nature, or if they do, nature can repair the damage over time; meanwhile other changes injure the environment and hamper its ability to sustain humankind and other living things. The ancients were sometimes aware than humans can harm the natural world. Seneca remarked, "If we evaluate the benefits of nature by the depravity of those who misuse them, there is nothing we have received that does not hurt us. . . . You will find nothing, even of obvious usefulness, such that it does not change over into its opposite through man's fault."[33] Other writers portrayed a balance between humankind and nature, a kind of Golden Rule in which good or bad actions were reciprocated. Xenophon (see chapter 4) recognized that Earth has her own justice, a law deeper than human enactments, written in the nature of things.[34]

The evidence examined in the preceding chapters leads to the judgment that the Greeks and Romans were responsible for bringing about many of the failures of nature that affected them. Most of the ecological factors that contributed to the downfall of ancient societies were the result of human activities. If the people involved had seen what was happening, and had taken effort to modify its effects, they might have been able to delay or lessen the environmental disasters they were bringing about.

Deforestation and its consequence, erosion, lead the list of these disasters. Loss of forests over vast tracts was evident to the Greeks and Romans, since they had in many cases disappeared within living memory.[35] The removal of the bulk of the Mediterranean forests was the most devastating effect of human activity. Ancient economies were affected by shortages and rising prices of wood due to deforestation, but the most damaging result was erosion on millions of acres of denuded slopes exposed to rains.[36] The effects of deforestation were amplified by the pasturing of herd animals everywhere the vegetation afforded opportunity. They overgrazed, destroying some native plant species and preventing regeneration of trees and shrubs. After the soil was removed, in some places down to bare rocks, neither forests nor farms could flourish. Soil carried down from highlands was deposited on more level areas, in lakes, or in the sea at the mouths of rivers, where it often formed marshlands, breeding grounds for mosquitoes that carried malaria and forced inhabitants to relocate in drier locales. The process also added to salinization, since the saline content of both ground and surface water increased when erosion accelerated in the headwaters that are their source. It was sometimes necessary to replace food plants with low salt tolerance, such as wheat, with other crops that have a higher tolerance but are less valuable, such as barley. In severely affected areas, agriculture ceased.

Greek and Roman farmers were skilled and acquainted with methods to alleviate salinization, erosion, deposition, and leaching of essential minerals. Practices on a small Mediterranean farm tended to produce a complex and resilient ecosystem, since topography was often varied, and farmers planted various crops where soil, drainage, and exposure was best for them. Sometimes portions were left forested. Such a system might be expected to persist. But as Rostovtzeff observed, "exhaustion of the soil" occurred because "men failed to support nature" (see chapter 8).[37] And this happened as a result of economic, military, and political pressures that prevented those who owned or worked the land from applying the knowledge they possessed. Simkhovitch, in his provocative essay "Rome's Fall Reconsidered," maintained that farmers did not improve or rehabilitate their land because they could not afford to do so.[38] He does not explain why this was so, but several reasons have been suggested here. Taxes were collected primarily from agriculture, either as monetary payments or portions of the harvest. Such taxes weighed heaviest in the years when they could be afforded least, and therefore encouraged depletion of the land. One typical result of pressures on agriculture was the collapse of small farmers. They often lost their land to great landowners, who preferred stock raising to growing crops and could sometimes survive local crises because they possessed other estates in distant places. But the replacement of farming by grazing reduced productivity, since animals consume plants and produce less food per unit of land, and large herds were subject to epizootics, with the result that less food became available for the general population. Where the big landowners raised grain, they planted it in wide swaths; such reliance on monoculture creates a simplified ecosystem vulnerable to insects and diseases of plants.

Everywhere in the Greco-Roman world, agriculture was the base of the economic structure. The inescapable outcome of the failure of humankind "to support nature" was that nature failed to support a large human population. Governments took measures to encourage population growth, such as making marriage and childbearing mandatory for citizens, but these enactments did nothing to remedy the underlying problems. Decreasing population and declining productivity interacted so as to make each other worse, since fewer agricultural workers meant less production, and less production could entail starvation. Diocletian's Edict of Prices reflects the serious level to which these factors had deteriorated by the late third century A.D. It was an attempt to counter monetary inflation resulting from the scarcity of foodstuffs and other commodities by setting price ceilings. The emperor was well intentioned, but his administration's understanding of the operations of economic forces was rudimentary, and the edict was ineffective. Rising prices, food shortages, and a severe labor shortage continued to threaten the Roman Empire. For these problems the agricultural crisis was responsible, and it arose from environmental situations that were, for the most part, anthropogenic.

The removal of many species of animals and plants from localities or major geographical areas, and the extinction of some forms of life, affected agriculture and other human activities in ways that were not suspected. Depletion and extinction did not happen just because animals were killed. Shaw notes an even more important cause: "The tens of thousands of such animals purposefully hunted down for the arena were, of course, a small proportion of the total that must have yielded to more mundane processes such as the systematic destruction of their habitat by the expansion of agricultural settlements."[39] The result of the removal of a species is the simplification of the ecosystem and its increased vulnerability to damage, since an ecosystem with many species possesses more ways of restoring its balance under stress than a simpler one does. The more species lost, the closer the living community is to catastrophe, so by eliminating species, the Greeks and Romans were weakening their economies. They were unaware of this, because it seemed to them that in killing predatory animals that sometimes attacked their herds, they were doing a good thing. But predators ate a far greater number of rodents and other animals that devour crops. Plagues of mice that the few remaining predators, including domestic cats and dogs, were unable to control were reported by Aristotle, and such population explosions did far more damage to agriculture than the predators could by forays into the flocks.[40]

Compared to the modern world, industry in ancient times did not make up as large a segment of the total economy, but it did have significant environmental consequences. In many cases, scars of ancient mining and quarrying are still visible, as on Mount Pentelicus near Athens, although they are dwarfed or effaced by similar modern operations. Even more destructive were demands on forests for wood and fuel for mining, smelting, metallurgy, and firing of ceramics.

Although pollution was not produced on anything like the modern scale, neither was there any technology to reduce effluents to the air or water, except for the construction of chimneys to disperse noxious smoke high in the air, as noted about the silver smelters of Spain.[41] The poison there was lead from silver ore; other industrial processes released dangerous wastes including arsenic, mercury, and ammonia. Those whose work brought them in contact with these materials were in special danger.[42] But other people unwittingly were exposed to toxins such as lead. Since lead poisoning is cumulative and long-lasting, people did not often connect its effects with the cause. It is not necessary to hold that it acted primarily on the cream of society to see such poisoning as an effective factor. Arsenic was an ingredient of paints and dyes, and mercury was often used in refining gold. If industry contaminated the population with poisons through food, water, air, and commonly handled objects, this could have been a cause contributing to the fall of the ancient world.

Numerous problems of cities had effects on the course of civilization; these were the centers of society, and if the head is not sound, the body will not prosper. Pollution of the air by smoke, dust, and odors from countless urban activities made life uncomfortable and unhealthy. Ancient cities relied for light and heat on open fires, smoking oil lamps, and charcoal braziers. Water pollution presented a danger in cities, where sewage and garbage fouled groundwater and made wells unsafe. Not every center had aqueducts like those that supplied Rome. Urban wastes generated health problems even in Rome, where the main sewer discharged into the Tiber, putting at risk not only those downstream, but the city itself when the river flooded and backed up untreated effluent. Athens used raw sewage as fertilizer for the fields, hardly an advisable practice from a public health standpoint even if it did represent recycling. Solid garbage was thrown into streets, where it attracted flies, rats, and other vermin, and rotted into the sludge that was so deep in some towns that stepping stones were provided for those who wished to cross the streets. Such places were a breeding ground for epidemics. Ancient cities devoured their own populations, as early modern ones did. Only constant immigration from the countryside allowed them to maintain their numbers and even to grow, like Rome during early imperial times.

Conclusion

Environmental changes as a result of human activities must be judged to be one of the causes in the decline of ancient Greek and Roman civilization, and in producing the stark conditions of the early Medieval centuries. The evidence in support of this statement comes from surviving documents of many kinds, the results of archaeological investigations, and the land itself, which bears the marks of its treatment at the hands of its inhabitants through the centuries. The processes described in this book had the cumulative effect of draining both natural resources and the people who depended on them, consequently weakening the human communities of that period. These effects can be seen in some of the earliest societies of the Mediterranean basin, but they were cumulative, and by late Roman imperial times had forced themselves into the awareness of the more astute leaders and writers.

All these factors were not present throughout the ancient world at the same time, of course. How could any civilization survive if most of its forests had been removed, its soil washed away, its cropland salinized, its water and air polluted, its cities become crowded, unsafe, and subject to disease, and its rural environs ravaged by war? The effects of each environmental problem were greater in some areas and less in others, and although one can speak with confidence about some times and places, unfortunately evidence is more often incomplete. Research into these topics is progressing, however, and questions regarding environmental and ecological processes in the ancient world cannot be ignored today as they were in the recent past.

What are the reasons for the failure of the Greeks and Romans to maintain a viable balance with the environment? There are at least four factors that determine how a society will relate to nature, and how sustainable that relationship will be. Each of these can be considered for the ancient Greeks and Romans.

First, the attitudes contained in the prevailing ethos of a society should have some effect on its actions. It would seem that the way people regard nature would influence their decisions about practices that affect the environment. The view of nature of the early Greeks and Romans was religious; they saw the environment as the realm of the gods. This led them to take great care in such activities as hunting and agriculture. Artemis would be invoked before a wild animal could be killed, and a fertilizing ceremony to Demeter would precede the planting of wheat. Such religious practices no doubt contained ecological wisdom (not to kill too many deer; to use fertilizer on crops), but they became mere rituals and lost their original connection to natural processes. Also, they yielded too easily to economic expediency, as the handy prayer advised by Cato for use whenever one wants to cut trees or cultivate ground in a sacred grove shows.[43]

In classical Greek times many leaders of thought embraced an attitude of skeptical rationality that explained the world in natural terms and ignored the gods. "Man is the measure of all things," said Protagoras.[44] One embracing this view would try to use reason as the guide to actions in the world. But at this period, so little was known about how natural processes work that rationality was of little use. Economic self-interest reared its head here, too; Thales reportedly used his researches into nature to corner the olive market one year. Aristotle regarded human reason as evidence of human superiority, announcing that the highest purpose of everything in nature was to serve man, the single rational animal.[45] Of course, more traditional attitudes survived among common folk, particularly in rural areas.

Attitudes in Roman times emphasized pragmatism. Whatever was practical and profitable was the rule in developing natural resources, but the rule was applied rather narrowly. The Romans had conquered the political world; they seem to have thought they had conquered nature as well. Here can be seen an important root of the modern ecologic crisis. To use nature as a slave by right of conquest, without considering her ability to meet the demands placed upon her, was short-sighted practicality. In late Roman times, Christianity became a dominant force. The Christian view held that nature was a trust placed by God in the hands of humans, who were to care for it as God's stewards. But monotheism also taught that God was separate from creation, and denied any inherent sacredness in nature. The first book of the Bible said that God had given man "dominion" over the Earth, and many Christians took that command as permission to do what they wished to the environment, rather than a call to responsibility. Most human activities were seen by the Romans before and during the Christian period as improvements in nature and pleasing to God.

Second, the way in which societies relate to nature is shaped by the knowledge of nature that they possess. A considerable body of knowledge is accumulated through trial and error by people who live close to the natural world as gatherers, hunters, herders, and agriculturalists. The ancestors of the Greeks and Romans imparted this knowledge to them in the form of myths, traditions, and commonsense injunctions. But such lore is full of inaccuracies and misunderstandings. To demonstrate its failures as a guide for ecological decisions, one could compare the similar case of ancient pharmacology, in which fairly good remedies were outnumbered by awful, ineffective concoctions. Agriculture could be carried on fairly well through use of tried-and-true methods as long as it was not disrupted by natural disasters, political and economic exactions, and war, but these disruptions were all too common.

The natural philosophers attempted to understand nature rationally, explaining the phenomena by reference to physical reality, not the gods. They asked some questions that are now regarded as ecological. But reason was doomed to failure in this endeavor to the extent that it was unsupported by observation and unchecked by experiment. Even such keen minds as Democritus, Epicurus, and Lucretius, who advanced the atomic theory, engaged in doctrinaire speculation rather than empirical research into the phenomena of nature. The ancients barely achieved science worthy of the name. Aristotle came close, and his disciple Theophrastus nearly invented the science of ecology, but they had no followers who advanced beyond them. Particularly was this true of the Romans, who admired and patronized Greek science but made few theoretical advances of their own. Pliny the Elder, typically, was a collector and compiler of information true and false, not an independent thinker. Many Christians thought that the study of physical phenomena was a waste of time because the material world is temporary. So science in general, and ecology in particular, remained undeveloped after a brief period in which the seeds were planted by the Peripatetic School and flourished, but bore little fruit.

Third, a society can find a sustainable balance with nature only if it possesses an appropriate technology. One is tempted to say that the ancient technology was more appropriate than the modern, since it was simpler, utilizing human and animal power for the most part, and could do less damage over similar periods of time. But Greeks and Romans brought their efforts to bear cumulatively over centuries, so much damage was done. Even relatively simple technologies can be destructive, as the ancient dependence on wood and charcoal for energy and the resultant inroads into the forests demonstrate. Ironically, the very technological achievements of the Romans that moderns admire most in retrospect are those that show most clearly their ability to alter and control nature in ways that were sometimes productive, but often destructive. Granted their proficiency, it is strange that they seem to have been on the verge of further inventions and a technological revolution that remained unachieved for unknown reasons; a slave economy, psychological resistance, a desire to preserve jobs, and failure to develop interchangeable parts have all been suggested as playing a role. Yet it would be pointless to criticize the Romans for not achieving the Industrial Revolution 1,500 years before it actually occurred. If they had developed their technology further without improving their attitudes toward and knowledge of nature, their impact on the natural environment would have been swifter and more destructive.

Fourth, a society can control and direct its effects on the environment only if it is organized in such a way as to be able to encourage or compel its members to act in certain ways. This is necessary because the attainment of goals that are desirable for the society as a whole entails sacrifices, even if they are small ones, on the part of individuals. For example, the owner of a herd of goats will not refrain from grazing his animals on a hillside where small trees are growing just because it would be good to have a forest there in a few years. He puts a marginal gain for himself ahead of a much larger gain for his community. So the state must exercise some degree of coercion. But too much coercion, ostensibly for the public good, can be extremely harmful to the environment if it is directed to exploitation and not informed by ecological understanding, as twentieth-century experience in the socialist countries demonstrates all too well.

Greek and Roman governments established policies affecting agriculture, forestry, mining, commerce, and so on, but citizens were allowed a tolerable latitude of choice within these guidelines. Huge works such as aqueducts, canals, and roads show that ancient states had ways of getting cooperation, but it can well be imagined that the common people evaded regulations if it seemed in their interest to do so. Greek citizens had carefully defined duties to the polis, and the polis concerned itself with the use of various categories of land, but many city-states were proud of the degree of freedom they allowed. The authorities of the Roman Empire attempted to interfere in and control the lives of its citizens to a greater extent, particularly in the days of Diocletian and afterward. No ancient autocracy remotely approached the ability of a modern state with computer technology to keep informed about its citizens and be sure that they perform their social duties. But they were able to do a lot, nonetheless. The environmental result of the considerable degree of social control exercised by ancient societies can be seen in their ability to reach out and use resources located at great distances. Athens imported grain from Egypt and from north of the Black Sea. Roman roads and ships brought timber from the Alps and Lebanon. Tin came to the Mediterranean from beyond the Pillars of Hercules.

A most damaging aspect of Greek and Roman social organization as it affected the environment was its direction toward war. A balance with nature is a condition of peace. Ancient cities and empires were warrior-dominated societies, never at peace for very long. Even the famous Pax Romana that lasted, with few breaks, for 200 years, did not end wars along the frontiers, and was followed by 50 years of war in the third century A.D. which left no major province untouched by campaigns and battles. War exacted a debilitating toll from agriculture, because military campaigns devastated the countryside, slaughtered farmers and their families, and requisitioned or destroyed crops and buildings. Farmers were conscripted and had to spend time fighting instead of caring for the land, so terraces and irrigation works were left neglected. The mere passage of armies living off the country and trampling the crops was a calamity, and calculated "environmental warfare," in which an enemy's natural resources and food supplies were demolished, was not uncommon.

Social organization and technology can be used either for positive or negative purposes ecologically. The Greeks and Romans used them in both ways, but unfortunately the trend over the centuries was destructive. Nonrenewable resources were consumed, and renewable resources were exploited faster than was sustainable. As a result, the lands where Western civilization received its formative impulse were gradually drained, losing their living and nonliving heritage. This was the fate of the natural environment and human populations alike, and it was not something that came irresistibly from outside with a climatic change or other natural disaster; it was the result of the unwise actions of the Greeks and Romans themselves, unwitting as they may have been. The problems of the societies that followed them were in part results of the necessity of attempting to flourish in an impoverished environment.

Ancient Sources Cited, with Abbreviations

Ael.	Aelian
NA	*De Natura Animalium*
VH	*Varia Historia*
Aesch. *Prom. Vinct.*	Aeschylus, *Prometheus Bound*
Ammian. Marc.	Ammianus Marcellinus, *History*
Anaxagoras	
Anaximander	
Anthol. Graec.	*Greek Anthology*
Apollod. *Bibl.*	Apollodorus, *Bibliotheca*
Apul. *Flor.*	Apuleius, *Florida*
Ar. *Av.*	Aristophanes, *Birds*
Arist.	Aristotle
Ath. Pol.	*Constitution of Athens*
Hist. An.	*History of Animals*
Metaph	*Metaphysics*
Mete.	*Meteorology*
Mir. Ausc.	*De Mirabilibus Auscultationibus* (pseud.)
Part. An.	*Parts of Animals*
Pol.	*Politics*
Resp.	*Respiration*
Arr.	Arrian
Anab.	*Anabasis of Alexander*
Cyn.	*Cynegetica* [Hunting]
Ath.	Athenaeus, *Deipnosophists*
Aur. Vict. *Caes.*	Aurelius Victor, *Caesares.*

Auson. *Mos.*	Ausonius, *Moselle*
Beda Ven.	Venerable Bede, *Ecclesiastical History of the English People*
Callim. *Dian.*	Callimachus, *Hymn to Diana*
Cato *Agr.*	Cato the Elder, *De Agricultura*
Cic.	Cicero
Ad Fam.	*Letters to Friends*
Amic.	*On Friendship*
Leg.	*On the Laws*
Leg. Agr.	*On the Agrarian Law*
Nat. D.	*On the Nature of the Gods*
Off.	*On Offices*
Rep.	*Republic*
Sen.	*On Old Age*
CIL	*Corpus of Latin Inscriptions*
Cod. Theod.	*Codex of Theodosius*
Columella *Rust.*	Columella, *De Re Rustica*
Ctesias	Ctesias, *Persica*
D.L.	Diogenes Laertius, *Lives of the Philosophers*
Democritus	
Dem.	Demosthenes
In Macart.	*On the Dead*
Phaen.	*Against Phaenippus*
Dig.	Justinian, *Corpus Iuris, Digest*
Dio Cass.	Dio Cassius, *Roman History*
Dio Chrys. *Or.*	Dio Chrysostom, *Orations*
Diod. Sic.	Diodorus Siculus, *World History*
Dion. Hal. *Ant. Rom.*	Dionysius of Halicarnassus, *Roman Antiquities*
Empedocles	
Eur.	Euripides
Alc.	*Alcestis*
Bacch.	*Bacchae*
Danae	*Danae*
Frontin. *Aq.*	Frontinus, *Aqueducts*
Gal. *Anat. Engch.*	Galen, *Anatomical Procedures*
Gell. *NA*	Aulus Gellius, *Attic Nights*
Hdn.	Herodian, *History*
Hdt.	Herodotus, *Histories*
Hero *Pneum.*	Hero, *Pneumatica*
Hes. *Op.*	Hesiod, *Works and Days*
Hippoc.	Hippocrates
Aeron Hydaton Topon	*Airs, Waters, Places*

Epidemica	*Epidemics*
Hom.	Homer
Il.	*Iliad*
Od	*Odyssey*
Hor.	Horace
Carm.	*Carmina*
Ep.	*Epistles*
Sat.	*Satires*
Hymn. Hom.	Homeric Hymns
ad Cererem	To Demeter
ad Venerem	To Aphrodite
IG	*Greek Inscriptions*
IGRR	*Greek Inscriptions pertaining to Roman Matters*
Juv.	Juvenal, *Satires*
Livy	Livy, *History of Rome*
Lucr.	Lucretius, *On the Nature of Things*
Macrob. *Sat.*	Macrobius, *Saturnalia*
Mart.	Martial, *Epigrams*
Nic. *Ther.*	Nicander, *Theriaca*
Oppian	Oppian
Cyn.	*Cynegetica*
Hal.	*Halieutica*
Oribasius, *Collectiones*	Oribasius, *Collectiones medicae*
Oros.	Orosius, *Against the Pagans*
Orphic Hymn to Pan	
Ov.	Ovid
Fast.	*Fasti*
Met.	*Metamorphoses*
Palladius	Palladius, *De Re Rustica*
Paus.	Pausanias, *Description of Greece*
Perses, *Anth. Pal.*	Perses, *Anthologia Palatina*
Philolaus	
Photius	Photius, *Bibliotheca*
Pind. *Nem.*	Pindar, *Nemean Odes*
Pl.	Plato
Criti.	*Critias*
Epin.	*Epinomis* (pseud.)
Leg.	*Laws*
Phd.	*Phaedo*
Phdr.	*Phaedrus*
Prt.	*Protagoras*
Rep.	*Republic*

Tht.	*Theaetetus*
Ti.	*Timaeus*
Pliny *Ep.*	Pliny the Younger, *Epistles*
Pliny *HN*	Pliny the Elder, *Natural History*
Plotinus *Enn.*	Plotinus, *Enneads*
Plut.	Plutarch
Alex.	*Alexander*
Ant.	*Anthony*
Cim.	*Cimon*
Crass.	*Crassus*
De Solert. An.	*On the Cleverness of Animals*
G. Gr.	*Gaius Gracchus*
Gal.	*Galba*
Lyc.	*Lycurgus*
Mor.	*Morali*
Sol.	*Solon*
Them.	*Themistocles*
Polyb.	Polybius, *Histories*
Procl. *Chrest.*	Proclus, *Chrestomathia*
Procop. *Pers.*	Procopius, *Persian Wars*
Prop.	Propertius, *Elegies*
Ptol.	Claudius Ptolemy
Alm.	*Almagesti*
Geog.	*Geography*
Tetr.	*Tetrabiblos*
Res Gestae	Augustus, *Res Gestae*
Sappho	
Sen.	Seneca
Ben.	*De Beneficiis*
Ep.	*Epistles*
Ep. Mor.	*Moral Epistles*
Q. Nat.	*Quaestiones Naturales*
S.H.A.	Scriptores Historiae Augustae
Aurel.	*Aurelian*
Hadr.	*Hadrian*
Marc.	*Marcus Aurelius*
Simpl. *in Phys.*	Simplicius, *Commentary on Aristotle's Physics*
Soph.	Sophocles
Ant.	*Antigone*
El.	*Electra*
Stat. *Silv.*	Statius, *Silvae*
Strabo	Strabo, *Geography*

Suet.	Suetonius, *Lives of the Twelve Caesars*
Aug.	Augustus
Claud.	Claudius
Nero	Nero
Tib.	Tiberius
Vesp.	Vespasian
Symmachus, *Epp.*	Symmachus, *Epistles*
Tac.	Tacitus
Ann.	Annals
Hist.	Histories
Thales	
Themist. *Or.*	Themistius, *Orations*
Theoc. *Id.*	Theocritus, *Idylls*
Theog.	Theognis, *Poems*
Theophr.	Theophrastus
Caus. Pl.	Causes of Plants [De Causis Plantarum]
De Ventis	Winds
Hist. Pl.	History of Plants [Enquiry into Plants]
Metaphysics	Metaphysics
Thuc.	Thucydides, *Peloponnesian War*
Tib.	Tibullus, *Elegies*
Val. Max.	Valerius Maximus
Varro	Varro
Rust.	De Re Rustica
Sat. Men.	Saturae Menippeae
Veg. *Ep. R. Mil.*	Vegetius, *Epitoma Rei Militaris*
Verg.	Virgil
Aen.	Aeneid
Ecl.	Eclogues
G.	Georgics
Vitr. *De Arch.*	Vitruvius, *On Architecture*
Xen.	Xenophon
An.	Anabasis
Cyn.	Cynegeticus [Hunting]
Cyr.	Cyropaedia [Education of Cyrus]
Eq.	Horsemanship
Hell.	Hellenica
Lac. Pol.	Constitution of Sparta
Oec.	Economics
Symp.	Symposium

Notes

Chapter 1. Introduction: Ecology in
the Greek and Roman Worlds

1. George Perkins Marsh, *Man and Nature* (New York, 1864), 10–11.
2. Paul Bigelow Sears, *Deserts on the March* (Norman: University of Oklahoma Press, 1935), 27–30; Walter C. Lowdermilk, *Conquest of the Land through 7,000 Years* (U.S. Department of Agriculture Information Bulletin no. 99), (Washington, D.C.: Government Printing Office, 1941; repr. 1953, 1975); and Lowdermilk, "Lessons from the Old World to the Americas in Land Use," *Smithsonian Report for 1943* (Washington, D.C.: Government Printing Office, 1944), 413–427.
3. Fairfield Osborn, *The Limits of the Earth* (Westport, Conn.: Greenwood Press, 1971), 11.
4. Pl. *Criti.* 111B–D.
5. Thuc. 4.108. Translations are my own unless otherwise noted.
6. Robert Sallares, *The Ecology of the Ancient Greek World* (Ithaca, N.Y.: Cornell University Press, 1991), 4.
7. I have searched the database *Thesaurus Linguae Graecae* for morphemes related to *ecology*, with the kind assistance of Dr. Theodore F. Brunner, Director of the *Thesaurus Linguae Graecae* Project at the University of California, Irvine. The database contains virtually all Greek literature from Homer to about A.D. 800.
8. Ernst Haeckel, *Generelle Morphologie der Organismen* (Berlin: n.p., 1866).
9. William A. McDonald and George R. Rapp, Jr., eds., *The Minnesota Messenia Expedition: Reconstructing a Bronze Age Regional Environment* (Minneapolis: University of Minnesota Press, 1972); Tjeerd H. Van Andel and Curtis N. Runnels, *Beyond the Acropolis: A Rural Greek Past* (Stanford:

Stanford University Press, 1987); Tjeerd H. Van Andel, Curtis N. Runnels, and Kevin O. Pope, "Five Thousand Years of Land Use and Abuse
in the Southern Argolid, Greece." *Hesperia* 55 (1986): 103–28.

*Chapter 2. The Environment: Life, Land, and Sea in
the Mediterranean Region*

1. Fernand Braudel, *La Méditerranée et le Monde Méditerranéen à
   l'Époque de Philippe II*, 2 vols. (Paris: Armand Colin, 1966).
2. Fernand Braudel, *The Mediterranean and the Mediterranean World in
   the Age of Philip II*, 2 vols. (New York: Harper and Row, 1972), 17–18.
3. See Henry Fanshawe Tozer, *Lectures on the Geography of Greece*
   (1882; Chicago: Ares, 1974), 142–51.
4. Arist. *Mete.* 2.6; 363.a.21.
5. Ibid. 2.6; 264.b.15.
6. Thomas J. M. Schopf, *Paleoceanography* (Cambridge: Harvard University Press, 1980), 79.
7. Aesch. *Prom. Vinct.* 371.
8. Richard Carrington, *The Mediterranean* (New York: Viking Press,
   1971), 31–35.
9. Theophr. *Hist. Pl.* 8.2.8.
10. Oleg Polunin and Anthony Huxley, *Flowers of the Mediterranean*
    (Boston: Houghton Mifflin, 1966), 5–13.
11. Strabo 2.2.3.
12. Tegwyn Harris, *The Natural History of the Mediterranean* (London:
    Pelham Books, 1982), 12–15.
13. James Macintosh Houston, *The Western Mediterranean World* (Lon-
    don: Longmans, Green, 1964), 112.
14. Harris, *Natural History of the Mediterranean,* 15–17.
15. Polunin and Huxley, *Flowers of the Mediterranean,* 12–13.
16. Russell Meiggs, *Trees and Timber in the Ancient Mediterranean World*
    (Oxford: Clarendon Press, 1982), 49–87.
17. Plotinus *Enn.* 3.2.15.
18. Ellen Churchill Semple, *The Geography of the Mediterranean Region*
    (New York: Henry Holt, 1931), 593.

Chapter 3. Ecological Crises in Earlier Societies

1. Richard E. Leakey and Roger Lewin, *Origins* (New York: E. P. Dutton,
   1977), 117; Donald C. Johanson and James Shreeve, *Lucy's Child:
   The Search for Our Beginnings* (New York: Morrow, 1989), 209.

2. Deut. 22:6.
3. Ake Hultkrantz, "The Owner of the Animals in the Religion of the North American Indians," in Belief and Worship in Native North America, ed. Christopher Vecsey (Syracuse: Syracuse University Press, 1981), 135–46.
4. Omer C. Stewart, "Fire as the First Great Force Employed by Man," in Man's Role in Changing the Face of the Earth, ed. Carl O. Sauer, Marston Bates, and Lewis Mumford (Chicago: University of Chicago Press, 1956), 115–33.
5. Michael A. Hoffman, Egypt before the Pharaohs: The Prehistoric Foundations of Egyptian Civilization (New York: Knopf, 1979), 85–90.
6. James Mellaart, Çatal Hüyük: A Neolithic Town in Anatolia (London: Thames and Hudson, 1967).
7. Theophr. Hist. Pl. 1.3.6.
8. Mark Nathan Cohen, Health and the Rise of Civilization (New Haven: Yale University Press, 1989), 116–22.
9. Anne H. Ehrlich and Paul R. Ehrlich, Earth (New York: Franklin Watts, 1987), 59.
10. Purushottam Singh, Neolithic Cultures of Western Asia (London: Seminar Press, 1974), 208–12; Erich Isaac, Geography of Domestication (Englewood Cliffs, N.J.: Prentice-Hall, 1970).
11. N. K. Sandars, trans., The Epic of Gilgamesh (Harmondsworth: Penguin Books, 1960), 94.
12. Thorkild Jacobsen and Robert M. Adams, "Salt and Silt in Ancient Mesopotamian Agriculture," Science 128 (1958): 1252.
13. Karl W. Butzer, Early Hydraulic Civilization in Egypt (Chicago: University of Chicago Press, 1976), 2, 56.
14. Adolf Erman, Life in Ancient Egypt (1894; New York: Dover, 1971), 425.
15. Hdt. 2.5.
16. Erman, Life, 425; from R. Lepsius, Denkmäler aus Aegypten und Aethiopen (Berlin, 1858), 3:175.d.
17. Pliny HN 18.47.167.
18. John Baines and Jaromir Malek, Atlas of Ancient Egypt (New York: Facts on File Publications, 1980), 14.
19. Butzer, Early Hydraulic Civilization in Egypt, 51–56.
20. Karl W. Butzer, "Long-Term Nile Flood Variation and Political Discontinuities in Pharaonic Egypt," in J. Desmond Clark and Steven A. Brandt, eds., From Hunters to Farmers: The Causes and Consequences of Food Production in Africa (Berkeley: University of California Press, 1984), 104–12.
21. John A. Wilson, The Culture of Ancient Egypt (Chicago: University of Chicago Press, 1951), 13.

22. John A. Wilson, "Egypt," in *Before Philosophy*, ed., Henri Frankfort, et al. (Baltimore: Penguin Books, 1949), 37–133.
23. "Joy over the Inundation," from the *Pyramid Texts*, Utterance 581, quoted in Adolf Erman, ed. *The Ancient Egyptians: A Sourcebook of Their Writings* (1927; New York: Harper and Row, 1966), 10.
24. Barry J. Kemp, *Ancient Egypt: Anatomy of a Civilization* (London: Routledge, 1989), 20.
25. Karl Wittfogel, *Oriental Despotism: A Comparative Study of Total Power* (New Haven: Yale University Press, 1957).
26. Butzer, *Early Hydraulic Civilization in Egypt*, 105; see also Michael A. Hoffman, *Egypt before the Pharaohs* (New York: Alfred A. Knopf, 1979).
27. First Intermediate Period tomb inscription, Siut, quoted in Hoffman, *Egypt*, 313, from Breasted, *Records of Ancient Egypt* (Chicago: University of Chicago Press, 1906), 1:188–89.
28. Ibid.
29. Gen. 41:1–37.
30. Kemp, *Ancient Egypt*, 192.
31. Butzer, *Early Hydraulic Civilization in Egypt*, 55–56.
32. Kemp, *Ancient Egypt*, 239.
33. Ibid., 25.
34. Wilson, *Culture of Ancient Egypt*, 183, quoted from G. A. and M. B. Reisner, *Zeitschrift für aegyptische Sprache und Altertumskunde* 69 (1933):34–35.
35. Herrmann Kees, *Ancient Egypt: A Cultural Topography* (Chicago: University of Chicago Press, 1961), 78–79.
36. Butzer, *Early Hydraulic Civilization in Egypt*, 86–87.
37. Kees, *Ancient Egypt*, 20.
38. Butzer, *Early Hydraulic Civilization in Egypt*, 26–27.
39. Isa. 18:1.
40. Kees, *Ancient Egypt*, 93–94.
41. Ibid., 95. The lion was sacred to Bastet as cat-goddess.
42. Hoffman, *Egypt before the Pharaohs*, 24.

Chapter 4. Concepts of the Natural World

1. Theoc. *Id.* 4.43.
2. Hom. *Od.* 14.457–58.
3. Hdt. 7.141.
4. *Hymn. Hom.* 5.35.
5. Hom. *Il.* 1.39; Eur. *Alc.* 578–81.

6. *Hymn. Hom.* 30.1.
7. *Hymn. Hom.* 14.4–5.
8. Xen. *Oec.* 5.12.
9. Procl. *Chrest.* 1. This fragment must be used with care because it is probably pseudonymous and dates from the fifth century A.D., but it may preserve an earlier story, and even if not, it represents the last phase of "pagan" Greco-Roman thought from a Neoplatonic source.
10. See J. Donald Hughes, "Artemis: Goddess of Conservation," *Forest and Conservation History* 34 (October 1990): 191–97.
11. *Hymn. Hom.* 19.5–11.
12. *Orphic Hymn to Pan*, lines 11–12.
13. See J. Donald Hughes, "Pan: Environmental Ethics in Classical Pantheism," in *Religion and Environmental Crisis*, ed. Eugene C. Hargrove (Athens: University of Georgia Press, 1986), 7–24.
14. Hom. *Od.* 2.181–82.
15. Hom. *Il.* 7.58–60.
16. Pl. *Phdr.* 229.b–c.
17. An exception is Hesiod's comment on his own land at Ascra: "Bad in winter, sultry in summer, and good at no time." (Hes. *Op.* 640).
18. Verg. *G.*2.173–74.
19. Vincent Joseph Scully, *The Earth, the Temple, and the Gods: Greek Sacred Architecture* (New Haven: Yale University Press, 1962).
20. Callim. *Dian.*
21. Hom. *Od.* 19.592–93.
22. Hdt. 1.174.
23. Strabo 14.2.5.
24. Robert Parker, *Miasma: Pollution and Purification in Early Greek Religion* (Oxford: Clarendon Press, 1983).
25. Hes. *Op.* 757–59; Suet. *Nero* 27.
26. Hom. *Il.* 16.384–92. A. T. Murray translation, Loeb Classical Library, modernized.
27. Hom. *Od.* 19.109–14.
28. Cato *Agr.* 139–40.
29. *Hymn. Hom. ad Cererem.*
30. Theopompus, in D.L. 1.116.
31. Hermann S. Schibli, *Pherekydes of Syros* (Oxford: Clarendon Press, 1990), 69–77.
32. Empedocles fr. 8–9, quoted later.
33. Philolaus, fr. 10.
34. Strabo 7.3.5; cf. Pl. *Leg.* 782.c.
35. Empedocles fr. 127, 117.

36. Pl. *Rep.* 10.614–21.
37. Pl. *Ti.* 30.d.
38. James Lovelock, *The Ages of Gaia: A Biography of Our Living Earth* (New York: W. W. Norton, 1988), 206.
39. Hom. *Od.* 15.295; *Il.* 2.757; 9.151.
40. Hom. *Il.* 8.555–59.
41. Sappho fr. 2.
42. Eur. *Danae* fr. 316.
43. Pl. *Phdr.* 230.b.
44. Pl. *Criti.* 118.b.
45. Cic. *Amic.* 19.68.
46. Pliny *Ep.* 1.9.6.
47. Verg. *Ecl.* 1.82.
48. Verg. *G.* 2.437–42.
49. Ibid. 2.485.
50. S.H.A. *Hadr.* 13.3. For the most complete collection of references to ancient ascents of mountains, see Henry Fanshawe Tozer, *A History of Ancient Geography*, 2d ed. (1897; New York: Biblo and Tannen, 1964), 314–37.
51. S.H.A. *Hadr.* 13.12.
52. D.L. 8.69; Sen. *Ep.* 79.2–3.
53. Strabo 6.2.8.
54. Paus. 10.32.7; cf. 10.5.1.
55. Thales fr. 12, 22.
56. Arist. *Pol.* 1.3.7. (1256.b.20).
57. Pl. *Phdr.* 230.d.
58. Arist. *Hist. An.* 8.1 (588.a.13–b.17); see also *Part. An.* 4.5 (681.a.12–14).
59. Anthony Preus, *Science and Philosophy in Aristotle's Biological Works* (Hildesheim: Georg Olms Verlag, 1975), 217.
60. Arist. *Pol.* 1.5 (1254.b.18–19); 1.8 (1256.b.15–26).
61. Theophr. *Metaphysics* 9 (34).
62. Cic. *Nat. D.* 2.13 (35).
63. Hes. *Op.* 277–79.
64. Empedocles f.17.
65. Ibid. ff. 8–9.
66. Anaxagoras fr. 6.
67. Anaximander fr. 11, 30.
68. Empedocles fr. 57–61.
69. Ibid. f. 72; Arist. *Resp.* 477.a.32; cf. Theophr. *Caus. Pl.* 1.22.2–3.
70. Hdt. 3.108.3–4.
71. Pl. *Prt.* 321.b.
72. George Sessions, "Spinoza and Jeffers: An Environmental Perspective," *Inquiry* 20 (1977): 481–528.

73. Arist. *Metaph.* 12.10.2 (107.a.17–20).
74. George Sarton, *A History of Science: Ancient Science through the Golden Age of Greece* (Cambridge: Harvard University Press, 1952), 565.
75. Arist. *Hist. An.* 9.1 (609.b.19–25).
76. Ibid. (610.a.34–35).
77. Ibid. 6.36 (580.b.10–29).
78. In Theophrastus's lost work *Peri tôn athroôs phainomenôn zôiôn*, described in Photius 527.b.11–528.a.39.
79. Photius 5.15 (547.b.15–32). The pea crab, *Pinnotheres pisum*, is often found in the mantle cavity of bivalved molluscs.
80. For a detailed discussion, see J. Donald Hughes, "Theophrastus as Ecologist," in *Theophrastean Studies, Volume III: On Natural Science, Physics and Metaphysics, Ethics, Religion, and Rhetoric*, ed. William W. Fortenbaugh and Robert W. Sharples (New Brunswick, N.J.: Transaction Books, 1988), 67–75.
81. Theophr. *Caus. Pl.* 1.9.3, 1.16.11, 2.3.7, 2.7.1, 3.6.6–7, etc.
82. Theophr. *Hist. Pl.* 3.2.5.
83. W. W. Tarn and G. T. Griffith, *Hellenistic Civilization* (London: Arnold, 1952), 307.
84. Thuc. 1.2.
85. Democritus fr. 154.
86. Hes. *Op.* 106–201.
87. Lucr. 5.247–836; see Clarence J. Glacken, *Traces on the Rhodian Shore* (Berkeley: University of California Press, 1967), 70–73.
88. Dio Chrys. *Or.* 7 ("Euboean Discourse").
89. Mart. 12.57.4–6.
90. Anaxagoras fr. 102.
91. Soph. *Ant.* 332–75.
92. Cic. *Nat. D.* 2.60 (152).
93. Strabo 17.1.3.
94. Sen. *Ben.* 4.5–6.
95. Pl. *Criti.* 111–b.
96. Cic. *Nat. D.* 2.34 (87).
97. Pliny *HN* 33.1.2.
98. Columella *Rust.* 1. pref. 1–3.
99. Hor. *Carm.* 3.1.36–37.

Chapter 5. Deforestation, Overgrazing, and Erosion

1. Pl. *Criti.* 111B–D.
2. Strabo 5.2.5.
3. Pliny *HN* 13.29; Varro *Rust.* 1.6.5; Theophr. *Hist. Pl.* 3.2.4,6; 3.3.2; 4.5.5.

4. Dem. *Phaen.* 42.7 (1040–41).
5. Livy 35.10.12.
6. Ibid. 35.41.10.
7. Sen. *Ep.* 90.9; Juv. 3.254–56.
8. Suet. *Claud.* 19.20; Tac. *Ann.* 13.51; Mikhail Rostovtzeff, *The Social and Economic History of the Hellenistic World,* 3 vols. (Oxford: Clarendon Press, 1941), 1:335–36.
9. Hdt. 5.23; Thuc. 6.90.
10. Xen. *Hell.* 1.1.24–25.
11. Veg. *Ep. R. Mil.* 27–30, 49, 82–85.
12. Alfred Zimmern, *The Greek Commonwealth,* 4th ed. (Oxford: Clarendon Press, 1924), 278.
13. Columella *Rust.* 11.1.12.
14. Theophr. *Hist. Pl.* 5.1.5–12.
15. Pliny *HN* 16.74, 76.
16. Auson. *Mos.* 362–64.
17. Columella *Rust.* 2.2.8, 11–12.
18. Pliny *HN* 17.3.
19. Varro *Rust.* 2. intro. 4.
20. Pl. *Leg.* 1.639A.
21. Macrob. *Sat.* 7.5–9.
22. J.R.A. Greig and J. Turner, "Some Pollen Diagrams from Greece and Their Archaeological Significance," *Journal of Archaeological Science* 1 (1974): 188.
23. Verg. *Aen.* 10.405–9.
24. Theophr. *Hist. Pl.* 5.3.7. These trees, called *citrus* in Pliny *HN* 13.29, are not citrus at all, but sandarac, a member of the cypress family providing finely patterned, pleasant-smelling wood. The botanical name is *Tetraclinis articulata* (formerly *Callitris quadrivalvis*). The species grows only in North Africa and places colonized by the Carthaginians, such as Malta and Cartagena.
25. Ov. *Fast.* 5.93–94.
26. Dion. Hal. *Ant. Rom.* 3.43.1.
27. Pliny *HN* 13.19; Diod. Sic. 8.5.2.
28. Livy 9.36.1.
29. These names can be found in Allan Chester Johnson, "Ancient Forests and Navies," *Transactions and Proceedings of the American Philological Association* 58 (1927): 199–209; Hdt. 7.183, 188; and Claudius Ptolemy, *Geography of Claudius Ptolemy,* trans. and ed. Edward Luther Stevenson (New York: New York Public Library, 1932), map of Macedonia, 87.
30. Nikolaos Athanasiadis, *Zur postglazialen Vegetationsentwicklung von Litochoro Katerinis und Pertouli Trikalon* (Basel: University of Basel

Press, 1975), esp. 125 30; Achilleas M. Gerasimidis, *Stathmologikes Sinthikes kai Metapagetodis Exelixi tis Blastitis sta Dasi Laila Serron kai Kataphigiou Pierion* (Thessaloniki: Aristotelian University of Thessaloniki. *Didaktoriki Diatrihi*, 1985), 106 24.

31. H. E. Wright, Jr., "Vegetation History," in *The Minnesota Messenia Expedition: Reconstructing a Bronze Age Regional Environment*, ed. William A. McDonald and George R. Rapp, Jr. (Minneapolis: University of Minnesota Press, 1972), 199.

32. Marcus Niebuhr Tod, *A Selection of Greek Historical Inscriptions*, 2 vols. (Oxford: Clarendon Press, 1933), 2:111. See Greig and Turner, "Some Pollen Diagrams," 191.

33. Katherine Patey, "Endangered Forests," *The Athenian* (November 1987):18–22.

34. George Perkins Marsh, *Man and Nature*, ed. David Lowenthal (Cambridge: Harvard University Press, 1965), 9.

35. Vitr. *De Arch.* 8.1.6–7.

36. Paus. 7.26.4.

37. Pliny *HN* 31.30.

38. Oros. 4.11.

39. John Kraft, "The General Picture of Erosion in the Mediterranean Area," and Colin Renfrew, "Erosion in Melos and the Question of the Younger Fill," papers presented at the symposium "Deforestation, Erosion, and Ecology in the Ancient Mediterranean and Middle East," Smithsonian Institution, National Museum of Natural History, Washington, D.C., April 19, 1978.

40. Pl. *Criti.* 111B.

41. Pl. *Phd.* 110E.

42. Paus. 8.24.5.

43. Russell Meiggs, *Roman Ostia* (Oxford: Clarendon Press, 1960).

44. Theophr. *Caus. Pl.* 5.14.5.

45. Russell Meiggs, *Trees and Timber in the Ancient Mediterranean World* (Oxford: Clarendon Press, 1982), see particularly Appendix 4, pp. 423–57.

46. Ibid., see esp. chapter 5, "Forests and Fleets," 116–53.

47. Pliny *HN* 16.74; Livy 28.45.15–21.

48. Diod. Sic. 14.42.4; Ath. 5.206F, 208E–F.

49. Thuc. 6.90.

50. Ibid. 4.108.

51. Cato *Agr.* 1.7.

52. Pliny *Ep.* 5.67.7–13.

53. Pliny *HN* 17.1.

54. Columella *Rust.* 1.3.7.

55. Arist. *Pol.* 6.5.4 (1321b); 7.11.4 (1331b).

56. Strabo 14.6.5.
57. Dion. Hal. *Ant. Rom.* 10.31.2.
58. Pl. *Leg.* 8.843E.
59. A. S. Hunt and C. C. Edgar, *Select Papyri*, 2 vols. (London: Harvard-Heinemann, 1934), vol. 2, no. 210.
60. Livy 28.45.18 ("ex publicis silvis").
61. Theophr. *Hist. Pl.* 5.8.1.
62. Cic. *Leg. Agr.* 1.3.
63. Mikhail Rostovtzeff, *The Social and Economic History of the Hellenistic World*, 3 vols. (Oxford: Clarendon Press, 1941), 1:299, 480–81; 3:1169–70.

Chapter 6. Wildlife Depletion: Hunting, Fishing, and the Arena

1. Hes. *Astr.* fr. 4 (Pseudo-Eratosthenes *Catast.* fr. 32); Ov. *Fasti* 5.539–41; Hyg. *Astr.* 2.26; Scholiast on Nic. *Ther.* 15.
2. *Anthol. Graec.* 4.202.
3. Dio Chrys. *Or.* 7 ("Euboean Discourse").
4. Hom. *Od.* 10.156–77; 12.297–396.
5. James George Frazer, *The Golden Bough: A Study in Magic and Religion* (New York: Macmillan, 1935), 8:221.
6. Diod. Sic. 22.5.
7. Arr. *Cyn.* 34.1–36.4.
8. Xen. *Cyn.* 5.14; cf. Arr. *Cyn.* 16.1–7.
9. Xen. *An.* 5.3.7–10.
10. See Hom. *Od.* 2.181–82.
11. John Pollard, *Birds in Greek Life and Myth* (London: Thames and Hudson, 1977), 15.
12. Paus. 8.38.5.
13. Apollod. *Bibl.* 3.9.2.
14. Under the Romans, perhaps due to the influence of the mock hunts (*venationes*, see later), wild animal sacrifices became less rare.
15. Apollod. *Bibl.* 3.30.
16. Hugh Lloyd-Jones, "Artemis and Iphigenia," *Journal of Hellenic Studies* 103 (1983): 99.
17. Eur. *Bacch.* 337–40.
18. Soph. *El.* 563–72.
19. Ibid.
20. Paus. 8.54.5.
21. Hdt. 8.41.2.
22. Plut. *De Solert. An.* 35.11.
23. Ael. *NA* 8.4.; Plut. *Mor.* 976A; Paus. 7.22.4.

24. Paus. 1.32.1.
25. Apollod. *Bibl.* 3.104–5.
26. Lilly Kahil, "The Mythological Repertoire of Brauron," chap. 15 in *Ancient Greek Art and Iconography*, ed. Warren G. Moon (Madison: University of Wisconsin Press), 237.
27. J. Donald Hughes, "Artemis: Goddess of Conservation," *Forest and Conservation History* 34 (October 1990): 191–97.
28. K. M. D. Dunbabin, *The Mosaics of Roman North Africa* (Oxford: Oxford University Press, 1978), no. 32.
29. Ar. *Av.* 529–30.
30. Ath. 5.198D–201C.
31. William Radcliffe, *Fishing from the Earliest Times* (London: J. Murray, 1921), 256.
32. Hor. *Sat.* 2.4.73; Mart. 3.77.5, 5.11.94.
33. Pliny *HN* 9.79.
34. Xen. *Cyn.* 12.1; John Kinloch Anderson, *Hunting in the Ancient World* (Berkeley: University of California Press, 1985), 17.
35. Xen. *Lac. Pol.* 2.7–8; Plut. *Lyc.* 12.1–2, 17–18; Ath. 4.141C.
36. Polyb. 5.84; Pliny *HN* 8.9.
37. H. H. Scullard, *The Elephant in the Greek and Roman World* (Ithaca, N.Y.: Cornell University Press, 1974), 24.
38. Hom. *Il.* 11.129, 544–56; 18.573–86.
39. Anderson, *Hunting in the Ancient World*, 15, 25.
40. Pl. *Leg.* 7.822D–824B.
41. Anderson, *Hunting in the Ancient World*, 76 80.
42. S.H.A. *Hadr.* 20.13. See Anderson, *Hunting in the Ancient World*, 169, n. 12.
43. Dio Cass. 69.10.3.
44. *Cod. Theod.* 15.11.1.
45. Hom. *Od.* 19.418–58.
46. Plut. *Ant.* 29.2.
47. Plut. *De Solert. An.* 9.
48. Xen. *An.* 1.2.7; *Cyr.* 1.4.4–15.
49. Varro *Rust.* 3.13.1–3.
50. Auson. *Mos.*
51. Ar. *Av.* 70; *Schol. in Aves* 489; Pollard, *Birds in Greek Life and Myth*, p. 108; George Jennison, *Animals for Show and Pleasure in Ancient Rome* (Manchester: Manchester University Press, 1937), 18.
52. Livy 39.22; Ludwig Friedländer, *Roman Life and Manners under the Early Empire*, 4 vols (London: George Routledge and Sons, 1909–13), 2:62.
53. Scullard, *The Elephant in the Greek and Roman World*, 250.
54. *Res Gestae* 22.3.

55. Friedländer, *Roman Life and Manners*, 2:66.
56. Ibid., 63; Jennison, *Animals in Ancient Rome*, 174.
57. Symmachus, *Epp.* 5.60, 62.
58. Edicts of Honorius and Theodosius, *Cod. Theod.* 15.11.1, 2.
59. Pliny *HN* 36.40; Jennison, *Animals in Ancient Rome*, 174.
60. Cic. *Ad. Fam.* 7.1.3; Dio Cass. 39.38.2–4; Pliny *HN* 8.7 (20–21); Anderson, *Hunting in the Ancient World*, 87.
61. Varro *Sat. Men.* 161, 293–96, 361; J. Aymard, *Essai sur les chasses romaines des origines à la fin du siècle des Antonins*, Fasc. 171 (Paris: Bibliothèque des Écoles Françaises d'Athenes et de Rome, 1951), 60–63; Anderson, *Hunting in the Ancient World*, 87.
62. Arr. *Cyn.* 16.6–8.
63. Pind. *Nem.* 3.51–52.
64. Anderson, *Hunting in the Ancient World*, 14.
65. Xen. *Eq.* 8.1–10; Perses *Anth. Pal.* 6.112.
66. Ctesias 4.26; Arist. *Hist. An.* 9.620A32; Arist. *Mir. Ausc.* 118.841B15; Anderson, *Hunting in the Ancient World*, xii.
67. Xen. *Cyn.* 11.1–4.
68. Ibid. 9.1–7.
69. Anderson, *Hunting in the Ancient World*, 5, 10.
70. Ibid. 14 n. 50, and 38–39, 158.
71. Xen. *Cyn.* 2.9; 9, 11–20.
72. Pollard, *Birds in Greek Life and Myth*, 104.
73. Xen. *An.* 1.5.2; Ael. *NA* 14.7.
74. Hom. *Od.* 10.124.
75. Radcliffe, *Fishing from the Earliest Times*, 10, 74, 236.
76. Mart. *Ep.* 5.18.7–8; Ael. *NA* 14.22; 15.1; Radcliffe, *Fishing from the Earliest Times*, 158.
77. Pl. *Leg.* 7.824C.
78. Oppian *Hal.* 3.29–31.
79. Radcliffe, *Fishing from the Earliest Times*, 242, refs. Aelian, Athenaeus, Pliny *HN*.
80. Radcliffe, *Fishing from the Earliest Times*, 231–33; Mikhail Rostovtzeff, *Social and Economic History of the Roman Empire*, 2d. ed., 2 vols. (Oxford: Clarendon Press, 1957), 1:287.
81. *Dig.* 44.3.7.
82. Bössneck and Driesch, cited in Anderson, *Hunting in the Ancient World*, 4 n. 10, and 157.
83. Hdt. 7.125–26.
84. Arist *Hist. An.* 6.31.579b7; 8.28.606b15.
85. Paus. 3.20.5; 8.23.6.
86. David Attenborough, *The First Eden: The Mediterranean World and Man* (Boston: Little, Brown and Co., 1987), 28–31.

87. Ammian. Marc. 18.7; 22.15.24; Themist. *Or.* 10, p. 140a.; William C. Brice, *The Environmental History of the Near and Middle East since the Last Ice Age* (New York: Academic Press, 1978), 141; Friedländer, *Roman Life and Manners* 2·67
88. Verg. *Ecl.* 5.29.
89. Ar. *Av.* 504–75.
90. J. A. Thomson, in Radcliffe, *Fishing from the Earliest Times*, 230.
91. Suet. *Tib.* 34; Pliny *HN* 9.30.
92. Ellen Churchill Semple, *The Geography of the Mediterranean Region: Its Relation to Ancient History* (New York: Henry Holt, 1931), 446–54.
93. George Sarton, *A History of Science: Ancient Science through the Golden Age of Greece*, 2 vols. (Cambridge: Harvard University Press, 1952), 1:537–38.
94. Ath. 5.198D–201C; Diod. Sic. 3.36.2–4. (For Ptolemy II, see W. W. Tarn and G. T. Griffith, *Hellenistic Civilization* (London: Arnold, 1952), 307. Tarn and Griffith argue from Callixenus that the "white bear" cannot have been an ordinary albino bear. On this subject see also Paus. 8.17.3–4. See also E. E. Rice, *The Grand Procession of Ptolemy Philadelphus* (Oxford: Oxford University Press, 1983).
95. Strabo 15.4.73; Dio Cass. 54.9.58; cf. *Res Gestae* 36; H. G. Rawlinson, *Intercourse between India and the Western World from the Earliest Times to the Fall of Rome* (Cambridge: University of Cambridge Press, 1926), 107–9.
96. Friedländer, *Roman Life and Manners*, 2:66, from Aur. Vict. *Caes.* 1.25.
97. Ga. *Anat. Engch.* 7.10.
98. Hom. *Il.* 23.288–84; *Od.* 17.290–327.
99. Friedländer, *Roman Life and Manners*, 2:67–68.
100. Jennison, *Animals in Ancient Rome*, 10–27, 99–121, 126–36.
101. Ov. *Met.* 15.60–143.
102. Plut. *Mor.* 962C–D.
103. Ibid. 996F.
104. This riposte was also directed at Odysseus's questionable parentage, since some ancient commentators say that Sisyphus seduced Odysseus's mother, Anticlea daughter of Autolycus, shortly before her marriage to Laertes, Odysseus's ostensible father.
105. Ibid. 999A, referring to Hes. *Op.* 277–79.

Chapter 7. Industrial Technology and Environmental Damage

1. Pliny *HN* 36.125.
2. Ibid. 33.1.2.

3. Hes. *Op.* 757–59; Vitr. *De Arch.* 8.6.10–11.
4. Aesch. *Prom. Vinct.*
5. Simpl. *in Phys.* 1110.5.
6. J. J. Coulton, "Lifting in Early Greek Architecture," *Journal of Hellenic Studies* 94 (1974): 1–19.
7. Thorkild Schiöler, "Bronze Roman Piston Pumps," *History of Technology* 5 (1980): 17–38.
8. Derek John de Solla Price, "Gears from the Greeks," *Transactions of the American Philosophical Society* 64, pt. 7 (1974): 5–68; Vitr. *De Arch.* 10.5.
9. Hero, *Pneum.* 2.6, 11.
10. Ibid., 1.43; John G. Landels, *Engineering in the Ancient World* (Berkeley: University of California Press, 1978), 29–30.
11. J. T. Schlebeker, "Farmers and Bureaucrats: Reflections on Technological Innovation in Agriculture," *Agricultural History* 51 (1977): 641–55.
12. Pliny *HN* 36.195; Suet. *Vesp.* 18.
13. Plut. *G. Gr.* 7; Keith Hopkins, "Roman Trade, Industry, and Labor," in *Civilization of the Ancient Mediterranean: Greece and Rome*, 3 vols., ed. Michael Grant and Rachel Kitzinger (New York: Charles Scribner's Sons, 1988), 2:759–60.
14. Hopkins, "Roman Trade, Industry, and Labor," 759.
15. Aesch. *Prom. Vinct.* 498–500, trans. by Philip Velacott (London: Penguin, 1961).
16. Lucr. 5.1242–66.
17. John F. Healy, "Mines and Quarries," in Grant and Kitzinger, eds., *Civilization of the Ancient Mediterranean: Greece and Rome*, 2:779.
18. Thuc. 4.105.
19. Strabo 15.1.30, C700.
20. 1 Maccabees 8:3.
21. Diod. Sic. 5.38.4.
22. Robert J. Forbes, *Studies in Ancient Technology*, 9 vols. (Leiden: E. J. Brill, 1957–64), 7:196; Healy, "Mines and Quarries," 781; see Constantin E. Conophagos, *Le Laurium antique et la technique grecque de la production de l'argent* (Paris: Olympe, 1980).
23. Diod. Sic. 5.38.
24. Hopkins, "Roman Trade, Industry, and Labor," 757.
25. Tac. *Ann.* 6.19.1; Plut. *Gal.* 5; Suet. *Tib.* 49; Strabo 3.2.10.
26. Forbes, *Studies in Ancient Technology*, 7:154–55.
27. Ibid., 192.
28. Livy 21.37.2–3.
29. Pliny *HN* 33.21.70. Just such an event is discussed later (see *HN* 33.21, 68–78).

30. Ibid. 31.28; 31.49.
31. See Robert H. J. Sellin, "The Large Roman Watermill at Barbegal (France)," *History of Technology* 8 (1983): 91–109; and Robert J. Spain, "The Second-Century Romano-British Watermill at Ickham, Kent," *History of Technology* 9 (1984): 143–80.
32. Healy, "Mines and Quarries," 789.
33. Forbes, *Studies in Ancient Technology*, 7:174–77.
34. Ibid. 193. Pliny *HN* 36.159 describes saws used in Gaul. Saws are also mentioned in Vitr. *De Arch.* 2.7.5–7.
35. Auson. *Mos.* 362–64.
36. See John B. Ward-Perkins, "Quarrying in Antiquity: Technology, Tradition, and Social Change," *Proceedings of the British Academy* (1972): 97–115.
37. Strabo 5.2.5, C222.
38. Sen. *Ep. Mor.* 86.
39. Forbes, *Studies in Ancient Technology*, 7:175.
40. Ibid. 3:170.
41. Hendrik Bolkestein, *Economic Life in Greece's Golden Age* (Leiden: E. J. Brill, 1958), 48–49.
42. Pliny *HN* 36. 194.
43. Roman Malinowski, "Ancient Mortars and Concretes: Aspects of Their Durability," *History of Technology* 7 (1982): 89–100.
44. Kenneth G. Holum, Robert L. Hohlfelder, Robert J. Bull, and Avner Raban, *King Herod's Dream: Caesarea on the Sea* (New York: W. W. Norton and Company, 1988), 101.
45. Hdt. 6.46.
46. Theodore A. Wertime, "The Furnace versus the Goat: The Pyrotechnologic Industries and Mediterranean Deforestation in Antiquity," *Journal of Field Archaeology* 10 (1983): 448; Forbes, *Studies in Ancient Technology*, 7:148–49.
47. Pliny *HN* 33.21.68–78.
48. Wertime, "The Furnace versus the Goat," 448.
49. Strabo 4 6.7.
50. Lucr. 6.810–15. See also Pliny *NH* 33.98.
51. Vitr. *De Arch.* 8.6.13.
52. Pliny *HN* 33.21.71.
53. Forbes, *Studies in Ancient Technology*, 7:141.
54. Ibid. 193.
55. Pliny *HN* 3.20.138; 33.21.78; Forbes, *Studies in Ancient Technology*, 7:153.
56. Strabo 9.1.23, C399.
57. Hes. *Op.* 428.
58. Hopkins, "Roman Trade, Industry, and Labor," 758–59; Michael

Grant, *Roman History from Coins* (Cambridge: Cambridge University Press, 1968), 83–85.

59. Wertime, "The Furnace versus the Goat," 452, from W. Rostocker and E. Gebhard, "The Reproduction of Roof Tiles for the Archaic Temple of Poseidon at Isthmia, Greece," *Journal of Field Archaeology* 8 (1981): 211–17.

60. Wertime, "The Furnace versus the Goat," 450, 452, from H. A. Koster and H. A. Forbes, "The Commons and the Market," paper presented at the symposium "Deforestation, Erosion, and Ecology in the Ancient Mediterranean and Middle East," Smithsonian Institution, National Museum of Natural History, Washington, D.C., April 19, 1978.

61. Anthony King, *Roman Gaul and Germany* (Berkeley: University of California Press, 1990), 125.

62. Forbes, *Studies in Ancient Technology*, 6:17–18.

63. Theophr. *Hist. Pl.* 5.9.1–6.

64. Hopkins, "Roman Trade, Industry, and Labor," 758.

65. Wertime, "The Furnace versus the Goat," 452.

66. Pliny *HN* 34.96–97; Forbes, *Studies in Ancient Technology*, 6:26–27.

67. Wertime, "The Furnace versus the Goat," 451–52.

68. Forbes, *Studies in Ancient Technology*, 6:18. See also R. J. Forbes, "Metallurgy," in *A History of Technology*, ed. Charles Singer, E. J. Holmyard, and A. R. Hall (Oxford: Oxford University Press, 1956), 2:59; Diod. Sic. 5.13; Strabo 5.2.6, C223.

69. Strabo 3.2.8, C146.

70. Vitr. *De Arch.* 8.6.11.

71. Clair C. Patterson, Tsaihwa J. Chow, and Masayo Murozumi, "The Possibility of Measuring Variations in the Intensity of Worldwide Lead Smelting during Medieval and Ancient Times Using Lead Aerosol Deposits in Polar Snow Strata," in *Scientific Methods in Medieval Archaeology*, ed. Rainer Berger (Berkeley: University of California Press, 1970), 339–50; Clair C. Patterson, C. Boutron, and R. Flegal, "Present Status and Future of Lead Studies in Polar Snow," in *Greenland Ice Core: Geophysics, Geochemistry, and the Environment*, ed. C. C. Langway, Jr., H. Oeschger, and W. Dansgaard (Washington, D.C.: American Geophysical Union, 1985), 101–4.

72. Vitr. *De Arch.* 8.6.10–11.

73. J. Scarborough, "The Myth of Lead Poisoning among the Romans: An Essay Review," *Journal of the History of Medicine and Allied Sciences* 39 (1984): 469–75; S. Colum Gilfillan, "Roman Culture and Dysgenic Lead Poisoning," *Mankind Quarterly* 5 (1965): 3–20.

74. Wertime, "The Furnace versus the Goat," 445–52.

Chapter 8. Agricultural Decline

1. Soph. *Ant.* 338–41; trans. Elizabeth Wyckoff in David Grene and Richmond Lattimore, eds., *Greek Tragedies* vol 1 (Chicago: University of Chicago Press, 1960), 192, slightly altered.
2. Hes. *Op.* 117–18, 176–77.
3. Lucr. 1157–68; Lucretius, *The Way Things Are*, trans. by Rolfe Humphries (Bloomington: Indiana University Press, 1968), 85.
4. Ellen Churchill Semple, *The Geography of the Mediterranean Region: Its Relation to Ancient History* (New York: Henry Holt and Co., 1931), 357.
5. J. Donald Hughes, "Land and Sea," in *Civilization of the Ancient Mediterranean: Greece and Rome*, 3 vols., ed. Michael Grant and Rachel Kitzinger (New York: Charles Scribner's Sons, 1988), 1:98–99, 108–13.
6. Pliny *HN* 17.33.
7. Hes. *Op.* 640.
8. Kenneth D. White, *Roman Farming* (Ithaca, N.Y.: Cornell University Press, 1970), 173.
9. Semple, *Geography of the Mediterranean Region*, 433.
10. Xen. *Symp.* 2.24.6.
11. Theophr. *Caus. Pl.* 1.10.4; 3.10.8; Theophr. *Hist. Pl.* 4.14.7; Xen. *Oec.* 19.18; cf. Columella *Rust.* 2.2.24–25.
12. Theophr. *Hist. Pl.* 4.14.9.
13. Varro *Rust.* 1.8.5.
14. Cato *Agr.* 11. A *jugerum* was about five-eighths of an acre.
15. Columella *Rust.* 4.25; see Kenneth D. White, *Agricultural Implements of the Roman World* (London: Cambridge University Press, 1967), 97.
16. Varro *Rust.* 1.2.6.
17. Dem. *In Macart.* 71.
18. Palladius 12.1.
19. Theophr. *Hist. Pl.* 2.8.4.
20. Pliny *HN* 15.102.
21. Columella *Rust.* 10.410–12.
22. Theophr. *Caus. Pl.* 4.5.4.; Humfrey Michell, *The Economics of Ancient Greece* (Cambridge: Cambridge University Press, 1957), 58.
23. Michell, *Economics of Ancient Greece*, 66.
24. Cato *Agr.* 30.
25. Theoc. *Id.* 5.140.
26. Ath. 9.387.
27. Theog. 864 (ca. 540 B.C.); Michell, *Economics of Ancient Greece*, 74.

28. Ael. *VH* 2.2.8.
29. Theophr. *Caus. Pl.* 3.20.8; for detailed description of ancient agricultural tools and machines, see White, *Agricultural Implements of the Roman World*; and by the same author, *Farm Equipment of the Roman World* (Cambridge: Cambridge University Press, 1975).
30. L. A. Moritz, *Grain-Mills and Flour in Classical Antiquity* (New York: Arno Press, 1979).
31. White, *Farm Equipment of the Roman World*, 15.
32. White, *Roman Farming*, 447.
33. Varro *Rust.* 1.19.2; White, *Roman Farming*, 36.
34. Pliny *HN* 18.296; Palladius 7.4.
35. White, *Roman Farming*, 453.
36. Lucr. 2.1111–25; Varro *Rust.* 1.9.2. praef.; Pliny *HN* 18.4; Columella *Rust.* 1. praef.; 2.1; Vladimir Grigorievitch Simkhovitch, "Rome's Fall Reconsidered," in *Toward the Understanding of Jesus, and Two Additional Historical Studies* (New York: Macmillan, 1921), p. 94.
37. Columella *Rust.* 3.3.
38. Ibid. praef. 1–3.
39. Pliny *HN* 18.192.
40. Cato *Agr.* 36; *IG* xi, 2, 161A, 43, 162A, 39, 278A, 20.
41. Michell, *Economics of Ancient Greece*, 53.
42. Theophr. *Hist. Pl.* 2.7.4; 7.5.1; Theophr. *Caus. Pl.* 3.9.2; Columella *Rust.* 2.14.5–6.
43. Strabo 8.16.6.
44. Hes. *Op.* 464; see White, *Roman Farming*, 177.
45. Theophr. *Caus. Pl.* 4.7.3; 4.8.1–3; Theophr. *Hist. Pl.* 8.11.8.
46. Verg. *G.* 1.73–75; Pliny *HN* 18.91.
47. Theophr. *Hist. Pl.* 7.3.3–4.
48. Theophr. *Caus. Pl.* 1.9.3; 2.13.5.
49. Xen. *Oec.* 5.12.
50. Ibid. 20.22–26. Cf. Moses I. Finley, *Studies in Land and Credit in Ancient Athens, 500–200 B.C.* (New Brunswick, N.J.: Rutgers University Press, 1952), 82, who says there are "not a dozen references in Greek literature to increasing the value of a farm or urban holding."
51. Cic. *Sen.* 15.
52. Gustave Glotz, *Ancient Greece at Work: An Economic History of Greece from the Homeric Period to the Roman Conquest* (London: Kegan Paul, 1930), 247.
53. Mikhail Rostovtzeff, *Social and Economic History of the Roman Empire*, 2 vols., 2d ed., (Oxford: Clarendon Press, 1957), 2:197.
54. Semple, *Geography of the Mediterranean Region*, 440–41.
55. Columella *Rust.* 2.8.3.

56. H. A. Koster, H. A. Forbes, and L. Foxhall, "Terrace Agriculture and Erosion: Environmental Effects of Population Instability in the Mediterranean," paper presented at the symposium "Deforestation, Erosion, and Ecology in the Ancient Mediterranean and Middle East," Smithsonian Institution, National Museum of Natural History, Washington, D.C., April 19, 1978.
57. Hom. *Il.* 21.257–62; *Od.* 7.129–30.
58. Strabo 8.6.7–8.
59. Pl. *Leg.* 6.761B–C; 8.844A–D.
60. Plut. *Them.* 31.
61. *Dig.* 8.3.17; 8.5.18.
62. Cic. *Leg. Agr.* 3.2.9; cf. Cic. *Ad Fam.* 15.18; Frontin. Ag. 9; *CIL*, vol. 15, 7696; cf. ibid. vol. 6, 1261; *ILS* 5793; William Emerton Heitland, *Agricola: A Study of Agriculture and Rustic Life in the Greco-Roman World from the Point of View of Labour* (Cambridge: Cambridge University Press, 1921), 293; White; *Roman Farming*, 158.
63. Semple, *Geography of the Mediterranean Region*, 455–57; Claudio Vita-Finzi, *The Mediterranean Valleys: Geological Changes in Historical Times* (Cambridge: Cambridge University Press, 1969).
64. Vitr. *De Arch.* 10.7.1–3.
65. Simkhovitch, "Rome's Fall Reconsidered," 124.
66. White, *Roman Farming*, 12; A. H. M. Jones, *The Later Roman Empire*, 2 vols. (Oxford: Oxford University Press, 1964), 2:1043–44.
67. Victor Davis Hanson, *The Western Way of War* (New York: Knopf, 1989), esp. chap. 4, "The Hoplite and His Phalanx: War in an Agricultural Society," 27–39.
68. Columella *Rust.* 2.1.5–6. Sheldon Judson, "Erosion Rates near Rome, Italy," *Science* 160 (1968): 144–46.
69. Lucr. 5.1247–49, 1370–71, trans. by Rolfe Humphries (see note 3 above).
70. Theophr. *Hist. Pl.* 6.3.2.
71. White, *Roman Farming*, 147.
72. Strabo 8.5.1.
73. Theophr. *Caus. Pl.* 5.14.2–6.
74. Semple, *Geography of the Mediterranean Region*, 444–53; White, *Roman Farming*, 160.
75. Livy 6.12.
76. *Cod. Theod.* 11.28.2.
77. Simkhovitch, "Rome's Fall Reconsidered," 116.
78. Reported of Hellenistic Cyprus by Eratosthenes, Strabo 14.6.5; of Rome in the second century A.D., Hdn. 2.4.6; and in the fifth century, *Cod. Theod.* 5.2.8, 5.11.12.
79. Pliny *HN* 18.7.

80. Sen. *Ep.* 89.
81. Cic. *Off.* 2.25.
82. P. D. A. Garnsey, "Grain for Rome," in *Trade in the Ancient Economy*, ed. P. D. A. Garnsey, K. Hopkins, and C. R. Whittaker (Berkeley: University of California Press, 1983), 118–19.
83. Suet. *Aug.* 46.
84. Karl Joachim Marquardt and Theodor Mommsen, eds., *Handbuch der römischen Alterthumer*, 7 vols., vol. 5, 2d ed.: *Römische Staatsverwaltung* by Karl Joachim Marquardt (Leipzig: S. Hirzel, 1881), 141–47.
85. Pl. (pseud.) *Epin.* 979A–B., trans. by A. E. Taylor, in *The Collected Dialogues of Plato*, ed. Edith Hamilton and Huntington Cairns (Princeton: Princeton University Press, 1961), 1522.

Chapter 9. Urban Problems

1. Hor. *Carm.* 3.29.12; 2.15.1–2.
2. Mart. 12.57.
3. Juv. 3.6–8, trans. by Rolfe Humphries, *The Satires of Juvenal* (Bloomington: Indiana University Press, 1958), 33.
4. Joseph Rykwert, *The Idea of a Town: The Anthropology of Urban Form in Rome, Italy and the Ancient World* (Cambridge: MIT Press, 1988), 27–72.
5. Plut. *Alex.* 26.2–4.
6. Hdt. 4.150–59.
7. Pl. *Leg.* 5.747D–E.
8. Hippoc. *Aeron Hydaton Topon* 3–6.
9. Arist. *Pol.* 7.10.1.
10. Vitr. *De Arch.* 1–6.
11. Leicester B. Holland, "Colophon," *Hesperia* 13 (1944): 91–171; R. E. Wycherley, *How the Greeks Built Cities* (New York: Macmillan, 1962), 33, 202.
12. Arist. *Pol.* 7.10.4, 1330b.
13. Rykwert, *The Idea of a Town*, 86–87.
14. Arist. *Pol.* 2.8.2, 1267b.
15. Wycherley, *How the Greeks Built Cities*, 19.
16. Ibid., 27–29; Anthony Kriesis, *Greek Town Building* (Athens: National Technical University, 1965), 70.
17. Ptol. *Alm.* 3.1.
18. Ar. *Av.* 1004–9.
19. Pl. *Criti.* 112A–E, 115A–C; *Leg.* 5.745B–E.

20. Pl. *Leg.* 6.779A–B.
21. Diod. Sic. 19.45; Vitr. *De Arch.* 2.8.42; Wycherley, *How the Greeks Built Cities*, 27; J. B. Ward-Perkins, *Cities of Ancient Greece and Italy: Planning in Classical Antiquity* (New York: George Braziller, 1974), 19
22. Konstantinos Apostolou Doxiadis, *Architectural Space in Ancient Greece*, trans. and ed. Jaqueline Tyrwhitt (Cambridge: MIT Press, 1972).
23. Ward-Perkins, *Cities of Ancient Greece and Italy*, 19–21.
24. Kriesis, *Greek Town Building*, 71–72.
25. Ibid., 69–70. The *decumanus* apparently was named after the gate farthest from the enemy, so-called because in Roman military camps, the tenth cohort of the legion was stationed there.
26. Cic. *Rep.* 2.10–11; Livy 5.54.4, 7.38.
27. See Moses I. Finley, "The Ancient City from Fustel de Coulanges to Max Weber and Beyond," *Comparative Studies in Society and History* 19 (July 1977): 305–27.
28. Arist. *Pol.* 2.5.
29. Pl. *Leg.* 4.704–5.
30. See Catherine Delano Smith, *Western Mediterranean Europe* (London: Academic Press, 1979), 166–76.
31. Pl. *Leg.* 4.704–5.
32. Pl. *Rep; Leg.* 5.745C.
33. Diod. Sic. 17.52.6; P. M. Fraser, *Ptolemaic Alexandria*, 3 vols. (Oxford: Clarendon Press, 1972), 1:90–91, n. 358 (2:171–72).
34. Cf. Edwin S. Ramage, "Urban Problems in Ancient Rome," in *Aspects of Graeco-Roman Urbanism: Essays on the Classical City*, ed. Ronald T. Marchese (Oxford: B.A.R., 1983), 64.
35. Vitr. *De Arch.* 2.8.17.
36. Hor. *Carm.* 2.15.1–2.
37. R. E. Wycherley, *The Stones of Athens* (Princeton: Princeton University Press, 1978), 245–46.
38. Pl. *Phdr.* 229A–E.
39. Strabo 17.1.10, C795.
40. Lewis Mumford, *The City in History: Its Origins, Its Transformations, and Its Prospects* (New York: Harcourt, Brace and World, 1961), 221.
41. Cic. *Leg. Agr.* 2.96; Mart. 5.22.5–8.
42. Tac. *Hist.* 1.8, 75; Juv. 3.5; 11.51.
43. Hor. *Sat.* 2.6.28; Juv. 3.243–48; Tib. 1.5.63–64; Mart. 3.46.5–6.
44. Juv. 3.254–91.
45. *CIL* I² 593, 56–67.
46. Suet. *Claud.* 25.2; S.H.A. *Marc.* 23.8; S.H.A. *Hadr.* 22.6.
47. Sen. *Ep.* 56.1–2, 4; Mart. 4; 12.57; Stat. *Silv.* 1.1.63–65.

48. Strabo 5.3.7; Aur. Vict. *Caes.* 13.13.
49. Juv. 3.7–8.
50. Ramage, "Urban Problems in Ancient Rome," 65.
51. Gell. *NA* 15.1.2.
52. Plut. *Crass.* 2.2–4.
53. Suet. *Aug.* 30.1.
54. Tac. *Ann.* 15.38.
55. Ibid. 15.43; Suet. *Nero* 16.1.
56. American School of Classical Studies at Athens, *Ancient Corinth: A Guide to the Excavations*, 6th ed. (Athens: American School of Classical Studies, 1954), 27–33, 38–40.
57. Plut. *Sol.* 23.5.
58. Vitr. *De Arch.* 8.1.
59. Hdt. 3.60.1.
60. R. J. Forbes, *Studies in Ancient Technology*, 9 vols. (Leiden: E. J. Brill, 1955), 1:159.
61. Wycherley, *How the Greeks Built Cities*, 210.
62. R. J. Forbes, "Hydraulic Engineering and Sanitation," in *A History of Technology*, 7 vols., ed. by Charles Singer et al. (London: Oxford University Press, 1956), 2:669; A. G. Drachmann, *Ktesibios, Philon, and Heron* (Copenhagen, 1948), 84.
63. H. Gräber, *Die Wasserleitungen von Pergamon* (Berlin: Abh. Akad. Wiss., 1887); Forbes, *Studies in Ancient Technology*, 1:160–61.
64. Frontin. *Aq.* 1.16.
65. Ibid. 2.65–73.
66. IGRR vol. 1, 1055; Oribasius 1.337.
67. John G. Landels, *Engineering in the Ancient World* (Berkeley: University of California Press, 1978), 41–42.
68. George F. W. Hauck, "The Roman Aqueduct of Nimes," *Scientific American* 260 (March 1989): 98–104.
69. Forbes, *Studies in Ancient Technology*, 1:166.
70. Thuc. 2.15.4–5; Wycherley, *How the Greeks Built Cities*, 220.
71. Forbes "Hydraulic Engineering and Sanitation," 2:664.
72. Arist. *Ath. Pol.* 43.1.
73. Plut. *Them.* 31.1.
74. Forbes, *Studies in Ancient Technology*, 1:165–66.
75. Forbes, "Hydraulic Engineering and Sanitation," 2:674.
76. Vitr. *De Arch.* 8.4.1–2; Guido Majno, *The Healing Hand: Man and Wound in the Ancient World* (Cambridge: Harvard University Press, 1975), 186–88.
77. Vitr. *De Arch.* 8.6.15; Hdt. 1.188.
78. Forbes, "Hydraulic Engineering and Sanitation," 2:672–73; Oribasius *Collectiones* 7.797.

79. Vitr. *De Arch* 8.6.10–11.
80. Forbes, *Studies in Ancient Technology*, 1:173; Forbes, "Hydraulic Engineering and Sanitation," 2:674.
81. Hauck, "The Roman Aqueduct of Nimes," 100
82. Athenian laws: Arist. *Pol.* 7; *Ath. Pol.* 50.2. Roman laws: *Dig.* 9.3.1 pr.
83. *CIL* 1.2².593.
84. Humfrey Michell, *The Economics of Ancient Greece* (Cambridge: Cambridge University Press, 1940), 33; Ellen Churchill Semple, *The Geography of the Mediterranean Region* (New York: Henry Holt and Co., 1931), 414.
85. Samuel Ball Platner, *Topography and Monuments of Ancient Rome* (Boston: Allyn and Bacon, 1911), 106.
86. Ibid., 75; Pliny *HN* 36.105.
87. Suet. *Vesp.* 23.
88. Tac. *Ann.* 15.18; Ramage, "Urban Problems in Ancient Rome," 72.
89. Frontin. *Aq.* 1.4.
90. Ramage, "Urban Problems in Ancient Rome," 70.
91. Suet. *Aug.* 30.1; S.H.A. *Aurel.* 27.3.
92. Suet. *Aug.* 37; Dio Cass. 57.14.8.
93. Hom. *Il.* 1.317; 8.183; 9.243; 18.207; 21.522, etc.
94. Hor. *Carm.* 3.29.11–12.
95. Frontin. *Aq.* 2.88; Tac. *Hist.* 2.94.
96. Mart. 12.57.
97. Cic. *Leg.* 2.28; Val. Max. 2.5.6; Hor. *Ep.* 1.7.5–9.
98. Livy 40.19.3; 40.36.14; 41.21.5; Suet. *Nero* 39.1; Suet. *Tit.* 8.3, 4.
99. Emily Vermeule, "The Afterlife: Greece," and John A. North, "The Afterlife: Rome," in *Civilization of the Ancient Mediterranean: Greece and Rome*, 3 vols., ed. Michael Grant and Rachel Kitzinger (New York: Scribner's, 1988), 993–94, 1001–2.
100. S. B. Platner and T. Ashby, *A Topographical Dictionary of Ancient Rome* (Oxford: Oxford University Press, 1929), 269.
101. Hom. *Od.* 6.390.
102. Paus. 2.1.7; 8.26.1.
103. Strabo 5.C235; Forbes, *Studies in Ancient Technology*, 2:135.
104. M. P. Charlesworth, *Trade Routes and Commerce of the Roman Empire* (Cambridge: Cambridge University Press, 1924), 18; Forbes, *Studies in Ancient Technology*, 2:139.
105. Forbes, *Studies in Ancient Technology*, 2:140–41.
106. Vitr. *De Arch.* 5.9.7.
107. Forbes, *Studies in Ancient Technology*, 2:150–51.
108. A. Lang, trans., *Theocritus, Bion and Moschus* (London: Macmillan, 1901).

109. Mart. 12.68; Juv. 3.1–4, 315–22; Ramage, "Urban Problems in Ancient Rome," 85; Hor. *Ep.* 1.14.17; Pliny *Ep.* 7.30.2.
110. Dion. Hal. *Ant. Rom.* 4.13.4; Pliny *HN* 3.67; Tac. *Hist.* 3.79.
111. J. Donald Hughes, "An Ecological Paradigm of the Ancient City," in Richard J. Borden, ed., *Human Ecology: A Gathering of Perspectives* (College Park: University of Maryland and The Society for Human Ecology, 1986), 214–20; Hughes, "The Effects of Classical Cities on the Mediterranean Landscape," *Ekistics* 42 (1976): 332–42.
112. Robert E. Park, Ernest W. Burgess, and Roderick D. McKenzie, *The City* (Chicago: University of Chicago Press, 1925).

Chapter 10. *Groves and Gardens, Parks and Paradises*

1. Sen. *Ep.* 4.12.3
2. *"Numen inest"*: Ov. *Fast.* 3.295–96.
3. Verg, *Aen.* 8.351–52.
4. Pliny *HN* 12.2.
5. Strabo 9.2.33.
6. Verg. *G.* 1.21–22.
7. Paus. 1.21.9.
8. Apul. *Flor.* 1.1.
9. Strabo 14.2.6; Paus. 2.37.1; 10.37.5–7.
10. Paus. 2.27.1.
11. Arr. *Anab.* 7.20.3–4. He named the island Icarus.
12. Paus. 7.22.1.
13. Pliny *HN* 12.5.
14. Paus. 8.24.4.
15. Verg. *Aen.* 6.258–59.
16. Paus. 7.27.3.
17. *Hymn. Hom. ad. Venerem* 257–72.
18. Paus. 2.28.7.
19. Ibid. 1.38.1; 3.21.5; 7.22.2; 8.10.4, 38.5, 54.5; Plut. *Mor.* 976A, C; 983–84.
20. Ov. *Fast.* 3.263–66; F. Sokolowski, "On the Episode of Onchestus in the Homeric *Hymn to Apollo,*" *Transactions and Proceedings of the American Philological Association* 91 (1960): 376–80.
21. Paus. 5.13.1–2, 15.6.
22. James George Frazer, *The Golden Bough: The Magic Art and the Evolution of Kings,* 2 vols., 3d ed. (New York: Macmillan, 1935), 1:45; 2:121–22.
23. Hdt. 6.75–80.

24. Frazer, *Golden Bough*, loc. cit.
25. Ov. *Met.* 8.738–878.
26. Marcus Niebuhr Tod, *A Selection of Greek Historical Inscriptions*, 2 vols. (Oxford: Clarendon Press, 1933), 2:110.
27. Verg. *G.* 1.14–15.
28. Paus. 5.13.3.
29. Harry Thurston Peck, ed., *Harper's Dictionary of Classical Literature and Antiquities* (New York: American Book Company, 1923), 686–88 (S.V. "Fratres Arvales").
30. Cato *Agr.* 139–40. See also chapter 4.
31. Frazer, *Golden Bough*, 2:122.
32. Columella *Rust.* 7.3.23.
33. Verg. *G.* 3.332–34.
34. Ov. *Fast.* 4.744–54, 757–60.
35. Pl. *Leg.* 6.761C–D; Paus. 3.11.2, 14.8.
36. Xen. *Oec.* 4.19.
37. Juv. 3.13–16.
38. Adolf Wilhelm, "Die Pachturkunden der Klytiden," *Jahreshefte des Österreichischen Archäologischen Institutes in Wien* 28 (1933): 197–221.
39. Mikhail Rostovtzeff, *Social and Economic History of the Hellenistic World*, 3 vols. (Oxford: Clarendon Press, 1941), 3:1613, n. 113.
40. J. Donald Hughes and Jim Swan, "How Much of the Earth Is Sacred Space?" *Environmental Review* 10 (1986): 247–59.
41. Strabo 9.2.33.
42. Hom. *Od.* 7.112–32.
43. Diod. Sic. 3–4; Ellen Churchill Semple, *The Geography of the Mediterranean Region: Its Relation to Ancient History* (New York: Henry Holt and Co., 1931), 490.
44. Theophr. *Hist. Pl.* 5.8.1.
45. Rostovtzeff, *Hellenistic World*, 1:357.
46. John E. Stambaugh, *The Ancient Roman City* (Baltimore: Johns Hopkins University Press, 1988), 168–69.
47. Varro *Rust.* 3.13.2–3.
48. J. Donald Hughes, "Mencius' Prescriptions for Ancient Chinese Environmental Problems," *Environmental Review* 13 (1989): 15–27.
49. Plut. *Cim.* 10.
50. Strabo 17.1.8–10.
51. Prop. 2.32.11–16; Stambaugh, *Ancient Roman City*, 41–42.
52. Hor. *Sat.* 1.8; Pierre Grimal, *Les Jardins Romains*, 2d ed. (Paris: Presses Universitaires de France, 1969), 152–57.
53. R. B. Lloyd, "Three Monumental Gardens on the Marble Plan,"

American Journal of Archaeology 86 (1982): 91–100; Stambaugh, *Ancient Roman City,* 72, 120–21.

54. Semple, *The Geography of the Mediterranean Region,* 495–96.

Chapter 11. Environmental Problems as Factors in the Decline of the Greek and Roman Civilizations

1. Sen. *Ep. Mor.* 71.15.
2. Brent D. Shaw, "Climate, Environment, and History: The Case of Roman North Africa," chap. 16 in T. M. L. Wigley, M. J. Ingram, and G. Farmer, eds., *Climate and History: Studies in Past Climates and Their Impact on Man* (Cambridge: Cambridge University Press, 1981), 382.
3. Pl. *Leg.* 6.782A.
4. Arist. *Mete.* 1.14. (351b).
5. Columella *Rust.* 1.1.4; Ptol. *Tetr.* 2.12–13.
6. M. J. Ingram, G. Farmer, and T. M. L. Wigley, "Past Climates and Their Impact on Man: A Review," chap. 1 in Wigley et al., eds., *Climate and History,* 16.
7. Hubert H. Lamb, "Climate at the Dawn of History," chap. 6 in *Climate, History, and the Modern World* (New York, Methuen, 1982), 104–16.
8. Lamb, *Climate, History, and the Modern World,* 136; Stephen C. Porter, "Glaciological Evidence of Holocene Climatic Change," chap. 3 in Wigley et al., *Climate and History,* 82.
9. Rhys Carpenter, *Discontinuity in Greek Civilization* (Cambridge: Cambridge University Press, 1966); cf. Lamb, *Climate, History, and the Modern World,* 139–43.
10. Lamb, *Climate, History, and the Modern World,* 148.
11. Doeke Eisma, "Stream Deposition and Erosion by the Eastern Shore of the Aegean," chap. 6 in Wigley et al., eds., *Climate and History,* 75–76.
12. Shaw, "Climate, Environment, and History," 379–403; see esp. 388.
13. Theophr. *Caus. Pl.* 5.14.2–3, trans. Benedict Einarson and George K. K. Link, *Theophrastus De Causis Plantarum,* 3 vols. (London: Heinemann, 1976–90), 3:151–55.
14. Theophr. *De Ventis* 13.
15. Theophr. *Caus. Pl.* 5.14.5.
16. Hom. *Il.* 1.10.
17. Paus. 8.38.8, 41.7–9.
18. Ibid. 2.32.6.
19. Hippoc. *Epidemica* 3.3.
20. Thuc. 2.47–55.

21. Diod. Sic. 11.14, 70; Hans Zinsser, *Rats, Lice, and History* (Boston: Little, Brown and Co., 1935), 125–26.
22. Livy 3.6; J. L. Cloudsley-Thompson, *Insects and History* (New York: St. Martin's Press, 1976).
23. Strabo 17.1.13; William Hardy McNeill, *Plagues and Peoples* (Garden City, N.Y.: Anchor Press, 1976), 114.
24. Suet. *Nero* 39.1.
25. J. F. Gilliam, "The Plague under Marcus Aurelius," *American Journal of Philology* 82 (1961): 225–51.

26. Beda Ven. 2.1.14–15.
27. Procop. *Pers.* 2.22.6–39, 23.1.
28. McNeill, *Plagues and Peoples*, 124.
29. Mirko Drazen Grmek, *Diseases in the Ancient Greek World* (Baltimore: Johns Hopkins University Press, 1989), 265–83.
30. Varro *Rust.* 1.12.2.
31. Columella *Rust.* 1.5.6.
32. W. H. S. Jones, *Malaria and Greek History* (Manchester: Manchester University Press, 1909).
33. Sen. *Q. Nat.* 5.18.15.
34. Xen. *Oec.* 5.12.
35. Pl. *Criti.* 111B–D.
36. Russell Meiggs, *Trees and Timber in the Ancient Mediterranean World* (Oxford: Clarendon Press, 1982), 423–57.
37. Mikhail Rostovtzeff, *Social and Economic History of the Roman Empire*, 2 vols., 2d ed. (Oxford: Clarendon Press, 1957), 2:197.
38. Vladimir Grigorievitch Simkhovitch, "Rome's Fall Reconsidered," in *Toward the Understanding of Jesus and Other Historical Studies* (New York: Macmillan, 1921), 84–139.
39. Shaw, "Climate, Environment and History," 387.
40. Arist. *Hist. An.* 6.36. (580).
41. Strabo 3.2.8.
42. Vitr. *De Arch.* 8.6.11.
43. Cato *Agr.* 139–40.
44. Pl. *Tht.* 152A.
45. Arist. *Pol.* 1.11.8. (1259a9); 1.3.7. (1254b).

Bibliography

Abel, Ernest L. *Ancient Views on the Origins of Life.* Rutherford, N.J.: Fairleigh Dickinson University Press, 1973.

Abrams, Philip, and E. A. Wrigley. *Towns in Societies: Essays in Economic History and Historical Sociology,* ed. Philip Cambridge. New York: Cambridge University Press, 1978.

Africa, Thomas W. *Science and the State in Greece and Rome.* Huntington, N.Y.: R. E. Krieger, 1968.

Ager, D. V., and M. Brooks. *Europe from Crust to Core.* London: John Wiley and Sons, 1977.

Allen, Katharine. *The Treatment of Nature in the Poetry of the Roman Republic.* Madison: University of Wisconsin Press, 1899.

American School of Classical Studies at Athens. *Ancient Corinth: A Guide to the Excavations,* 6th ed. Athens: American School of Classical Studies, 1954.

——. *Garden Lore of Ancient Athens.* Princeton: American School of Classical Studies, 1963.

Amouretti, Marie-Claire. *Le Pain et l'huile dans la Grece antique: De l'araire au moulin* (Les Annales Littéraires de l'Université de Besançon, 328; Centre de Recherche d'Histoire Ancienne, v. 67). Paris: Belles Lettres, 1986.

Anderson, John Kinloch. *Hunting in the Ancient World.* Berkeley: University of California Press, 1985.

André, Jacques. *L'Alimentation et la cuisine à Rome.* Paris: Librarie C. Klincksieck, 1961.

Angel, J. Lawrence. "Ecology and Population in the Eastern Mediterranean." *World Archaeology* 4 (1972): 88–105.

235

Bibliography

Ashby, Thomas. *The Aqueducts of Ancient Rome.* Oxford: Oxford University Press, 1935.

———. *The Roman Campagna in Classical Times.* London: Ernest Benn, 1970.

Athanasiadis, Nikolaos. *Zur postglazialen Vegetationsentwicklung von Litochoro Katerinis und Pertouli Trikalon.* Basel: University of Basel Press, 1975.

Attenborough, David. *The First Eden: The Mediterranean World and Man.* Boston: Little, Brown and Co., 1987.

Aubouin, Jean. "Alpine Tectonics and Plate Tectonics: Thoughts about the Eastern Mediterranean." In *Europe from Crust to Core,* edited by D. V. Ager and M. Brooks. London: John Wiley and Sons, 1977.

Austin, Michel M. "Greek Trade, Industry, and Labor." In *Civilization of the Ancient Mediterranean: Greece and Rome,* 3 vols., edited by Michael Grant and Rachel Kitzinger. New York: Charles Scribner's Sons, 1988. 2:723–52.

Austin, Michel M., and Pierre Vidal-Naquet. *Economic and Social History of Ancient Greece: An Introduction.* Berkeley: University of California Press, 1977.

Aymard, J. *Essai sur les chasses romaines des origines à la fin du siècle des Antonins.* Fasc. 171. Paris: Bibliothèque des Écoles Françaises d'Athenes et de Rome, 1951.

Baines, John, and Jaromir Malek. *Atlas of Ancient Egypt.* New York: Facts on File Publications, 1980.

Balsdon, John Percy Vyvian Dacre. *Life and Leisure in Ancient Rome.* New York: McGraw-Hill, 1969.

Baumann, Hellmut. *Die Griechische Pflanzenwelt in Mythos, Kunst und Literatur.* Munich: Hirmer Verlag, 1982.

Baynes, N. H. "Decline of the Roman Empire in Western Europe: Some Modern Explanations." *Journal of Roman Studies* 33 (1943): 29–35.

Bender, Helmut. "Historische Umweltforschung aus der Sicht der provinzialrömischen Archäologie." In *Siedlungsforschung: Archäologie-Geschichte-Geographie, Band 6,* edited by Klaus Fehn et al. Bonn: Verlag Siedlungsforschung, 1988.

Bergquist, Birgitta. *The Archaic Greek Temenos: A Study of Structure and Function.* Lund, Sweden: Gleerup, 1967.

Bernard, Michelle. "Recent Advances in Research on the Zooplankton of the Mediterranean Sea." *Oceanography and Marine Biology* 5 (1967): 231–56.

Bernardo, Aurelio. "The Economic Problems of the Roman Empire." *Studia et Documenta Historiae et Juris* 31 (1965): 110–70.

Beug, Hans-Juergen. "On the Forest History of the Dalmatian Coast." *Review of Paleobotany and Palynology* 2 (1967): 271–79.

Biel, Erwin R. *Climatology of the Mediterranean Area*. University of Chicago, Institute of Meteorology: Miscellaneous reports, no. 13. Chicago: University of Chicago Press, 1944.

Biese, Alfred. *Die Entwicklung des Naturgefühls bei den Griechen und Römern*. 2 vols. Kiel: Lipsius und Tischer, 1882–84.

Birge, Darice Elizabeth. "Sacred Groves in the Ancient Greek World." Ph.D. dissertation, University of California, Berkeley, 1982.

Birot, Pierre, Pierre Gabert, and Jean Dresch. *La Méditeranée et le Moyen Orient*. 2 vols. Paris: Presses Universitaires de France, 1964.

Blake, Marion E. *Ancient Roman Construction in Italy from Nerva through the Antonines*. Philadelphia: American Philosophical Society, 1973.

————. *Ancient Roman Construction in Italy from the Prehistoric Period to Augustus*. Washington, D.C.: Carnegie Institution, 1947.

————. *Ancient Roman Construction in Italy from Tiberius through the Flavians*. Washington, D.C.: Carnegie Institution, 1959.

Boak, Arthur E. R. *Manpower Shortage and the Fall of the Roman Empire in the West*. Ann Arbor: University of Michigan Press, 1955.

Bokser, Baruch M. "Approaching Sacred Space." *Harvard Theological Review* 78 (1985): 279–99.

Bolkestein, Hendrik, ed. *Economic Life in Greece's Golden Age*. Leiden: E. J. Brill, 1958.

Borgeaud, Philippe. *The Cult of Pan in Ancient Greece*. Chicago: University of Chicago Press, 1988.

Bottema, Sietse. *Late Quaternary Vegetation History of Northwestern Greece*. Groningen: V. R. B. Offsetdrukkerij, 1974.

Bötticher, C. *Über den Baukultus der Hellenen und Römer*. Berlin, 1856.

Bourne, F. C. "Reflections on Rome's Urban Problems." *Classical World* 62 (1969): 205–9.

Bradford, Ernle. *Mediterranean: Portrait of a Sea*. London: Hodder and Stoughton, 1971.

Bradford, John. *Ancient Landscapes in Europe and Asia*. London: G. Bell and Sons, 1957.

Braudel, Fernand. *La Méditerranée et le Monde Méditerranéen à l'Époque de Philippe II*. 2 vols. Paris: Armand Colin, 1966. *The Mediterranean and the Mediterranean World in the Age of Philip II*, trans. by Sian Reynolds. New York: Harper and Row, 1972.

Brice, William Charles. "The History of Forestry in Turkey." *Istanbul Üneversitesi Orman Faciltesi Dergisi*, Series A. 20 (1955): 29–38.

————, ed. *Environmental History of the Near and Middle East since the Last Ice Age*. New York: Academic Press, 1978.

Bromehead, Cyril Edward Nowell. "The Early History of Water Supply." *Classical Journal* 99 (1942): 142–51, 183–96.

Brothwell, Don R. "Foodstuffs, Cooking, and Drugs." In *Civilization of the*

Ancient Mediterranean, 3 vols., edited by Michael Grant and Rachel Kitzinger. New York: Charles Scribner's Sons, 1988. 1:247–64.

Brothwell, Don R., and Patricia Brothwell. *Food in Antiquity: A Survey of the Diet of Early Peoples*. New York: Praeger, 1969.

Brumbaugh, Robert Sherrick. *Ancient Greek Gadgets and Machines*. New York: Crowell, 1966.

Bryson, R. A., and T. J. Murray. *Climates of Hunger: Mankind and the World's Changing Weather*. Madison: University of Wisconsin Press, 1977.

Buck, Robert John. *Agriculture and Agricultural Practice in Roman Law*. Historia; Einzelschriften, Heft 45. Wiesbaden: F. Steiner, 1983.

Bunting, Brian T. "Soils of Mediterranean and Humid Subtropical Areas." In *The Geography of Soil*. Chicago: Aldine, 1965. 179–86.

Burford, Alison. "Crafts and Craftsmen." In *Civilization of the Ancient Mediterranean: Greece and Rome*, 3 vols., edited by Michael Grant and Rachel Kitzinger. New York: Charles Scribner's Sons, 1988. 1:367–88.

———. *Craftsmen in Greek and Roman Society*. Ithaca, N.Y.: Cornell University Press, 1972.

———. "Heavy Transport in Classical Antiquity." *Economic History Review* 13 (1960):1–18.

Burns, A. "Ancient Greek Water Supply." *Technology and Culture* 15 (1974): 389–412.

Butler, Alfred Joshua. *Sport in Classic Times*. Los Altos, Calif.: W. Kaufmann, 1975.

Butzer, Karl W. *Early Hydraulic Civilization in Egypt: A Study in Cultural Ecology*. Chicago: University of Chicago Press, 1976.

———. *Environment and Archaeology*. Chicago: Aldine, 1964.

———. "Long-Term Nile Flood Variation and Political Discontinuities in Pharaonic Egypt." In *From Hunters to Farmers: The Causes and Consequences of Food Production in Africa*, edited by J. Desmond Clark and Steven A. Brandt. Berkeley: University of California Press, 1984. 102–12.

Caputo, M., and Pieri, L. "Eustatic Sea Variation in the Last 2000 years in the Mediterranean." *Journal of Geophysical Research* 81 (1976): 5787–90.

Carcopino, Jerome. *Daily Life in Ancient Rome*, ed. Henry T. Rowell, trans. E. O. Lorimer. New Haven: Yale University Press, 1940.

Carpenter, Rhys. *Discontinuity in Greek Civilization*. Cambridge: Cambridge University Press, 1966.

Carrington, Richard. *The Mediterranean: Cradle of Western Culture*. New York: Viking Press, 1971.

Carter, Francis W., ed. *An Historical Geography of the Balkans*. New York: Academic Press, 1977.

Cartledge, Paul. *Sparta and Lakonia: A Regional History, 1300–362 B.C.* London: Routledge and Kegan Paul, 1979.

Cartwright, Frederick Fox. *Disease and History.* New York: Crowell, 1972.

Cary, Max. *The Geographic Background of Greek and Roman History.* Oxford: Clarendon Press, 1949.

Casson, Lionel. *Travel in the Ancient World.* London: George Allen and Unwin, 1974.

Casson, Stanley. *Macedonia, Thrace, and Illyria: Their Relations to Greece from the Earliest Times Down to the Time of Philip, Son of Amyntas.* Oxford: Oxford University Press, 1926.

Castagnoli, F. *Ippodamo di Mileto e l'urbanistica a pianta ortogonale.* Rome: De Luca, 1956.

Chappell, J. E. "Climatic Change Reconsidered: Another Look at the 'Pulse of Asia.' " *Geographic Review* 60 (1970): 347–73.

Charlesworth, M. P. *Trade Routes and Commerce of the Roman Empire.* Cambridge: Cambridge University Press, 1924.

Chloros, N. "Forstwissenschaftliche Leistungen der Altgriechen." *Forstwissenschaftliches Centralblatt* 5 (1885): 15–23.

Clairborne, Robert. *Climate, Man, and History.* New York: Norton, 1970.

Clark, John Graham Desmond. "Water in Antiquity." *Antiquity* 18 (1944): 1–15.

Clark, Kenneth. *Animals and Men.* New York: William Morrow, 1977.

Clausing, Roth. "The Roman Colonate: The Theories of its Origin." (Studies in History, Economics, and Public Law, edited by the Faculty of Political Science of Columbia University, vol. 117, no. 1; whole no. 260). New York: Columbia University, 1925.

Cloudsley-Thompson, J. L. *Insects and History.* New York: St. Martin's Press, 1976.

Cockle, Helen. "Pottery Manufacture in Roman Egypt: A New Papyrus." *Journal of Roman Studies* 71 (1981): 87–97.

Cohen, Mark Nathan. *Health and the Rise of Civilization.* New Haven: Yale University Press, 1989.

Collingwood, R. G. *The Idea of Nature.* New York: Oxford University Press, 1945.

Collis, John Stewart. *The Triumph of the Tree.* New York: Viking Press, 1954.

Conophagos, Constantin E. *Le Laurium antique et la technique grecque de la production de l'argent.* Paris: Olympe, 1980.

Coulton, J. J. "Greek Building Techniques." In *Civilization of the Ancient Mediterranean: Greece and Rome,* 3 vols., edited by Michael Grant and Rachel Kitzinger. New York: Charles Scribner's Sons, 1988. 1:277–98.

———. "Lifting in Early Greek Architecture." *Journal of Hellenic Studies* 94 (1974):1–19.

Crawford, Dorothy J. "Food: Tradition and Change in Hellenistic Egypt." *World Archaeology* 11 (1979):136–46.

Cunliffe, Barry W. *Fishbourne: A Roman Palace and Its Garden.* Baltimore: Johns Hopkins University Press, 1971.

Dale, Tom, and Vernon Gill Carter. *Topsoil and Civilization.* Norman: University of Oklahoma Press, 1955.

Darby, H. C. "The Clearing of the Woodland in Europe." In *Man's Role in Changing the Face of the Earth,* edited by William L. Thomas. Chicago: University of Chicago Press, 1956. 183–216.

Davies, Oliver. *Roman Mines in Europe.* Oxford: Oxford University Press, 1935.

Deacon, Margaret. "The Ancient World." In *Scientists and the Sea.* London: Academic Press, 1971. 3–19.

de Camp, L. Sprague. *The Ancient Engineers.* Cambridge: MIT Press, 1970.

Decker, Frank Norton. *Historical Background: Arts, Skills and Needs of Ancient and Modern Farming.* Syracuse: Syracuse University Press, 1961.

Dembeck, Hermann. *Animals and Men.* Garden City, N.Y.: Natural History Press, 1965.

Detienne, Marcel, and Jean-Pierre Vernant. *The Cuisine of Sacrifice among the Greeks,* trans. Paula Wissing. Chicago: University of Chicago Press, 1989.

Dewey, J. F., W. C. Pitman, III, W. B. F. Ryan, and J. Bonnin. "Plate Tectonics and the Evolution of the Alpine System." *Geological Society of America Bulletin* 84 (1973): 3137–80.

Di Castri, Francesco. "Mediterranean-Type Shrublands of the World." In *Ecosystems of the World 11: Mediterranean-Type Shrublands,* edited by Francesco di Castri, David W. Goodall, and Raymond L. Specht. Amsterdam: Elsevier Scientific Publishing Company, 1981. 1–52.

Di Castri, Francesco, and Harold A. Mooney. *Mediterranean Type Ecosystems: Origin and Structure.* Heidelberg: Springer-Verlag, 1973.

Dombrowski, Daniel A. *The Philosophy of Vegetarianism.* Amherst: University of Massachusetts Press, 1984.

Doxiadis, Konstantinos Apostolou. *Architectural Space in Ancient Greece,* trans. and ed. by Jaqueline Tyrwhitt. Cambridge: MIT Press, 1972.

———. *The Method for the Study of the Ancient Greek Settlements.* Athens: Athens Center of Ekistics, 1972.

Drachmann, Aage Gerhardt. *Ktesibios, Philon, and Heron: A Study in Ancient Pneumatics.* Copenhagen: E. Munksgaard, 1948.

———. *The Mechanical Technology of Greek and Roman Antiquity: A Study of the Literary Sources.* Madison: University of Wisconsin Press, 1963.

Dumezil, Georges. *Camillus: A Study of Indo-European Religion as Roman*

History, ed. Udo Strutynski. Berkeley: University of California Press, 1980.

Dunbabin, K. M. D. *The Mosaics of Roman North Africa*. Oxford: Oxford University Press, 1978.

Duncan-Jones, Richard P. *The Economy of the Roman Empire: Quantitative Studies*. 2d ed. Cambridge: Cambridge University Press, 1982.

Eck, Diana L. "The City as a Sacred Center." *Journal of Developing Societies* 2 (1986): 149–281.

Edgerton, W. Dow. "Sacred Space (Thematic Issue)." *Chicago Theological Seminary Register* 75 (1985): 1–19.

Ehrenberg, Victor. *The People of Aristophanes*. Oxford: B. Blackwell, 1951.

Ehrlich, Anne H., and Paul R. Ehrlich. *Earth*. New York: Franklin Watts, 1987.

Eisma, Doeke. "Stream Deposition by Erosion by the Eastern Shore of the Aegean." In *Climate and History: Studies in Past Climates and Their Impact on Man*, edited by T. M. L. Wigley, M. J. Ingram, and G. Farmer. Cambridge: Cambridge University Press, 1981.

Emberger, L. "La Végétation de la région Méditerranéenne." *Revue Générale Botanique* 32 (1930): 461–662, 705–21.

Erim, Kenan T. *Aphrodisias: City of Venus Aphrodite*. New York: Facts on File, 1986.

Erman, Adolf. *Life in Ancient Egypt*. London: Macmillan, 1894. Repr. New York: Dover, 1971.

———, ed. *The Ancient Egyptians: A Sourcebook of Their Writings*. London: Methuen, 1927. Repr. New York: Harper and Row, 1966.

Eubanks, J. "Navigation on the Tiber." *Classical Journal* 25 (1930): 683–95.

Evans, J. K. "Wheat Production and Its Social Consequences in the Roman World." *Classical Quarterly* 31 (1981): 428–42.

Evenari, Michael, Leslie Shanan, and Naphtali Tadmor. *The Negev: The Challenge of a Desert*. 2d ed. Cambridge: Harvard University Press, 1982.

Fairclough, Henry Rushton. *The Attitude of the Greek Tragedians toward Nature*. Toronto: Rowsell, 1897.

———. *Love of Nature Among the Greeks and Romans*. New York: Longmans, Green, 1930.

Farnell, Lewis Richard. *The Cults of the Greek States*. 5 vols. Oxford: Clarendon Press, 1896.

Faure, Gabriel. *Gardens of Rome*. London: N. Kaye, 1960.

Fernow, Bernhard E. *A Brief History of Forestry in Europe, the United States, and Other Countries*. Toronto: Toronto University Press, 1907.

Finley, Moses I. "The Ancient City from Fustel de Coulanges to Max Weber and Beyond." *Comparative Studies in Society and History* 19 (July 1977): 305–27.

————. *The Ancient Economy.* 2d ed. Berkeley: University of California Press, 1985.

————. *Economy and Society in Ancient Greece.* New York: Viking Press, 1982.

————. *Studies in Land and Credit in Ancient Athens, 500–200 B.C.* New Brunswick, N.J.: Rutgers University Press, 1952.

————. ed. *Studies in Roman Property.* Cambridge: Cambridge University Press, 1976.

Fleming, N. C. *Archaeological Evidence for Eustatic Change of Sea Level and Earth Movements in the Western Mediterranean during the Last 2000 Years.* Geological Society of America, Special Paper no. 109, 1969.

————. "Holocene Earth Movements and Eustatic Sea Level Change in the Peloponnese." *Nature* 217 (1968): 1031–32.

Fontenrose, Joseph. *Orion: The Myth of the Hunter and the Huntress.* University of California Classical Studies, vol. 23. Berkeley and Los Angeles: University of California Press, 1981.

Forbes, H. A., and H. A. Koster. "Fire, Axe and Plow: Human Influence in Local Plant Communities in the Southern Argolid." *Annals of the New York Academy of Sciences* 268 (1976): 109–26.

Forbes, Robert J. "Hydraulic Engineering and Sanitation." In *A History of Technology,* 7 vols., edited by Charles Singer et al. London: Oxford University Press, 1956. 2:663–94.

————. "Land Transport and Road-Building." In *Studies in Ancient Technology,* vol. 2. Leiden: E. J. Brill, 1955. 126–86.

————. *Studies in Ancient Technology.* 9 vols. Leiden: E. J. Brill, 1955–64.

————. "Water Supply." In *Studies in Ancient Technology,* vol. 1. Leiden: E. J. Brill, 1955. 145–89.

Forster, E. S. "Trees and Plants of Herodotus." *Classical Review* 56 (1942): 57–63.

Fowler, W. Warde. *The City-State of the Greeks and Romans.* London: Macmillan, 1893.

————. *Social Life at Rome in the Age of Cicero.* London: Macmillan, 1908.

Foxhall, Lynn, and H. A. Forbes. "Sitometreia: The Role of Grain as a Staple Food in Classical Antiquity." *Chiron* (Munich) 12 (1982).

Frankfort, Henri et al., ed. *Before Philosophy.* Baltimore: Penguin Books, 1949.

Fraser, P. M. *Ptolemaic Alexandria.* 3 vols. Oxford: Clarendon Press, 1972.

Frazer, James George. *The Golden Bough: A Study in Magic and Religion.* 12 vols., 3d ed. New York: Macmillan, 1935.

Freeman, Kathleen. *Greek City-States.* New York: W. W. Norton, 1950.

Friedländer, Ludwig. *Roman Life and Manners under the Early Empire.* 4 vols. London: George Routledge and Sons, 1909–13.

Fussell, George Edwin. "Farming Systems of the Classical Era." *Technology and Culture* 8 (1967); 16–44.

Fustel de Coulanges, Numa Denis. *La Cité antique.* Strasbourg, 1864.

Gage, Jean. "Sur les origines du culte de Janus [Trees in Religion]." *Revue de l'Histoires des Religions* 195 (1979): 3–33.

Gale, N. H., and Stos-Gale, Z. A. "The Sources of Mycenaean Silver and Lead." *Journal of Field Archaeology* 9 (1982): 467–85.

Gallant, Thomas W. *Risk and Survival in Ancient Greece: Reconstructing the Rural Domestic Economy.* Stanford, Calif.: Stanford University Press, 1991.

Gamulin-Bride, Helena. "The Benthic Fauna of the Adriatic Sea." *Oceanography and Marine Biology* 5 (1967): 535–68.

Garnsey, Peter D. A. "Peasants in Ancient Roman Society." *Journal of Peasant Studies* 3 (1976): 221–35.

Garnsey, Peter D. A., K. Hopkins, and C. R. Whittaker, eds. *Trade in the Ancient Economy.* Berkeley: University of California Press, 1983.

Geikie, Archibald. *The Love of Nature among the Romans.* London: John Murray, 1912.

Gerasimidis, Achilleas M. *Stathmologikes Sinthikes kai Metapagetodis Exelixi tis Blastisis sta Dasi Laila Serron kai Kataphigiou Pierion.* Thessaloniki: Aristotelian University of Thessaloniki (*Didaktoriki Diatribi*), 1985.

Gilfillan, S. Colum. "Roman Culture and Dysgenic Lead Poisoning." *Mankind Quarterly* 5 (1965): 3–20.

Gilliam, J. F. "The Plague under Marcus Aurelius." *American Journal of Philosophy* 82 (1961): 225–51.

Glacken, Clarence J. *Traces on the Rhodian Shore.* Berkeley: University of California Press, 1967.

Glotz, Gustave. *Ancient Greece at Work: An Economic History of Greece from the Homeric Period to the Roman Conquest.* London: Kegan Paul, 1930.

Glover, Terrot R. *The Challenge of the Greek and Other Essays.* Freeport, N.Y.: Books for Libraries Press, 1972.

Gothein, Marie Luise. "Der grieschische Garten." *Mitteilungen des deutschen archäologischen Instituts, Athenische Abteilung* 34 (1909): 100–144.

———. *A History of Garden Art,* ed. by Walter P. Wright, trans. by M. A. Archer-Hind. London: J. M. Dent and Sons, 1928.

Goulandris, Niki A., and Constantine M. Goulimis. *Wild Flowers of Greece,* ed. by W. T. Stearn. New York: Academic Press, 1969.

Gow, Andrew Sydenham Farrer. "The Ancient Plough." *Journal of Hellenic Studies* 34 (1914): 249–75.

Gräber, H. *Die Wasserleitungen von Pergamon.* Berlin: Abhandlung Akademischer Wissenschaften, 1887.

Graham, A. J. *Colony and Mother City in Ancient Greece.* Manchester, U.K.: Manchester University Press, 1964.

Graham, J. W. "The Greek House and the Roman House." *Phoenix* 20 (1966): 3–31.

Grant, Michael. *The Ancient Mediterranean.* New York: Scribner's, 1969.

———. *Cities of Vesuvius: Pompeii and Herculaneum.* New York: Macmillan, 1971.

———. *The Roman Forum.* New York: Macmillan, 1970.

———. *Roman History from Coins.* Cambridge: Cambridge University Press, 1968.

Green, Kevin. *The Archaeology of the Roman Economy.* Berkeley: University of California Press, 1986.

Greig, J. R. A., and J. Turner. "Some Pollen Diagrams from Greece and Their Archaeological Significance." *Journal of Archaeological Science* 1 (1974): 177–94.

Grimal, Pierre. *Les Jardins Romains.* 2d ed. Paris: Presses Universitaires de France, 1969.

———. *Roman Cities,* trans. and ed. G. Michael Woloch. Madison: University of Wisconsin Press, 1983.

Grmek, Mirko Drazen. *Diseases in the Ancient Greek World.* Baltimore: Johns Hopkins University Press, 1989.

Guggisberg, C. A. W. *Man and Wild Life.* London: Evans Brothers, 1970.

Guthrie, W. K. C. *In the Beginning: Some Greek Views on the Origins of Life and the Early State of Man.* Ithaca, N.Y.: Cornell University Press, 1957.

Haeckel, Ernst. *Generelle Morphologie der Organismen.* Berlin, 1866.

Hammond, Mason. *The City in the Ancient World.* Cambridge: Harvard University Press, 1972.

Hansen, Mogens Herman. *Demography and Democracy: The Number of Athenian Citizens in the Fourth Century B.C.* Herning, Denmark: Systime, 1986.

Hanson, Victor Davis. *The Western Way of War.* New York: Knopf, 1989.

Harris, Tegwyn. *The Natural History of the Mediterranean.* London: Pelham Books, 1982.

Harris, W. V. "Roman Terracotta Lamps: The Organization of an Industry." *Journal of Roman Studies* 70 (1980): 126–45.

Harrison, Fairfax, ed. and trans. *Roman Farm Management: The Treatises of Cato and Varro Done into English, with Notes of Modern Instances, by a Virginia Farmer.* New York: Macmillan, 1913.

Hartwell, Kathleen. "Nature in Theocritus." *Classical Journal* 17 (1922): 181–90.

Hauck, George F. W. "The Roman Aqueduct of Nimes." *Scientific American* 260 (March 1989): 98–104.

Haywood, Richard Mansfield. *The Myth of Rome's Fall*. New York: Crowell, 1958.

Healy, John F. "Mines and Quarries." In *Civilization of the Ancient Mediterranean: Greece and Rome*, 3 vols., edited by Michael Grant and Rachel Kitzinger. New York: Charles Scribner's Sons, 1988. 2:779–94.

———. *Mining and Metallurgy in the Greek and Roman World*. London: Thames and Hudson, 1978.

———. "Mining and Processing Gold Ore in the Ancient World." *Journal of Metals* 31, no. 8 (1979): 11–16.

———. "Pliny the Elder and Ancient Mineralogy." *Interdisciplinary Science Reviews* 6 (1981): 112–30.

Heitland, William Emerton. *Agricola: A Study of Agriculture and Rustic Life in the Greco-Roman World from the Point of View of Labour*. Cambridge: Cambridge University Press, 1921.

Hill, Ida Carleton Thallon. *The Ancient City of Athens: Its Topography and Monuments*. Chicago: Argonaut, 1969.

Hodges, Henry. *Technology in the Ancient World*. London: Allen Lane, 1970.

Hoffman, Michael A. *Egypt before the Pharaohs: The Prehistoric Foundations of Egyptian Civilization*. New York: Alfred A. Knopf, 1979.

Hohlfelder, Robert L. "Sebastos, the Harbor Complex of Caesarea Maritima, Israel." In *Oceanography: The Past*, edited by Mary Sears and Daniel Merriman. New York: Springer-Verlag, 1980.

Holland, Leicester B. "Colophon." *Hesperia* 13 (1944): 91–171.

Holum, Kenneth G., Robert L. Hohlfelder, Robert J. Bull, and Avner Raban. *King Herod's Dream: Caesarea on the Sea*. New York: W. W. Norton, 1988.

Hopkins, Keith. "Roman Trade, Industry, and Labor." In *Civilization of the Ancient Mediterranean: Greece and Rome*, 3 vols., edited by Michael Grant and Rachel Kitzinger. New York: Charles Scribner's Sons, 1988. 2:753–78.

Hopper, Robert J. *Trade and Industry in Classical Greece*. London: Thames and Hudson, 1979.

Horden, Peregrine, and Nicholas Purcell. *The Mediterranean World: Man and Environment in Antiquity and the Middle Ages*. Oxford: Basil Blackwell, 1988.

Horle, Josef. *Catos Hausbucher: Analyse seiner Schrift De Agricultura nebst Wiederherstellung seines Kelterhauses und Gutshofes* (Studien zur Geschichte und Kultur des Altertums, 15 Bd., 3. und 4. Hft.). Paderborn, Germany: F. Schoningh, 1929. Repr. New York: Johnson Reprint Corp., 1968.

Horn, R. C. "The Attitude of the Greeks toward Natural Scenery." *Classical Journal* 11 (1916): 302–18.

Houston, James Macintosch. *The Western Mediterranean World: An Introduction to Its Regional Landscapes*. London: Longmans, Green, 1964.

Hubbell, Harry M. "Ptolemy's Zoo." *Classical Journal* 31 (1935): 68–76.

Hughes, J. Donald. "Artemis: Goddess of Conservation." *Forest and Conservation History* 34 (October 1990): 191–97.

———. "An Ecological Paradigm of the Ancient City." In *Human Ecology: A Gathering of Perspectives*, edited by Richard J. Borden. College Park: University of Maryland and The Society for Human Ecology, 1986. 214–20.

———. "The Effect of Classical Cities on the Mediterranean Landscape." *Ekistics* 42 (1976): 332–42.

———. "Forests and Cities in the Classical Mediterranean." In *Perspectives in Urban Geography*, vol. 10, *Morphology of Towns*, edited by C. S. Yadav. New Delhi: Concept Publishing Company, 1987. 203–23.

———. "How the Ancients Viewed Deforestation." *Journal of Field Archaeology* 10 (1983): 437–45.

———. "Land and Sea." In *Civilization of the Ancient Mediterranean: Greece and Rome*, 3 vols., edited by Michael Grant and Rachel Kitzinger. New York: Charles Scribner's Sons, 1988. 1:89–133.

———. "Mencius' Prescriptions for Ancient Chinese Environmental Problems." *Environmental Review* 13 (1989): 15–27.

———. "Pan: Environmental Ethics in Classical Polytheism." In *Religion and Environmental Crisis*, edited by Eugene C. Hargrove. Athens: University of Georgia Press, 1986. 7–24.

———. "Sacred Groves: The Gods, Forest Protection, and Sustained Yield in the Ancient World." In *History of Sustained-Yield Forestry: A Symposium*, edited by Harold K. Steen. Durham, N.C.: Forest History Society, 1984.

———. "Sustainable Agriculture in Ancient Egypt." *Agricultural History* 66 (1992): 12–22.

———. "Theophrastus as Ecologist." In *Theophrastean Studies, Volume III: On Natural Science, Physics and Metaphysics, Ethics, Religion, and Rhetoric*, edited by William W. Fortenbaugh and Robert W. Sharples. Rutgers University Studies in Classical Humanities. New Brunswick, N.J.: Transaction Books, 1988. 67–75.

Hughes, J. Donald, and Jim Swan. "How Much of the Earth Is Sacred Space?" *Environmental Review* 10 (1986): 247–59.

Hughes, J. Donald, and J. V. Thirgood. "Deforestation, Erosion, and Forest Management in Ancient Greece and Rome." *Journal of Forest History* 26 (1982): 60–75.

Hull, Denison Bingham. *Hounds and Hunting in Ancient Greece*. Chicago: University of Chicago Press, 1964.

Hultkrantz, Ake. "The Owner of the Animals in the Religion of the North

American Indians." In *Belief and Worship in Native North America*, edited by Christopher Vecsey. Syracuse: Syracuse University Press, 1981. 135–46.

Humphreys, Sarah C. *Anthropology and the Greeks*. London: Routledge and Kegan Paul, 1978.

Hunt, A. S., and C. C. Edgar. *Select Papyri*. 2 vols. London: Harvard-Heinemann, 1934.

Huntington, Ellsworth. "Climatic Changes and Agricultural Decline as Factors in the Fall of Rome." *Quarterly Journal of Economics* 31 (1917): 173–208.

Huxley, A. J. *Flowers in Greece: An Outline of the Flora*. London: Royal Horticultural Society, 1965.

Hyams, Edward. *Soil and Civilization*. London: Thames and Hudson, 1952.

Hyde, W. W. "The Ancient Appreciation of Mountain Scenery." *Classical Journal* 11 (1915): 70–84.

Imhof-Blumer, Friedrich, and Otto Keller. *Tier- und Pflanzenbilder auf Münzen und Gemmes des klassischen Altertums*. Leipzig: n.p., 1889.

Isaac, Erich. *The Geography of Domestication*. Englewood Cliffs, N.J.: Prentice-Hall, 1970.

Jacobsen, Thorkild, and Robert M. Adams. "Salt and Silt in Ancient Mesopotamian Agriculture." *Science* 128 (1958): 1251–58.

James, Edwin Oliver. *From Cave to Cathedral: Temples and Shrines of Prehistoric, Classical, and Early Christian Times*. New York: F. A. Praeger, 1965.

———. *The Tree of Life: An Archaeological Study*. Leiden: E. J. Brill, 1966

Jameson, Michael H. "Agriculture and Slavery in Classical Athens." *Classical Journal* 73 (1977): 122–45.

Jashemski, Wilhelmina Mary Feemster. *The Gardens of Pompeii: Herculaneum and the Villas Destroyed by Vesuvius*. New Rochelle, N.Y.: Caratzas Bros., 1979.

———. "Pompeii and Mount Vesuvius, A.D. 79." In *Volcanic Activity and Human Ecology*, edited by Payson D. Sheets and Donald K. Grayson. New York: Academic Press, 1979

Jasny, Naum. "Competition Among Grains in Classical Antiquity." *American Historical Review* 47, no. 4 (1941): 747–64.

———. "The Daily Bread of the Ancient Greeks and Romans." *Osiris* 9 (1950): 228–53.

Jennison, George. *Animals for Show and Pleasure in Ancient Rome*. Manchester: Manchester University Press, 1937.

Johanson, Donald C., and James Shreeve. *Lucy's Child: The Search for Our Beginnings*. New York: Morrow, 1989.

Johnson, Allan Chester. "Ancient Forests and Navies." *Transactions and Proceedings of the American Philological Association* 58 (1927): 199–209.

Jones, Arnold Hugh Martin. *Ancient Economic History*. London: H. K. Lewis, 1948.

———. *The Decline of the Ancient World*. New York: Holt, Rinehart, and Winston, 1966.

———. *The Greek City from Alexander to Justinian*. Oxford: Clarendon Press, 1967.

———. *The Later Roman Empire*. 2 vols. Oxford: Oxford University Press, 1964.

———. *The Roman Economy: Studies in Ancient Economic and Administrative History*, ed. by P. A. Brunt. Totowa, N.J.: Rowman and Littlefield, 1974.

Jones, C. P. *The Roman World of Dio Chrysostom*. Cambridge: Harvard University Press, 1978.

Jones, Nicholas F. *Public Organization in Ancient Greece: A Documentary Study*. Philadelphia: American Philosophical Society, 1987.

Jones, W. H. S. *Malaria and Greek History*. Manchester: Manchester University Press, 1909.

———. *Malaria: A Neglected Factor in the History of Greece and Rome*. Cambridge: Macmillan and Bowes, 1907.

Jordan, Borimir, and Perlin, John. "On the Protection of Sacred Groves." In *Studies Presented to Sterling Dow on his Eightieth Birthday*, edited by Alan L. Boegehold et al. Durham, N.C.: Duke University Press, 1984.

Judson, Sheldon. "Erosion and Deposition of Italian Stream Valleys during Historic Time." *Science* 140 (1963): 898–899.

———. "Erosion Rates near Rome, Italy." *Science* 160 (1968): 1444–46.

———. "Stream Changes during Historic Time in East-Central Sicily." *American Journal of Archaeology* 67 (1963): 287–89.

Kahil, Lilly. "The Mythological Repertoire of Brauron." In *Ancient Greek Art and Iconography*, edited by Warren G. Moon. Madison: University of Wisconsin Press, 1983. 231–44.

Kees, Herrmann. *Ancient Egypt: A Cultural Topography*. Chicago: University of Chicago Press, 1961.

Kehoe, Dennis P. *The Economics of Agriculture on Roman Imperial Estates in North Africa*. Göttingen: Vanderhoeck and Ruprecht, 1988.

Keller, Otto. *Die antike Tierwelt*. 2 vols. Leipzig: Wilhelm Engelmann, 1909–13.

Kemp, Barry J. *Ancient Egypt: Anatomy of a Civilization*. London: Routledge, 1989.

Kerenyi, Karl. "Il Dio Cacciatore." *Dioniso* 15 (1952): 131–42.

Kiechle, Franz. *Sklavenarbeit und technischer Fortschritt im römischen Reich*. Wiesbaden: F. Steiner, 1969.

Körner, Otto. *Die Homerische Thierwelt: Ein Beitrag zur Geschichte der Zoologie*. Berlin, 1880.

Koster, H. A., and H. A. Forbes. "The Commons and the Market." Paper presented at symposium "Deforestation, Erosion, and Ecology in the Ancient Mediterranean and Middle East," Smithsonian Institution, National Museum of Natural History. Washington, D.C., April 19, 1978.

Koster, H. A., H. A. Forbes, and L. Foxhall. "Terrace Agriculture and Erosion: Environmental Effects of Population Instability in the Mediterranean." Paper presented at the symposium "Deforestation, Erosion, and Ecology in the Ancient Mediterranean and Middle East," Smithsonian Institution, National Museum of Natural History, Washington, D.C., April 19, 1978.

Kounas, Dionysios A., ed. *Studies on the Ancient Silver Mines at Laurion.* Lawrence, Kan.: Coronado Press, 1972.

Kraft, John. "The General Picture of Erosion in the Mediterranean Area." Paper presented at the symposium "Deforestation, Erosion, and Ecology in the Ancient Mediterranean and Middle East," Smithsonian Institution, National Museum of Natural History, Washington, D.C., April 19, 1978.

Kreissig, Heinz. *Wirtschaft und Gesellschaft im Seleukidenreich.* Berlin: Akademie-Verlag, 1978.

Kriesis, Anthony. *Greek Town Building.* Athens: National Technical University, 1965.

Lamb, Hubert H. *The Changing Climate.* London: Methuen, 1966.

————. *Climate: Present, Past, and Future.* Vol. 1, *Fundamentals and Climate Now*; vol. 2, *Climatic History and the Future.* London: Methuen, 1972–77.

————. *Climate, History, and the Modern World.* New York: Methuen, 1982.

————. "Climate, Vegetation, and Forest Limits in Early Civilized Times." *Philosophical Transactions of the Royal Society* A, 276 (1974): 193–230.

————. "The Climatic Background to the Birth of Civilization." *Advancement of Science* (September 1968): 103–120.

Lanciani, Rodolfo Amadeo. *Ancient and Modern Rome.* New Haven: Yale University Press, 1940.

Landels, John G. "Engineering." In *Civilization of the Ancient Mediterranean: Greece and Rome,* 3 vols., edited by Michael Grant and Rachel Kitzinger, New York: Charles Scribner's Sons, 1988. 1:323–52.

————. *Engineering in the Ancient World.* Berkeley: University of California Press, 1978.

Lang, Mabel. *Waterworks in the Athenian Agora.* Princeton: American School of Classical Studies at Athens (Excavations of the Athenian Agora, Picture Book no. 11), 1968.

Leakey, Richard E., and Roger Lewin. *Origins.* New York: E. P. Dutton, 1977.

Lee, Norman E. *Harvests and Harvesting through the Ages.* Cambridge: Cambridge University Press, 1960.

Le Gall, J. C. *Le Tibre dans l'Antiquité.* Paris: Presses Universitaires de France, 1953.

Legon, R. P. "The Megarian Decree and the Balance of Greek Naval Power." *Classical Philology* 68 (1973): 161–71.

Le Houèrou, H. N. "The Impact of Man and His Animals on Mediterranean Vegetation." In *Ecosystems of the World,* edited by F. di Castri et al. Amsterdam: Elsevier Science Publishers, 1981. 479–521.

Lenz, Harald Othmar. *Botanik der alten Griechen und Römer.* Wiesbaden: Martin Sändig, 1966.

Lloyd, R. B. "Three Monumental Gardens on the Marble Plan." *American Journal of Archaeology* 86 (1982): 91–100.

Lloyd-Jones, Hugh. "Artemis and Iphigeneia." *Journal of Hellenic Studies* 103 (1983): 87–102.

Loisel, Gustave. *Histoire des ménageries de l'antiquité à nos jours.* 3 vols. Paris, 1912.

Lonsdale, Steven. *Animals and the Origins of Dance.* London: Thames and Hudson, 1981.

Lord, Russell. *The Care of the Earth.* New York: Thomas Nelson and Sons, 1962.

Lovelock, James. *The Ages of Gaia: A Biography of Our Living Earth.* New York: W. W. Norton, 1988.

Lowdermilk, Walter C. *Conquest of the Land through 7,000 Years.* (U.S. Dept. of Agriculture Information Bulletin no. 99). Washington, D.C.: Government Printing Office, 1941; repr. 1953, 1975.

———. "Lessons from the Old World to the Americas in Land Use." *Smithsonian Report for 1943.* Washington, D.C.: Government Printing Office, 1944. 413–27.

Lowry, S. T. "The Classical Greek Theory of Natural Resource Economics." *Land Economics* 41 (1965): 292–98.

Ludwig, Emil. *The Mediterranean: Saga of a Sea.* New York: McGraw-Hill, 1942.

Lukermann, F. "The Concept of Location in Classical Geography." *Annals of the Association of American Geographers* 51 (1961): 194–210.

Macarthur, William. "The Athenian Plague: A Medical Note." *Classical Quarterly* 48 (1954): 171–74.

McDonald, William A., and George R. Rapp, Jr., eds. *The Minnesota Messenia Expedition: Reconstructing a Bronze Age Regional Environment.* Minneapolis: University of Minnesota Press, 1972.

MacDougall, Elisabeth Blair, ed. *Ancient Roman Villa Gardens: Dumbarton Oaks Symposium on Ancient Roman Gardens.* Washington, D.C.: Dumbarton Oaks Research Library and Collection, 1987.

McNeill, William Hardy. *Plagues and Peoples*. Garden City, N.Y.: Anchor Press, 1976.

Maddin, Robert, ed. *The Beginning of the Use of Metals and Alloys*. Cambridge: Massachusetts Institute of Technology, 1988.

Majno, Guido. *The Healing Hand: Man and Wound in the Ancient World*. Cambridge: Harvard University Press, 1975.

Makkonen, Olli. "Ancient Forestry: An Historical Study." *Acta Forestalia Fennica* 82 (1968): 1–84; 95 (1969): 1–46.

Malinowski, Roman. "Ancient Mortars and Concretes: Aspects of Their Durability." *History of Technology* 7 (1982): 89–100.

Mannhardt, Wilhelm. *Wald- und Feldkulte*. 2 vols. (bd. 1: Der Baumkultus der Germanen und ihrer Nachbarstämme, bd. 2: Antike Wald- und Feldkulte. Berlin: Gebrüder Bornträger, 1875–77.

Manns, O. "Jagd: Über die Jagd bei den Griechen." *Progr. Cassel* (1888): 7–38; (1889): 3–20; (1890): 3–21.

Marres, P. "Les Garrigues Languedociennes: Le Milieu et l'Homme." *Actes du 86ème Congrès Nationale des Sociétés Savantes* (Montpellier, 1961), 201–16.

Marsh, George Perkins. *Man and Nature*. New York, 1864. Repr. edited by David Lowenthal. Cambridge: Harvard University Press, 1965.

Martinengo-Cesaresco, Evelyn Lilian Hazeldine Carrington. *The Outdoor Life in Greek and Roman Poets, and Kindred Studies*. London: Macmillan, 1911.

Matthews, Kenneth D. *Cities in the Sand, Leptis Magna and Sabratha in Roman Africa*. Philadelphia: University of Pennsylvania Press, 1957.

Meiggs, Russell. *Roman Ostia*. Oxford: Clarendon Press, 1960.

———. "Sea-borne Timber Supplies to Rome." *Memoirs of the American Academy in Rome* 36 (1980): 185–96.

———. *Trees and Timber in the Ancient World*. Oxford: Clarendon Press, 1983.

Mellaart, James. *Çatal Hüyük: A Neolithic Town in Anatolia*. London: Thames and Hudson, 1967.

Michell, Humfrey. *The Economics of Ancient Greece*. Cambridge: Cambridge University Press, 1940.

Mikesell, Marvin W. "The Deforestation of Mt. Lebanon." *Geographical Review* 59 (1969): 1–28.

Moritz, L. Alfred. *Grain-Mills and Flour in Classical Antiquity*. Oxford: Clarendon Press, 1958.

Morris, Anthony Edwin James. *History of Urban Form: Before the Industrial Revolutions*. 2d ed. New York: Wiley, 1979.

Mossé, Claude. *The Ancient World at Work*. New York: Norton, 1969.

Mumford, Lewis. *The City in History: Its Origins, Its Transformations, and Its Prospects*. New York: Harcourt, Brace and World, 1961.

Murphey, R. "The Decline of North Africa Since the Roman Occupation: Climatic or Human?" *Annals of the Association of American Geographers* 41 (1951): 116–32.

Nash, Ernest. *A Pictorial Dictionary of Ancient Rome.* 2 vols., 2d ed. London: Thames and Hudson, 1968.

Neev, David. *The Geology of the Southeastern Mediterranean Sea.* Jerusalem: Geological Survey of Israel, 1976.

Neeve, P. W. de. *Peasants in Peril: Location and Economy in Italy in the Second Century B.C.* Amsterdam: J. C. Gieben, 1984.

Newbigin, Marion Isabel. *The Mediterranean Lands.* London: Christophers, 1924.

———. *Southern Europe.* 3d ed. London: Methuen, 1949.

Noble, Joseph Veach. *The Techniques of Painted Attic Pottery.* New York: Thames and Hudson, 1988.

North, John A. "The Afterlife: Rome." In *Civilization of the Ancient Mediterranean: Greece and Rome,* 3 vols., edited by Michael Grant and Rachel Kitzinger. New York: Scribner's, 1988. 3:1001–2.

Oleson, John Peter. *Bronze Age, Greek, and Roman Technology: A Select, Annotated Bibliography.* New York: Garland, 1986.

———. *Greek and Roman Mechanical Water-Lifting Devices: The History of a Technology.* Toronto: University of Toronto Press, 1984.

Ölschlager, Max. *The Idea of Wilderness: From Prehistory to the Age of Ecology.* New Haven: Yale University Press, 1991.

Olson, L. "Cato's Views on the Farmer's Obligation to the Land." *Agricultural History* 19 (1945): 129–32.

Osborn, Fairfield. *The Limits of the Earth.* Westport, Conn.: Greenwood Press, 1971.

Packer, James E. "Roman Building Techniques." In *Civilization of the Ancient Mediterranean: Greece and Rome,* 3 vols., edited by Michael Grant and Rachel Kitzinger. New York: Charles Scribner's Sons, 1988. 1:299–322.

Palgrave, Francis T. *Landscape in Poetry from Homer to Tennyson.* London: Macmillan, 1897.

Palmer, R. E. "Notes on Some Ancient Mine Equipment and Systems." *Transactions of the Institute of Mining and Metallurgy* 36 (1926): 299–310.

Palmer, R. E. A. "Jupiter Blaze, Gods of the Hills, and the Roman topography of *CIL* VI 377." *American Journal of Archaeology* 80 (1976): 43–56.

Paris, Ginette. "Artemis and Ecology." In *Pagan Meditations.* Dallas: Spring Publications, 1986. 109–10.

Park, Robert E., Ernest W. Burgess, and Roderick D. McKenzie. *The City.* Chicago: University of Chicago Press, 1925.

Parker, Robert. *Miasma: Pollution and Purification in Early Greek Religion.* Oxford: Clarendon Press, 1983.

Parry, Adam M. "Landscape in Greek Poetry." *Transactions of the American Philological Association* 87 (1956): 1–29. Repr. in *The Language of Achilles and Other Papers*. Oxford: Clarendon Press, 1989. 8–35.

Patey, Katherine. "Endangered Forests." *The Athenian* (November 1987): 18–22.

Patterson, Clair C., C. Boutron, and R. Flegal. "Present Status and Future of Lead Studies in Polar Snow." In *Greenland Ice Core: Geophysics, Geochemistry, and the Environment*, edited by C. C. Langway, Jr., H. Oeschger, and W. Dansgaard. Washington, D.C.: American Geophysical Union, 1985, 101–4.

Patterson, Clair C., Tsaihwa J. Chow, and Masayo Murozumi. "The Possibility of Measuring Variations in the Intensity of Worldwide Lead Smelting During Medieval and Ancient Times Using Lead Aerosol Deposits in Polar Snow Strata." In *Scientific Methods in Medieval Archaeology*, edited by Rainer Berger. Berkeley: University of California Press, 1970. 339–50.

Pavlovskis, Zoja. *Man in an Artificial Landscape: The Marvels of Civilization in Imperial Roman Literature*. Leiden: Brill, 1973.

Peck, Harry Thurston, ed. *Harper's Dictionary of Classical Literature and Antiquities*. New York: American Book Company, 1923.

Pérès, J. M. "The Mediterranean Benthos." *Oceanography and Marine Biology* 5 (1967): 449–534.

Perlin, John. *A Forest Journey: The Role of Wood in the Development of Civilization*. New York: W. W. Norton, 1989.

Perlman, Paula. "Plato Laws 833C–834D and the Bears of Brauron." *Greek, Roman, and Byzantine Studies* 24 (1983): 115–130.

Philippson, Alfred. *Das Mittelmeergebiet: Seine Geographische und Kulturelle Eigenart*. 2d ed. Leipzig: Teubner, 1907.

Philpot, J. H. *The Sacred Tree, or the Tree in Religion and Myth*. New York: Macmillan, 1897.

Pirazzoli, P. A. "Sea Level Variation in the Northeastern Mediterranean during Roman Times." *Science* 194 (1976): 519–21.

Platner, Samuel Ball. *Topography and Monuments of Ancient Rome*. Boston: Allyn and Bacon, 1911.

Platner, Samuel Ball, and Thomas A. Ashby. *A Topographical Dictionary of Ancient Rome*. Oxford: Oxford University Press, 1929.

Pollard, John Richard Thornhill. *Birds in Greek Life and Myth*. London: Thames and Hudson, 1977.

Polunin, Oleg, and Anthony Huxley. *Flowers of the Mediterranean*. Boston: Houghton Mifflin, 1966.

Polunin, Oleg, and B. E. Smythies. *Flowers of Southwest Europe*. London: Oxford University Press, 1973.

Pons, A. "The History of the Mediterranean Shrublands." In *Ecosystems of* the World 11: Mediterranean-Type Shrublands, edited by Francesco di Castri, David W. Goodall, and Raymond L. Specht. Amsterdam: Elsevier Scientific Publishing Company, 1981. 131–38.

Porteous, Alexander. Forest Folklore, Mythology, and Romance. London: Allen & Unwin, 1928.

Prager, Frank D. "Vitruvius and the Elevated Aqueducts." History of Technology 3 (1978): 105–21.

Preus, Anthony. Science and Philosophy in Aristotle's Biological Works. Hildesheim: Georg Olms Verlag, 1975.

Price, Derek John de Solla. "Gears from the Greeks." Transactions of the American Philosophical Society 64, pt. 7 (1974): 5–68.

Raban, Avner. "The Siting and Development of Mediterranean Harbors in Antiquity." In Oceanography: The Past, edited by Mary Sears and Daniel Meriman. New York: Springer-Verlag, 1980. 750–64.

Rackham, Oliver. "Land-use and the Native Vegetation of Greece." In Archaeological Aspects of Woodland Ecology, edited by Martin Bell and Susan Limbrey. Symposia of the Association for Environmental Archaeology, no. 2. Oxford: B.A.R., 1982. 177–98.

―――. "Observations on the Historical Ecology of Boeotia." Annual of the British School at Athens 78 (1983): 291–351.

Radcliffe, William. Fishing from the Earliest Times. London: J. Murray, 1921.

Ramage, Edwin S. "Urban Problems in Ancient Rome." In Aspects of Graeco-Roman Urbanism: Essays on the Classical City, edited by Ronald T. Marchese. Oxford: B.A.R., 1983. 61–92.

Randsborg, Klavs. The First Millennium A.D. in Europe and the Mediterranean: An Archaeological Essay. Cambridge: Cambridge University Press, 1991.

Rawlinson, H. G. Intercourse between India and the Western World from the Earliest Times to the Fall of Rome. Cambridge: Cambridge University Press, 1926.

Reckford, Kenneth J. "Some Trees in Virgil and Tolkien." In Perspectives of Roman Poetry: A Classics Symposium, edited by G. Karl Galinsky. Austin: University of Texas Press, 1974. 57–91.

Regnault, Félix. "Du rôle du dépeuplement, du déboisement et de la malaria dans la décadence de certaines nations." Revue Scientifique 52 (1914): 46–59.

―――. "La Décadence de la Grèce expliquée par la déforestation et l'impaludisme." Presse Med. (1909): 729–31.

Renfrew, Colin. "Erosion in Melos and the Question of the Younger Fill." Paper presented at the symposium "Deforestation, Erosion, and Ecology in the Ancient Mediterranean and Middle East," Smithsonian Institution, National Museum of Natural History, Washington, D.C., April 19, 1978.

Rice, E. E. *The Grand Procession of Ptolemy Philadelphus.* Oxford: Oxford University Press, 1983.

Richmond, John Anthony. *Chapters on Greek Fish-lore.* Hermes, Zeitschrift für klassische Philologie Einzelschriften, Heft 28. Wiesbaden: F Steiner, 1973.

Rickman, Geoffrey E. *The Corn-Supply of Ancient Rome.* Oxford: Clarendon Press, 1980.

————. *Roman Granaries and Store Buildings.* Cambridge: Cambridge University Press, 1971.

Rikli, Martin Albert. *Das Pflanzenkleid der Mittelmeerländer.* 3 vols. Bern: Hans Huber, 1943.

Robin, G. de Q., ed. *The Climatic Record in Polar Ice Sheets: A Study of Isotopic and Temperature Profiles in Polar Ice Sheets Based on a Workshop Held in the Scott Polar Research Institute, Cambridge.* Cambridge: Cambridge University Press, 1983.

Robinson, Henry Schroeder. *The Urban Development of Ancient Corinth.* Athens: American School of Classical Studies, 1965.

Rostocker, W., and E. Gebhard. "The Reproduction of Roof Tiles for the Archaic Temple of Poseidon at Isthmia, Greece." *Journal of Field Archaeology* 8 (1981): 211–17.

Rostovtzeff, Mikhail Ivanovich. *A Large Estate in Egypt in the Third Century B.C.* New York: Arno Press, 1979.

————. *The Social and Economic History of the Hellenistic World.* 3 vols. Oxford: Clarendon Press, 1941.

————. *The Social and Economic History of the Roman Empire.* 2 vols., 2d ed. Oxford: Clarendon Press, 1957.

Rouner, Leroy S., ed. *On Nature.* Notre Dame, Ind.: University of Notre Dame Press, 1984.

Roux, Georges. *Ancient Iraq.* London: Allen and Unwin, 1964.

Royds, Thomas Fletcher. *The Beasts, Birds, and Bees of Virgil: A Naturalist's Handbook to the Georgics.* Oxford: Blackwell, 1914.

Ruck, Carl A. P. "The Wild and the Cultivated in Greek Religion." In *On Nature,* edited by Leroy S. Rouner. Notre Dame, Ind.: University of Notre Dame Press, 1984. 79–95.

Rykwert, Joseph. *The Idea of a Town: Anthropology of Urban Form in Rome, Italy and the Ancient World.* Cambridge: MIT Press, 1988.

Sagan, Dorion, and Lynn Margulis. "Gaia and Philosophy." In *On Nature,* edited by Leroy S. Rouner. Notre Dame, Ind.: University of Notre Dame Press, 1984. 60–75.

Sallares, Robert. *The Ecology of the Ancient Greek World.* Ithaca, N.Y.: Cornell University Press, 1991.

Sandars, N. K., trans. *The Epic of Gilgamesh.* Harmondsworth: Penguin Books, 1960.

Sarton, George. *A History of Science: Ancient Science through the Golden Age of Greece.* 2 vols. Cambridge: Harvard University Press, 1952.

———. *Introduction to the History of Science.* 3 vols. Washington, D.C.: Carnegie Institution, 1927. 1:107.

Sauer, Carl O., Marston Bates, and Lewis Mumford, eds. *Man's Role in Changing the Face of the Earth.* Chicago: University of Chicago Press, 1956.

Sawyer, J. S., ed. *World Climate from 8000 to 0 B.C.* London: Royal Meteorological Society, 1966.

Scarborough, John. "The Myth of Lead Poisoning among the Romans: An Essay Review." *Journal of the History of Medicine and Allied Sciences* 39 (1984): 469–75.

Schibli, Hermann S. *Pherekydes of Syros.* Oxford: Clarendon Press, 1990.

Schiöler, Thorkild. "Bronze Roman Piston Pumps." *History of Technology* 5 (1980): 17–38.

Schlebeker, J. T. "Farmers and Bureaucrats: Reflections on Technological Innovation in Agriculture." *Agricultural History* 51 (1977): 641–55.

Schopf, Thomas J. M. *Paleoceanography.* Cambridge: Harvard University Press, 1980.

Scullard, Howard Hayes. *The Etruscan Cities and Rome.* Ithaca, N.Y.: Cornell University Press, 1967.

———. *The Elephant in the Greek and Roman World.* Ithaca, N.Y.: Cornell University Press, 1974.

Scully, Vincent Joseph. *The Earth, the Temple, and the Gods: Greek Sacred Architecture.* New Haven: Yale University Press, 1962.

Sears, Paul Bigelow. *Deserts on the March.* Norman: University of Oklahoma Press, 1935.

Seidensticker, August. *Waldgeschichte des Alterthums.* 2 vols. Frankfurt: Trowitzsch und Sohn, 1886.

Sellin, Robert H. J. "The Large Roman Watermill at Barbegal (France)." *History of Technology* 8 (1983): 91–109.

Semple, Ellen Churchill. *The Geography of the Mediterranean Region: Its Relation to Ancient History.* New York: Henry Holt and Co., 1931.

Sereni, Emilio. *Storia del paesaggio agrario italiano.* Bari: Laterza, 1961.

Sessions, George. "Spinoza and Jeffers: An Environmental Perspective." *Inquiry* 20 (1977): 481–528.

Shaw, Brent D. "Climate, Environment, and History: The Case of Roman North Africa." In *Climate and History: Studies in Past Climates and Their Impact on Man,* edited by T. M. L. Wigley, M. J. Ingram, and G. Farmer. Cambridge: Cambridge University Press, 1981.

Sheets, Payson D., and Donald K. Grayson, eds. *Volcanic Activity and Human Ecology.* New York: Academic Press, 1979.

Shepard, Paul. *Man in the Landscape.* New York: Alfred A. Knopf, 1967.

Shepard, Paul, and Barry Sanders. *The Sacred Paw: The Bear in Nature, Myth, and Literature.* New York: Viking, 1985.

Shrewsbury, J. F. D. "The Plague of Athens." *Bulletin of the History of Medicine* 24 (1950): 1–25.

Simkhovitch, Vladimir Grigorievitch. "Rome's Fall Reconsidered." In *Toward the Understanding of Jesus and Other Historical Studies.* New York: Macmillan, 1921. 84–139.

Singer, Charles, E. J. Holmyard, and A. R. Hall, eds. *A History of Technology,* vol. 2. Oxford: Oxford University Press, 1956.

Singh, Purushottam. *Neolithic Cultures of Western Asia.* London: Seminar Press, 1974.

Sjoberg, Gideon. *The Preindustrial City: Past and Present.* New York: Free Press, 1960.

Sklawunos, K. G. "Über die Holzversorgung Griechenlands in Altertum." *Forstwissenschaftliches Zentralblatt* 52 (1930): 868–91.

Smith, Catherine Delano. *Western Mediterranean Europe.* London: Academic Press, 1979.

Smith, Norman A. F. "Attitudes to Roman Engineering and the Question of the Inverted Siphon." *History of Technology* 1 (1976): 1–26.

Snell, Leonard J. "Effects of Sedimentation on Ancient Cities of the Aegean Coast, Turkey." *Bulletin of the International Association of Scientific Hydrology* 8 (1963): 71–73.

Sokolowski, F. "On the Episode of Onchestus in the Homeric Hymn to Apollo." *Transactions and Proceedings of the American Philological Association* 91 (1960): 376–80.

Sonnenfeld, Peter, ed. *Tethys: The Ancestral Mediterranean.* Stroudsburg, Penn.: Hutchinson Ross, 1981.

Sourvinou-Inwood, Christiane. "Myths of the First Temples at Delphi." *Classical Quarterly,* n.s. 29 (1979): 231–51.

———. *Studies in Girls' Transitions: Aspects of the Arkteia and Age Representation in Attic Iconography.* Athens: Kardamitsa, 1988.

Soutar, George. *Nature in Greek Poetry.* London: Oxford University Press, 1939.

Spain, Robert J. "The Second-Century Romano-British Watermill at Ickham, Kent." *History of Technology* 9 (1984): 143–80.

———. "The Cultivation of Millet in Roman Italy." *Papers of the British School at Rome* 51 (1983): 1–15.

Stadter, Philip A. *Arrian of Nicomedia.* Chapel Hill: University of North Carolina Press, 1980.

Stambaugh, John E. *The Ancient Roman City.* Baltimore: Johns Hopkins University Press, 1988.

Stanley, Daniel J., ed. *The Mediterranean Sea: A Natural Sedimentation Laboratory.* Stroudsburg, Penn.: Dowden, Hutchinson, and Ross, 1972.

257

Starr, Chester G. *The Economic and Social Growth of Early Greece, 800–500 B.C.* New York: Oxford University Press, 1977.

Stevens, Courtenay Edward. "Agriculture and Rural Life in the Later Empire." In *Cambridge Economic History of Europe.* 6 vols., 2d ed. Cambridge: Cambridge University Press, 1966. 1:92–124.

Storoni Mazzolani, Lidia. *The Idea of the City in Roman Thought: From Walled City to Spiritual Commonwealth,* trans. by S. O'Donnell. Bloomington: Indiana University Press, 1970.

Strong, Donald Emrys. *Greek and Roman Gold and Silver Plate.* Ithaca, N.Y.: Cornell University Press, 1966.

Strong, Donald Emrys, and David Brown, eds. *Roman Crafts.* New York: New York University Press, 1976.

Tarn, W. W., and G. T. Griffith. *Hellenistic Civilization.* London: Arnold, 1952.

Taylor, Lily Ross. "Caesar's Agrarian Legislation and His Municipal Policy." In *Studies in Roman Economic and Social History in Honor of Allan Chester Johnson,* edited by P. R. Coleman-Norton. Princeton: Princeton University Press, 1951.

Tcherikover, Avigdor. *Die hellenistischen Städtegrundungen von Alexander dem Grossen bis auf die Römerzeit.* New York: Arno Press, 1973.

Tengstrom, Emin. *Bread for the People: Studies of the Corn-Supply of Rome During the Late Empire.* Lund, Sweden: P. Astrom, 1974.

Thirgood, J. V. *Man and the Mediterranean Forest: A History of Resource Depletion.* London: Academic Press, 1981.

Thompson, D'Arcy Wentworth. *A Glossary of Greek Birds.* Oxford: Oxford University Press, 1936.

Thomson, J. Oliver. *History of Ancient Geography.* Cambridge: Cambridge University Press, 1948.

Tod, Marcus Niebuhr. *A Selection of Greek Historical Inscriptions.* 2 vols. Oxford: Clarendon Press, 1933.

Tomlinson, Richard Allan. *Greek Sanctuaries.* New York: St. Martin's Press, 1976.

Toutain, Jules Francois. *The Economic Life of the Ancient World.* Trans. M. R. Dobie. New York: Barnes and Noble, 1951.

Toynbee, Arnold J. "The Roman Revolution from the Flora's Point of View." In *Hannibal's Legacy: The Hannibalic War's Effect on Roman Life.* 2 vols. London: Oxford University Press, 1965. 2:585–99.

Toynbee, Jocelyn M. C. *Animals in Roman Life and Art.* Ithaca, N.Y.: Cornell University Press, 1973.

Tozer, Henry Fanshawe. *A History of Ancient Geography.* 2d ed. Cambridge: Cambridge University Press, 1897. Repr. New York: Biblo and Tannen, 1964.

————. *Lectures on the Geography of Greece*. 1882. Repr. Chicago: Ares, 1974.

Trotta-Treyden, Hans von. "Die Entwaldung in den Mittelmeerländern, mit einem Anhang über den heutigen Waldstand." In *Petermann's Geographische Mitteilungen aus Justus Perthes Geographischer Anstalt*. Gotha: Petermann, 1916. 248–53.

Tsoumis, George. "Depletion of Forests in the Mediterranean Region: A Historical Review from Ancient Times to the Present." *Scientific Annals of the Department of Forestry and Natural Environment, Aristotelian University of Thessaloniki* 28 (1988): 283–300.

Turrill, W. B. *The Plant-Life of the Balkan Peninsula*. Oxford: Clarendon Press, 1929.

UNESCO. *Mediterranean Forests and Maquis: Ecology, Conservation, and Management*. Paris, 1977.

Usher, Abbott Payson. *A History of Mechanical Inventions*. 2d ed. Cambridge: Harvard University Press, 1954.

Van Andel, Tjeerd H., and Curtis N. Runnels. *Beyond the Acropolis: A Rural Greek Past*. Stanford: Stanford University Press, 1987.

Van Andel, Tjeerd H., Curtis N. Runnels, and Kevin O. Pope. "Five Thousand Years of Land Use and Abuse in the Southern Argolid, Greece." *Hesperia* 55 (1986): 103–28.

Vermeule, Emily. "The Afterlife: Greece." In *Civilization of the Ancient Mediterranean: Greece and Rome*, 3 vols., edited by Michael Grant and Rachel Kitzinger. New York: Scribner's, 1988. 2:993–94.

Vidal-Naquet, Pierre. *The Black Hunter: Forms of Thought and Forms of Society in the Greek World*. Baltimore: Johns Hopkins University Press, 1983.

Vita-Finzi, Claudio. *The Mediterranean Valleys: Geological Changes in Historical Times*. Cambridge: Cambridge University Press, 1969.

————. "Roman Dams in Tripolitania." *Antiquity* 35 (1961): 77–95.

Wacher, J. S. *The Towns of Roman Britain*. Berkeley: University of California Press, 1975.

Walker, Donald S. *The Mediterranean Lands*. London: Methuen, 1965.

Ward-Perkins, John B. *Cities of Ancient Greece and Italy: Planning in Classical Antiquity*. New York: George Braziller, 1974.

————. *Landscape and History in Central Italy*. Oxford: Blackwell, 1964.

————. "Quarrying in Antiquity: Technology, Tradition, and Social Change." *Proceedings of the British Academy* (1972): 97–115.

Weber, Max. *The Agrarian Sociology of Ancient Civilizations*, trans. by R. I. Frank. Atlantic Highlands, N.J.: Humanities Press, 1976.

————. *The City*. New York: Free Press, 1958.

———. *Römische Agrargeschichte in ihrer Bedeutung für das Staats- und Privatrecht*. New York: Arno Press, 1979.

Wedeck, Harry Ezekiel. *Humor in Varro, and Other Essays*. Oxford: B. Blackwell, 1929.

Wegener, Wilhelm. *Die Tierwelt bei Homer*. Königsberg, 1887.

Wertime, Theodore A. "The Furnace versus the Goat: The Pyrotechnologic Industries and Mediterranean Deforestation in Antiquity." *Journal of Field Archaeology* 10 (1983): 445–52.

Wertime, Theodore A., and James D. Muhly, eds. *The Coming of the Age of Iron*. New Haven: Yale University Press, 1980.

Wertime, Theodore A., and S. Wertime, eds. *Early Pyrotechnology: The Evolution of the Fire Using Industries*. Washington, D.C.: Smithsonian, 1982.

Wheeler, R. E. M. *Rome Beyond the Imperial Frontiers*. London, 1954.

White, Kenneth D. *Agricultural Implements of the Roman World*. London: Cambridge University Press, 1967.

———. *A Bibliography of Roman Agriculture*. Reading: University of Reading (Institute of Agricultural History), 1970.

———. *Farm Equipment of the Roman World*. Cambridge: Cambridge University Press, 1975.

———. "Farming and Animal Husbandry." In *Civilization of the Ancient Mediterranean: Greece and Rome*, 3 vols., edited by Michael Grant and Rachel Kitzinger. New York: Charles Scribner's Sons, 1988. 1:211–46.

———. *Greek and Roman Technology*. Ithaca, N.Y.: Cornell University Press, 1984.

———. *Roman Farming*. Ithaca, N.Y.: Cornell University Press, 1970.

———. "Wheat-Farming in Roman Times." *Antiquity* 37 (1963): 207–12.

Wigley, T. M. L., M. J. Ingram, and G. Farmer, eds. *Climate and History: Studies in Past Climates and Their Impact on Man*. Cambridge: Cambridge University Press, 1981.

Wilhelm, Adolf. "Die Pachturkunden der Klytiden." *Jahresheft des Österreichischen Archäologischen Institutes in Wien* 28 (1933): 197–221.

Wilsdorf, Helmut. *Bergleute und Hüttenmännern im Altertum bis zum Ausgang der römischen Republik*. Berlin: Freiburger Forschungshefte, 1952.

Wilson, John A. *The Culture of Ancient Egypt*. Chicago: University of Chicago Press, 1951.

———. "Egypt." In *Before Philosophy*, edited by Henri Frankfort et al. Baltimore: Penguin Books, 1949. 37–133.

Windley, Brian F. *The Evolving Continents*. London: John Wiley and Sons, 1977.

Winters, Robert K. *The Forest and Man*. New York: Vantage Press, 1974.

Wittfogel, Karl. *Oriental Despotism: A Comparative Study of Total Power*. New Haven: Yale University Press, 1957.

Wycherley, R. E. *How the Greeks Built Cities.* New York: Macmillan, 1962.
———. *The Stones of Athens.* Princeton: Princeton University Press, 1978.
Yeo, Cedric A. "The Overgrazing of Ranch Lands in Ancient Italy." *Transactions and Proceedings of the American Philological Association* 79 (1948): 275–307.
Yoshino, Masatoshi M., ed. *Local Wind Bora.* Tokyo: University of Tokyo Press, 1976.
Young, Rodney. "An Industrial District of Ancient Athens." *Hesperia* 20 (1951): 135–288.
Zeuner, Frederick E. *A History of Domesticated Animals.* New York: Harper and Row, 1963.
Zimmern, Alfred. *The Greek Commonwealth: Politics and Economics in Fifth Century Athens.* 4th ed. Oxford: Oxford University Press, 1924.
Zinsser, Hans. *Rats, Lice, and History.* Boston: Little, Brown and Co., 1935.

Index

263

ANCIENT SOCIETY AND HISTORY

The series Ancient Society and History offers books, relatively brief in compass, on selected topics in the history of ancient Greece and Rome, broadly conceived, with a special emphasis on comparative and other nontraditional approaches and methods. The series, which includes both works of synthesis and works of original scholarship, is aimed at the widest possible range of specialist and nonspecialist readers.

Published in the Series:

Eva Cantarella, *Pandora's Daughters: The Role and Status of Women in Greek and Roman Antiquity*

Alan Watson, *Roman Slave Law*

John E. Stambaugh, *The Ancient Roman City*

Géza Alföldy, *The Social History of Rome*

Giovanni Comotti, *Music in Greek and Roman Culture*

Christian Habicht, *Cicero the Politician*

Mark Golden, *Children and Childhood in Classical Athens*

Thomas Cole, *The Origins of Rhetoric in Ancient Greece*

Maurizio Bettini, *Anthropology and Roman Culture: Kinship, Time, Images of the Soul*

Suzanne Dixon, *The Roman Family*

Stephen L. Dyson, *Community and Society in Roman Italy*

Tim G. Parkin, *Demography and Roman Society*

Alison Burford, *Land and Labor in the Greek World*

Alan Watson, *International Law in Archaic Rome: War and Religion*

Steven H. Lonsdale, *Dance and Ritual Play in Greek Religion*

J. Donald Hughes, *Pan's Travail: Environmental Problems of the Ancient Greeks and Romans*

C. R. Whittaker, *Frontiers of the Roman Empire: A Social and Economic Study*

Pericles Georges, *Barbarian Asia and the Greek Experience*

Nancy Demand, *Birth, Death, and Motherhood in Classical Greece*

Printed in the United States
19987LVS00002B/169-183